ANCIENT INDIAN TRADITION & MYTHOLOGY

Translated by
A BOARD OF SCHOLARS

Edited by
Prof. J. L. SHASTRI

VOLUME 24

ANCIENT INDIAN TRADITION AND MYTHOLOGY SERIES

[PURĀṆAS IN TRANSLATION]

Volumes Released

ŚIVA 1-4
LIṄGA 5-6
BHĀGAVATA 7-11
GARUḌA 12-14
NĀRADA 15-19
KŪRMA 20-21
BRAHMĀṆḌA 22-26
AGNI 27-30
VARĀHA 31-32
BRAHMA 33-36
VĀYU 37-38
PADMA 39-48
SKANDA, PARTS I-XXI, 49-69
VĀMANA 72

Volumes Under Preparation

SKANDA, PARTS XXII-XXIII, 70-71
BHAVIṢYA
BRAHMAVAIVARTA
DEVĪBHĀGAVATA
KĀLIKĀ
MĀRKAṆḌEYA
MATSYA
VIṢṆU
VIṢṆUDHARMOTTARA

THE BRAHMĀṆḌA PURĀṆA

Translated and Annotated by
DR. G.V. TAGARE

PART III

MOTILAL BANARSIDASS PUBLISHERS
PRIVATE LIMITED ● DELHI

Reprint: Delhi, 2000, 2007
First Edition : Delhi, 1983

ISBN: 978-81-208-0356-5

MOTILAL BANARSIDASS
41 U.A. Bungalow Road, Jawahar Nagar, Delhi 110 007
8 Mahalaxmi Chamber, 22 Bhulabhai Desai Road, Mumbai 400 026
203 Royapettah High Road, Mylapore, Chennai 600 004
236, 9th Main III Block, Jayanagar, Bangalore 560 011
Sanas Plaza, 1302 Baji Rao Road, Pune 411 002
8 Camac Street, Kolkata 700 017
Ashok Rajpath, Patna 800 004
Chowk, Varanasi 221 001

UNESCO COLECTION OF REPRESENTATIVE WORKS— Indian Series
This book has been accepted in the Indian Translation Series of the UNESCO Collection of Representative Works, jointly sponsored by the United Nations Educational Scientific and Cultural Organization (UNESCO) and the Government of India

PRINTED IN INDIA
BY JAINENDRA PRAKASH JAIN AT SHRI JAINENDRA PRESS,
A-45 NARAINA, PHASE-I, NEW DELHI 110 028
AND PUBLISHED BY NARENDRA PRAKASH JAIN FOR
MOTILAL BANARSIDASS PUBLISHERS PRIVATE LIMITED,
BUNGALOW ROAD, DELHI 110 007

PUBLISHER'S NOTE

The purest gems lie hidden in the bottom of the ocean or in the depth of rocks. One has to dive into the ocean or delve into the rocks to find them out. Similarly, truth lies concealed in the language which with the passage of time has become obsolete. Man has to learn that language before he discovers that truth.

But he has neither the means nor the leisure to embark on that course. We have, therefore, planned to help him acquire knowledge by an easier course. We have started the series of *Ancient Indian Tradition and Mythology* in English Translation. Our goal is to universalize knowledge through the most popular international medium of expression. The publication of the Purāṇas in English translation is a step towards that goal.

PREFACE

The present volume contains the *Brahmāṇḍa Purāṇa*, Part III (Chapters 44-74) of the third section, *Upodghātapāda*, of the text *in English Translation*. This is the Twenty-fourth volume in the Series which we have planned on *Ancient Indian Tradition and Mythology*.

The project of the Series was envisaged and financed in 1970 by Lala Sundar Lal Jain of Messrs Motilal Banarsidass. Hitherto twentythree volumes of the Series (comprising English translation of *Śiva, Liṅga, Bhāgavata, Garuḍa, Nārada, Kūrma* and *Brahmāṇḍa Purāṇas*) have been published and released for sale.

The present Volume continues the story of Paraśurāma from the previous volume. It records the visit of Paraśurāma to the hermitage of his father Jamadagni and his review of the battle with king Kārttavīrya ending in the latter's death, his visit to lord Brahmā who advised him to see lord Śiva who gave him the protective mantra *Trailokya-Vijaya* which he repeated for practice at the holy place named Puṣkara.

In the next visit to lord Śiva Paraśurāma meets stiff resistance from Vināyaka, son of lord Śiva. Vināyaka as a guard is posted at the gate. He would not allow Paraśurāma to enter the palace at that unusual hour. But in the excess of devotion for the lord, Paraśurāma can no longer wait and a furious combat ensues between Vināyaka and Paraśurāma wherein the former loses his tusk.

Pārvatī is extremely in rage. She threatens to desert Śiva if the insult is not avenged. All entreaties are of no avail till Rādhā and Kṛṣṇa arrive to intervene. Rādhā succeeds in appeasing Pārvatī. Thus, an unpleasant situation created by ugly incident is changed for the better.

Such incidents are no main parts of the story. They appear to have been inserted later on for establishing harmony among the mutually opposing religious sects. The emergence of Rādhā as a powerful celebrity who could pacify Pārvatī when others had failed is, in fact, the most significant factor that has been introduced for accomplishing the religious integration of different sects.

As a part of the main story, Jamadagni episode presents persons of different character. Jamadagni, by nature, is a peace-loving sage. He is not happy at the cruel slaughter of innocent Kṣatriyas. He advises Paraśurāma to perform penance for twelve years. Paraśurāma agrees to the proposal and starts penance at the mount Mahendra. Meanwhile, Śūra, son of Kārttavīrya, goes to the forest on hunting expedition. He enters the hermitage of Jamadagni and kills the sage. Reṇukā wife of Jamadagni, immolates herself on the pyre.

After completing his course of penance, Paraśurāma returns to the hermitage of his father. On knowing about the tragic death of his parents he is extremely pained. He goes to Māhiṣmatī and kills Śūra. Thereafter, he goes to the mount Mahendra and performs penance. Taking advantage of his absence, the Haihayas gather forces, devastate Bhārgavas and their allies. When Paraśurāma returns, he is informed of their activities. He repeats his expeditions twentyone times and slaughters Kṣatriyas. He catches hold of twelve thousand kṣatriya kings, kills them at Kurukṣetra, fills up five tanks with their blood and offers libations thereof to his deceased forefathers who, however, advise him to desist from violence. Paraśurāma performs a horse-sacrifice, donates all conquered land as gift to his preceptor Kaśyapa.

The rise of the power of Haihayas known as Tālajaṅghas shows that the effect of Rāma's conquests was temporary. Tālajaṅghas recovered their kingdom and drove out the ruler of Ayodhyā who due to blood-relation with Jamadagni was an ally of Paraśurāma.

Furthermore, the account shows that the sages were equipped with the knowledge of military science. For instance, king Sagara of Ayodhyā had received his military training under Aurva and attained proficiency in the fire missiles. As a result of this he had extended his dominion as far as Afghanistan. This volume contains the story of Sagara in detail, refers to his horse sacrifice wherein his progeny was destroyed by the fire of sage Kapila's anger. There are references to Bhagīratha who had brought Gaṅgā from the Himalayas to the northern plains of the country and sanctified the ashes of his ancestors with her holy waters.

The character of Paraśurāma is portrayed as militant, remorseless, aggressive revengeful and violent. His expeditions against the Haihayas, his conquests of the Earth repeated twentyone times, his filling up five tanks at Kurukṣetra with the blood of Kṣatriya rulers show how far his fury had reached to avenge the death of his father. As for further accounts of his exploits, mention may be made of how he had recovered the submerged land from the sea.

Furthermore, the Section presents the account of some prominent royal dynasties from the birth of Vaivasvata Manu to the Future Sāvarṇa Manu. These accounts are common in all Purāṇas and they seem to be the part of Ur-Purāṇa.

Chapters 61, 62 relate to the science of Music. Here the text is full of corrupt readings and obscurities. The corresponding text in the Vāyu Purāṇa is comparatively better and we have accepted readings from the Vāyu Purāṇa. This has facilitated the work of translation. Still, a lot of confusion will persist till the original text is restored which at present is not possible for want of manuscripts. Besides, the Volume deals with the history of kings of Ikṣvāku dynasty, marks the extent of their dominions, mentions how an important member of their dynasty attained Brahmanhood, states the names of kṣatriyas who attained the status of sages by means of penance (See p. 850), records some interesting legends such as the legend of famous physician king Dhanvantari, the founder of Āyurveda (Indian Medical Science), the episode of the city of Varanasi, how it was colonized by the Rākṣasa Kṣemaka, how it prospered by the blissful patronage of Nikumbha—a prominent member among the attendants of Lord Mahādeva and further how it became desolate by the curse of that very goblin, and still further, how lord Mahādeva took up his abode in the city and restored its prestine glory.

The section contains the story of king Yayāti, requesting his sons to exchange their youth for a period of 1000 years for his old age. This episode of mythological character is the greatest contribution to the history of pre-Vedic period. The five sons of Yayāti—Yadu, Turvasu, Druhyu, Anu and Pūru are historical personages well known to the Ṛgveda. The Puranic records maintain the oldest tradition of this dynasty. Ch. 69 of this section recounts the line of Yadu, the eldest son of Yayāti—the line which was sanctified by its association with lord Kṛṣṇa, son of Vasudeva and the foster-child of Nanda.

The concluding chapters include the history of some royal dynasties and high personages such as Bārhadrathas, Pradyotas, Śiśunāgas, Nandas, Mauryas and Kāṇvas. For the detailed description of these dynasties the reader is referred to Introduction to Vol. xxii, Part I of this Purāna.

Acknowledgement of Obligations

It is our pleasant duty to put on record our sincere thanks to Dr. R. N. Dandekar and the UNESCO authorities for their kind encouragement and valuable help which render this work more useful than it would otherwise have been. We are extremely grateful to Dr. G. V. Tagare for his critical Introduction, lucid translation and comprehensive annotations. We thank Shri T. V. Parameshwar Iyer for his valuable assistance in the preparation of this work. We should also express our gratitude to all those persons who have offered suggestions for improving the same.

—Editor

CONTENTS

PART III

SECTION III UPODGHĀTAPĀDA (*Continued*)

CHAPTERS

ABBREVIATIONS

Common and self-evident abbreviations such as ch(s)—chapter(s), p—page, pp—pages, v—verse, vv—verses, Ftn—footnote, Hist. Ind. Philo—History of Indian Philosophy are not included in this list.

ABORI	*Annals of the Bhandarkar Oriental Research Institute*, Poona.
AGP	S. M. Ali's *The Geography of Purāṇas*, PPH, New Delhi, 1973.
AIHT	*Ancient Indian Historical Tradition*, F. E. Pargiter, Motilal Banarsidass (MLBD), Delhi.
AITM	*Ancient Indian Tradition and Mythology* Series, MLBD, Delhi, 1972 onwards.
AP	*Agni Purāṇa*, Guru Mandal Edition (GM), Calcutta, 1957.
Arch. S. Rep.	Archaeological Survey Report.
AV	*Atharva Veda*, Svadhyaya Mandal, Aundh.
Bd. P.	*Brahmāṇḍa Purāṇa*, MLBD, Delhi 1973.
BG	*Bhagavadgitā*.
Bh. P.	*Bhāgavata Purāṇa*, Bhagavat Vidyapeeth, Ahmedabad.
Br.	*Brāhmaṇa* (preceded by name such as *Śatapatha*).
Bs. P.	*Bhaviṣya Purāṇa*, Vishnu Shastri Bapat, Wai.
Bv. P.	*Brahma Vaivarta Purāṇa*, GM, 1955-57.
CC	*Caturvarga Cintāmaṇi* by Hemādri.
CVS	*Caraṇa Vyūha Sūtra* by Śaunaka; Com. by Mahidāsa.
DB	*Devi Bhāgavata*, GM, 1960-61.

De or GDAMI	*The Geographical Dictionary of Ancient and Mediaeval India*, N. L. De, Orienta Reprint, Delhi, 1971.
Dh. S.	*Dharma Sūtra* (preceded by the author's name such as Gautama).
ERE	*Encyclopaedia of Religion and Ethics*—Hastings.
GP	*Garuḍa Purāṇa*, Ed. R. S. Bhattacharya, Chowkhamba, Varanasi, 1964.
GS	*Gṛhya Sūtra* (Preceded by the name of the author such as Āpastamba)
HD	*History of Dharma Śāstra* by P. V. Kane, G.O.S.
IA	*The Indian Antiquary*.
IHQ	*The Indian Historical Quarterly*.
KA	*Kauṭilīya Arthaśāstra*.
KP	*Kūrma Purāṇa*, Venkateshwara Press Edt. Bombay, also Kashiraj Trust Edt., Varanasi 1971.
LP	*Liṅga Purāṇa*, GM, 1960; also MLBD, Delhi, 1981.
Manu	*Manu Smṛti*.
Mbh.	*Mahābhārata*, Gītā Press, Gorakhpur, VS 2014.
MKP	*Mārkaṇḍeya Purāṇa*.
MN	*Mahābhārata Nāmānukramaṇi*, Gītā Press, Gorakhpur, VS 2016.
Mt. P.	*Matsya Purāṇa*, GM, 1954.
MW	*Monier Williams* Sk. English Dictionary MLBD, Delhi, 1976.
NP	*Nāradīya or Nārada Purāṇa*, Venkateshwar Press, Bombay.
PCK	*Bhāratavarṣiya Prācīna Caritrakośa*, Siddheshwar Shastri, Poona, 1968.
Pd. P.	*Padma Purāṇa*, GM, 1957-59.
PE	*Puranic Encyclopaedia* by V. Mani, English, MLBD, Delhi, 1975.

PJ.	*Purāṇa* (Journal of the Kashirāj Trust), Varanasi.
PR or PRHRC	*Puranic Records on Hindu Rites and Customs* R. C. Hazra, Calcutta, 1948.
ṚV	*Ṛg Veda*, Svadhyaya Mandal, Aundh
Śat. Br	*Śatapatha Brāhmaṇa.*
SC or SMC	*Smṛti Candrikā*—Devanna Bhatta.
SEP	*Studies in Epics and Purāṇas* by A. D. Pusalkar Bharatiya Vidya Bhavan(BVB), Bombay.

CHAPTER FORTYFOUR

The Story of Paraśurāma

Vasiṣṭha said :

1. Thus the scholarly scion of the family of Bhṛgu, of righteous Soul, proceeded (homeward) accompanied by Akṛtavraṇa, seeing on the way many lands and territories, O king.

2. Seeing Bhārgava on the way, everywhere all the Kṣatriyas hid themselves in their eagerness and anxiety to save their lives.

3. Then, O leading king, Rāma reached the hermitage of his father, that echoed with the sound of the Vedic Mantras and that was abounding in animals of tranquil nature.

4. It was a place where the animals (though mutually inimical by nature, like lions, deer, cows, elephants, cats and mice, roamed about in joy simultaneously, leaving off their fear.

5. On seeing the smoke arising from the Agnihotra rites, O ruler of the Earth, the peacocks cry aloud and dance delightedly (as if they have seen a cloud).

6. In the evening hours, the ground there was rendered slushy (?) with water by Brāhmaṇas who used to offer water libations facing the setting Sun.

7. The Vedas, Scriptures and Saṁhitās were joyously recited there, by the resident disciples strictly adhering to the vow of celibacy.

8. Surveying the luxurious wealth of the hermitage with great delight in his mind, O king, Rāma entered it accompanied by Akṛtavraṇa.

9. On being welcomed and honoured by the Brāhmaṇas and their sons who uttered such words as "Be victorious", "Obeisance to you", Rāma became greatly delighted.

10. Entering the inner precincts of the hermitage, his own house, Rāma saw his father, Jamadagni, the very storehouse of Penance.

11. The sage was one capable of chastising or blessing. He was seated there like Bhṛgu himself. Rāma prostrated him-

self at his feet touching the ground with eight parts (of his body).

12. "I am Rāma, your slave"—Uttering this, O lord of the Earth, Rāma, the leader of good people, duly touched his feet.

13. Then he made obeisance to the feet of his mother. With palms joined in reverence, he made the following statement which made them delighted.

Rāma said :

14. Due to the potentiality of your penance, O father, Kārttavīrya who was extremely inassailable (to his enemies) was killed in battle along with his sons, armies and vehicles.

15. Punishment was sternly meted out by me to (that king) who committed an offence against you, on being urged by his wicked minister, O leading sage.

16. After bowing down to you, I approached Brahmā. After duly bowing down to him I intimated to him my purpose of seeing him.

17. On hearing the report from the beginning, that lord advised me. "Go to the eternal region of God Śiva for the realization of your object".

18. After hearing his words, O father, I bowed down to Pitāmaha (god Brahmā) and went to Śivaloka with a desire to see Hara.

19. On entering it, O holy Sir, Lord Śiva accompanied by his consort Umā, Śiva who bestows the objects desired by us, was duly saluted by me.

20. In his presence the whole of my history was reported by me. With great concentration of mind, he heard everything.

21. Hearing it and pondering over everything, the merciful lord gave me a *Kavaca* (an esoteric *mantra* as a coat of mail) named *Trailokyavijaya* (conqueror of the three worlds). It is the bestower of success in everything.

22-23. On obtaining it, I bowed down to him and went to Puṣkara. There I practised the *Kavaca* and became delighted in my mind. After killing Kārttavīrya in the battle, I went to

Śivaloka once again. There Skanda and Vināyaka were seen by me at the entrance.

24-25. O sage conversant with Dharma, I attempted to enter after bowing down to them.

On seeing me entering hurriedly, Gaṇeśa suddenly prevented me saying—"This is not the proper time". Therefore, O father, a wordy warfare took place between me and him. Then the seizure of each other's hands and tugging at them followed. Thereafter, the hurling of the axe took place, O delighter of the family of 'Bhṛgu'.

26-29. Coming to know of it, he (Vināyaka) seized me with his hand and whirled me upwards and downwards. Then I was brought back (to my original place). On seeing him, the axe was hurled by me with great anger. His tusk was felled down when the lord came there. Pārvatī became angry. Then Kṛṣṇa came there accompanied by Rādhā. She (Pārvatī) was appeased by him and she granted me a boon. Kṛṣṇa went away after making me friendly with him (Gaṇeśa).

30. Thereafter, I bowed down to Pārvatī and the Supreme Lord Śiva, the sovereign of the Devas and have now come to your presence accompanied by Akṛtavraṇa."

Vasiṣṭha said :

31. After saying this, O lord of the Earth, Rāma, the scion of the family of Bhṛgu, stopped. Jamadagni then said to Rāma, the slayer of enemies.

Jamadagni said :

32. You have been affected by the sin of slaughtering Kṣatriyas. In order to remove the sin thereof, it behoves you to perform expiation duly".

33. On being told thus, Rāma, the most excellent one among intelligent persons, requested his father—"It behoves you to point out to me the proper expiation thereof".

Jamadagni said :

34. "Perform a penance for twelve years making your body emaciated by means of holy rites and observances and subsisting only on greens, roots and fruits for your diet".

Vasiṣṭha said :

35. On being told thus, the leading member of the family of Bhṛgu, bowed down to him as well as to his mother, O king, and went for performing penance accompanied by Akṛtavraṇa.

36-37. He, the destroyer of enemies, went to the excellent mountain Mahendra.[1] He built a hermitage there and performed a penance very difficult to be performed by others.

Rāma of noble mind spent some years there performing holy rites and observances and the worship of the deities.

CHAPTER FORTYFIVE

The Story of Paraśurāma (continued)

Vasiṣṭha said :—

1. Then once Śūra (i.e. Kārttavīrya's son) who had escaped to the Himalayan forests—went to the forest for hunting along with Śūrasena and others and accompanied by the armies of four different units.

2. After entering the great forest, they killed different kinds of animals. Overwhelmed by thirst at midday, they went to the river Narmadā.

3. Taking their bath there and drinking the waters of the river, they got rid of their fatigue. While going away they saw the hermitage of Jamadagni on the way.

4. On seeing the charming hermitage, they asked sages coming that way—"whose hermitage is this?" In that they were urged by the inevitable future result of their actions.

5. They replied : "Jamadagni of great penance lives in this hermitage. He is a sage of quiescent soul and his son Rāma is the most excellent one among the wielders of weapons."

6. On hearing it and because Rāma's name was mentioned, they were overcome with fear at the outset.

1. The range of hills extending from Orissa to Madurai district. It includes the Eastern Ghat and the range extending from Northern Circars to Gondwana—De, p. 119.

Remembering their previous ruthless enmity, they were exceedingly enraged.

7. Then they conferred with one another—"Since our father has been killed by Paraśurāma, why should we not take revenge by killing the father of the slayer of our father? Direct us now."

8. After saying this, they entered the hermitage with swords in their hands, as the heroic sages had gone to different places. They killed Jamadagni.

9. After killing him, they took away his head like the ruthless Niṣadas (hunters). Those wicked ones then returned to their capital along with their armies.

10. On seeing their father killed, the sons of that noble-souled sage lamented, O great king. Afflicted by grief they stood surrounding him,

11. On seeing her husband fallen on the ground after being killed, Reṇukā immediately fell down senseless like a creeper struck down by the thunderbolt.

12. After falling unconscious, she was burnt by the fire of grief in her mind. Like one whose consciousness is lost, she became separated from her vital airs. She died instantaneously.

13. The sons who had regained consciousness saw that she did not utter any word. They became immersed in the ocean of grief and fell down senseless on the ground.

14. Other sages who were living in that penance-grove, came there. They too were equally grieved but they consoled the sons of the sage.

15. After being consoled by the groups of sages the sons of Jamadagni duly cremated the bodies of their parents at their instance.

16. They performed all the obsequies that should be performed later on after the death of parents. They were afflicted day and night by the sorrow, due to the death of their parents.

17. In due course of time, at the end of the period of twelve years, Rāma returned from his penance. Accompanied by his friend, he went to the hermitage of his father.

CHAPTER FORTYSIX

The Story of Paraśurāma (Continued)

Vasiṣṭha said :—

1-3. While coming along the path, Rāma heard the details (of his father's murder) from the beginning, from the sages such as the attempt (on his father's life) by the princes, the passing away of his parents, the murder of his father and the removal of the head of his father by them.

On hearing of the death of his mother due to his father's death, Rāma of powerful arms, became miserable and grieved and he lamented. Akṛtavraṇa who had been equally grieved consoled him.

4. Through reasons pointed out in the scriptures, through hints of his heroism and capacity and through cogent arguments and popular examples he alleviated Rāma's grief.

5. On being consoled, the highly intelligent scion of the family of Bhṛgu, regained his courage. He proceeded ahead, desirous of seeing his brothers. He was accompanied by his friend.

6. Himself, reduced in physical strength due to misery he saw them (his brothers). He bowed down to them who too were equally miserable. Continuously experiencing grief and anger, he stayed with them for three days.

7. His fierce wrath (due to the recurring) recollection of the death of his father developed soon so much that it became capable of annihilating the worlds.

8. Being truthful to his vow, he reaffirmed in his heart the pledge taken by him formerly for the sake of his mother. He prepared himself for the massacre of all Kṣatriyas.

9-10. Bhārgava resolved thus—"After killing all those born of Kṣatriya race, I will perform the libation offerings to my parents with the blood from their bodies". He indicated his desire to all his brothers. Being permitted by them and having concluded all the obsequies, he started from his house.

11. Accompanied by Akṛtavraṇa, he went to Māhiṣmatī. Standing in a park at the outskirts of that city, he remembered Mahodara.

12. He sent to Rāma a chariot, bow etc. and all the necessary requisites for fighting along with Sahasāha.

13. Rāma, the conqueror of enemies, became ready (for the battle) well-accoutred. He got into the chariot. He took up his bow along with the arrows and blew his conch presented by Rudra.

14. He made a twanging sound with the bowstring, making heaven and Earth tremble as it were. Sahasāha, the most excellent one among the charioteers, drove the chariot.

15. On account of the sounds of the chariot as well as the bow-string of (Rāma) who was furious due to the slaughter of his parents, the entire city, the people and elephants became agitated.

16. On coming to know that Rāma, the destroyer of all Kṣatriyas, had come, the sons of the king became deeply agitated and they made full preparations for fighting with him.

17. Then, O king, the heroic princes Śūrasena and others (seated) in five chariots, made their endeavour to fight with Rāma. They were accompanied by other kings as well.

18. Equipped with armies consisting of four different units, those leading Kṣatriyas confronted Rāma like the locusts approching fire.

19. With his single chariot, Bhārgava restrained them as they rushed on. Being a hero of boundless valour, he fought with all the kings in the battle.

20. A battle took place once again between Rāma and the kings, wherein the infuriated sage of high intellect, killed a hundred kings.

21. After killing Śūrasena and others along with their armies and vehicles, he made the entire group of Kṣatriyas fall on the ground in a moment.

22. The kings who survived, whose wishes had been frustrated and whose vehicles and armies had been killed fled in all directions.

23. After routing the armies, killing the enemies and winning the battle, Rāma killed hundreds of kings and heroes by means of the fire from his excellent arrows.

24. Overwhelmed with fury and desirous of burning the entire city, Bhārgava discharged a missile that had a lustre similar to that of Kālāgni (the fire of world-destruction).

25. The fire from that missile burned the city along with elephants, horses and men. The flames enveloped the clusters of the entire rampart-wall of the city.

26. On seeing the city being burned and desirous of saving his own life, Prince Vītihotra became frightened and fled quickly for the sake of life.

27. After burning the entire city by means of fire from the missile, and after killing the enemies Rāma appeared like the god of Death, the destroyer who devours all the worlds.

28. Accompanied by Akṛtavraṇa and Sahasâha he went ahead making the Earth tremble, as it were, by means of the (rumbling) sound of the chariot.

29. After killing all the Kṣatriyas on the surface of the Earth, Rāma became calm. Then he went to the mountain Mahendra determining in his mind that he should perform penance.

30. In the meantime, in thirtytwo years (?) Kṣatriyas rose into prominence. Therefore, he returned (from penance) and took the vow of killing them.

31. Kṣatriya kings were begotten of the widowed wives of those Kṣatriyas by Brāhmaṇas. Again he (Rāma) killed hundreds and thousands of such kings.

32. In two years, Rāma made the Earth devoid of Kṣatriyas once again. At the end of it he performed penance of twenty-four years duration once again.

33. Again, O king, enlightened Kṣatriyas were procreated by the Brāhmaṇas. Rāma killed them entirely like the god of death, the destroyer on the Earth.

34. In the course of so many years some kings were born. Killing them Rāma roamed over the Earth continuously for two years.

35. Enough (of this repetition of incidents) O leading king. The Earth was rendered Kṣattriya-less by Rāma who remembered the death of his father. He cleared the earth of Kṣattriyas for all twentyone times.

36. Since his mother beat her own breast twentyone times, Kṣatriyas on the Earth were exterminated by Rāma as many times.[1]

CHAPTER FORTYSEVEN

The Story of Paraśurāma (Continued)

Vasiṣṭha said :—

1. "Thereafter, Rāma captured alive twelve thousand kings who had unmeasured splendour and who were duly coronated.

2. That sage of great splendour took these thousands of kings along with the sages to the pilgrimage centre Kurukṣetra which is full of penance (i.e. sages performing penance).

3. The leading member of the family of Bhṛgu caused five lakes to be dug there. All around them, he got built holy bathing ghats of comfortable access.

4. Bhārgava killed the kings there. With the blood flowing out of their bodies he filled those five lakes.

5. The valorous son of Jamadagni duly bathed in them and performed the rite of offering libations to the manes in accordance with the scriptures carefully.

6. He performed Śrāddha and other rites. O leading king, of his departed father and mother as mentioned in the scriptures in the company of Brāhmaṇas.

7. Surmounting all unfavourable circumstances thus, he stayed in the holy centre of Kurukṣetra abounding in austerities. He was alertly engaged in the worship of Pitṛs.

8. Thenceforward, the holy spot created by the son of Jamadagni in the penance grove of Kurukṣetra became the most excellent of all excellent sacred places.

1. This seems to be the refrain of the traditional ballad of Paraśurāma.

9. The place where the most excellent one among the members of the family of Bhṛgu caused the everlasting satisfaction to the manes has come to be known as *Syamantapañcaka* or *Samantapañcaka.* It is well known in all the three worlds.

10. It is the place where all his Pitṛs were fully propitiated by him by means of holy baths, charitable gifts, penance *Homas*, feeding of the Brāhmaṇas and offerings of libations.

11-13a. The Pitṛs obtained everlasting satisfaction and the eternal world of the Pitṛs. The holy centre named *Samantapañcaka* is well known in the world as destructive of all sins and developed by means of great merit. All the sins of men who go there are removed even from a great distance like a dry leaf in a strong wind.

13b-15a. The opportunity to go to that pilgrim centre is never obtained by bad men, O great king, even after hundreds of births.

The sacred spot *Samantapañcaka* in Kuruksetra is extremely sanctifying. A man who takes his holy bath there is (on a par with) a man who bathes in all holy rivers and tanks.

15b-17a. Having fulfilled all his religious acts very well, Rāma felt completely satisfied in regard to his desires. The highly intelligent sage stayed there for some time with great self-restraint.

Then, at the end of a year, the son of Jamadagni of great self control, went to Gayā accompanied by the Brāhmanas in order to offer the balls of rice to the Pitṛs.

17b-20a. After going there, the suppressor of enemies propitiated the Brāhmaṇas, greeted and honoured on behalf of the *Pitṛs* in the *Śrāddha* in accordance with the scriptures.

There is another holy spot there pertaining to Śiva, remembered as Candrapāda. A pilgrim centre that causes the satisfaction of the *Pitṛs* like that, does not exist in the world.

The *Pitṛs* who are worshipped there by persons belonging to their families, even to the slightest extent in accordance with their capacity, will attain everlasting access to their goal through the offerings of balls of rice and similar objects.

20b-23a. When the Brāhmaṇas had been fully propitiated on behalf of the *Pitṛs* Rāma who had devotion into the *Pitṛs* duly offered the ball of rice.

Thereupon, all the *Pitṛs* beginning with Jamadagni came from the *Pitṛloka* and accepted the reverent worship performed by him.

Delighted in their minds they approached the delighter of the members of the family of Bhṛgu (i.e. Paraśurāma). All those *Pitrs* remained invisible in the sky and addressed him :

The Pitṛs said :

23b-26a. "O heroic one, a great deed has been accomplished by you which is difficult for others to do. You have duly and very well propitiated us. But still you have not given us everlasting pleasure; since it was after massacred Kṣatriyas that you have achieved your aim.

Due to the potentiality of this holy centre as well as to your own devotion, we have been met by you and worshipped. But we have not enjoyed everlasting benefits.

26b-28. Hence, for the sake of destroying the sin of slaughter of heroes as well as other sins you should perform the due expiatory rites and perpetual Dharma. Henceforth, desist from killing the Kṣatriyas.

They are not directly responsible for the offence against your father since the universe is not uncontrolled. It was on account of that, that the murder of your father was committed formerly.

29. Who is competent to kill whom ? Who is competent to save whom in this world ? In these two affairs everyone can at best be the instrumental cause alone in regard to everyone else.

30-31. Certainly every one acts in accordance with his previous Karman. There is no doubt in this regard that the people became powerful befitting the proper time.

Without (the intercession) of the fate, no living being on the Earth is capable of oppressing other living beings, dear one, because every one does his own action in accordance with his ability.

32. Hence, give up your furious anger towards the Kṣatriyas. With a desire to do what is pleasing to us, regain quietism (restraint of passions). That indeed is our great strength. Welfare unto you".

Vasiṣṭha said:—

33. After telling this to Bhārgava all the *Pitṛs* vanished. He too respectfully accepted their proposals.

34. Accompanied by Akṛtavraṇa, Rāma joyfully went from that place to Siddhavanāśrama.

35. After staying there along with the Brāhmaṇas, O king, the noble-minded most excellent scion of the family of Bhṛgu, resolved to perform penance.

36. He sent off Sahasāha along with his chariot, the bows and other necessary requisites after making him agree to come again (if and when necessary).

37-38. Going all over the world, he took holy plunges in all pilgrim-spots and performed the worship of *Pitṛs*, Devas and others.

In this manner, O leading king, the delighter of the family of Bhṛgu went round the Earth three times, following the popular convention.

39. Then once again, O king, he went to Mahendra, the excellent mountain in order to perform penance. He was surrounded by the Brāhmanas then.

40. Conversant with Dharma, he made there a permanent abode for himself, O king, as it was a place inhabited by Sages and Siddhas.

41. Sages living in all the holy centres, the expounders of the Brahman with perfect Self-Control, came there desirous of seeing him as he performed penance.

42. Those groups of sages saw him with his mind attached to austerities like a fire that had become calm after burning down a forest of dead trees in the form of Kṣatriya completely.

43. On seeing those divine sages full of the power of penance come, Bhārgava honoured and welcomed them by means of conventional requisites such as *Arghya* etc.

44. After enquiries about their mutual welfare (they themselves) engaged in fascinating stories and anecdotes that were meritorious and leading to great advancement and prosperity.

45. Then, with the approval of these sages of purified souls, he began preparations for performing a horse-sacrifice,[1] the greatest of all sacrifices.

46-47. He collected the necessary requisites (for the sacrifice). He was accompanied by (sages like) Aurva, Viśvāmitra, Bharadvāja, Mārkaṇḍeya and others. With their approval, he made Kāśyapa as his preceptor and performed the great sacrifice called horse-sacrifice, O king.

48. In that sacrifice of Rāma who had realized the Ātman, the Adhvaryu was Kāśyapa, the Udgātṛ was the sage Gautama and the Hotṛ was Viśvāmitra.

49-52a. The great sage Mārkaṇḍeya did the work of Brahmā. Bharadvāja, Agniveśya and other sages who had thoroughly mastered the Vedas and the Vedāṅgas performed other rites in their due order.

Accompanied by his sons, disciples and disciples of his disciples and assisted by other sages, O king, the holy Bhṛgu performed the work of *Sadasya* (i.e. *Sadasaspati*, the President of the sacrificial assembly).

The leading scion of the family of Bhṛgu (i.e. Paraśurāma) concluded all rites along with these sages and duly worshipped Brahmā along with his preceptor.

52b-54. A beautiful girl was duly adorned with ornaments to represent the Earth. The leading member of the

---

1. One is surprised to find how Paraśurāma who was never anointed as a king nor was married at any time became eligible to perform Aśvamedha. For Āpastamba (XX.1.1) and Lāṭyāyana (IX.10.17) Śrauta Sūtras have specifically prescribed this for a crowned king. Out of the four queens required of a king, one must be a crowned queen (Lāṭyāyana Śrauta Sūtra IX.10.1-2).

The wives of the kings are to go round the horse when killed. The crowned queen is to unite with the dead horse under the cover of a mantle (*Āpastmba* XXII. 11.3-4). Was this Aśvamedha episode introduced to explain why Paraśurāma gave all the conquered Land to Kaśyapa ?

family of Bhṛgu invoked the Earth consisting of hundreds of cities and villages, having oceans for its garments and garlands, and including mountains, forests and parks and granted the same to Kāśyapa except the excellent mountain (Mahendra). Rāma reserved it for his own residence thereafter, O leading king.

55-56. He worshipped Kāśyapa in accordance with the injunctions of the sacred texts, by means of gold, gems, jewels, garments, horses, elephants, food and other things. He concluded the sacrifice (*Yajña*). At the end of the *Yajña* he had his ceremonial bath called *Avabhṛtha*. Then with the sage's permission, he performed the rite of Abandonment of wealth (by distribution of monetary gifts).

57. After giving the promise of freedom from fear to all living beings, the delighter of the family of Bhṛgu began to perform penance there itself on the excellent mountain.

58. All the sages of praiseworthy holy rites who had acted as *Sadasyas* (members of the sacrificial assembly) and sacrificial priests (*Ṛtviks*) took leave of him and returned the way they had come.

59. After they had gone, the holy lord (Rāma) began the performance of a great penance and lived happily there itself in the company of Akṛtavraṇa.

60-61. The Earth belonging to Kāśyapa and having many rulers over it performed the holy observance called *Dīpapratiṣṭhā* (Establishment of lamps)., with the permission of Mārīca (i.e. Kāśyapa) for the suppression of all miseries. The rite had been recounted by Viṣṇu himself. *Dharaṇī* (The Earth-goddess) became perfectly rid of all miseries.

62. Thus the appearance of the son of Jamadagni has been narrated. On hearing this story, a man is rid of all sins.

63. In the course of the story, the prowess of Kārttavīrya whose splendour had become renowned in the world, had been duly narrated without being too brief or too prolix.

64. That king Kārttavīrya had such great potentiality and influence on the Earth that there will never be a man like him in future. A man like him has never been heard of in the past.

65. Since he had formerly solicited from Dattātreya the boon of death at the hands of *Uttamapuruṣa* (Lord Viṣṇu or an excellent person), he attained salvation on being killed in battle by Rāma.

66. His fifth son who had been well-known by the name Jayadhvaja, O king, had a powerful son named Tālajaṅgha.

67. He had a hundred sons who were excellent archers. They were known as 'Tālajaṅghas'. The eldest among them was vītihotra.

68. The senior Tālajaṅgha lived for a long time in the middle of Himalayan forests along with his sons Vītihotra and others as well as Haihaya and other kings.

69. Formerly, when he was fleeing, Tālajaṅgha was hit on his back by an arrow of Rāma. With an excruciating pain he fell senseless on the ground.

70. By chance, Vītihotra who was also fleeing saw him. Taking him in his chariot, he fled speedily.

71. All of them lived on the Himalayas, afflicted by great fear. They had a lot of sufferings and they had only greens, roots and fruits for food.

72. Thereafter, when Rāma calmed down with his mind engrossed in penances, Tālajaṅgha along with his sons regained his kingdom.[1]

73. The excellent king, the suppressor of his enemies, established the city once again as before, stayed there and protected his own kingdom.

74. Recollecting the previous enmity, O great king, Tālajaṅgha attacked your city along with his sons, followers and armies.

75. Accompanied by his army consisting of four units, that king approached the city of Ayodhyā, making the Earth tremble as it were and yelled loudly.

---

1. The rise of the power of Haihayas (Tālajaṅghas) after the retirement of Paraśurāma from active life, shows the temporary effect of Paraśurāma's conquests. Tālajaṅghas not only recovered their kingdom but establishing their dominance on the Indo-gangetic plain, they drove out the ruler of Ayodhyā who, due to blood relation with Jamadagni, was an ally of Paraśurāma.

76. Your father, even though of futile authority, came out of the city. Although he was very old, he fought like a young man with all those kings.

77-78. Though the old king killed many elephants, horses and soldiers, and destroyed many chariots, he was defeated by his enemies. Hence he decided to flee.

Abandoning his city and kingdom along with the treasury, army and vehicles, he entered the forest accompanied by your mother who was pregnant.

79-80. He was staying on the outskirts of the hermitage of Aurva. He had been weighed down by old age and was overwhelmed with grief and fury. He was looked at helplessly by your mother with her throat choked with tears. Thus like a helpless person, O leading king, he passed away to the heavenly world from this world.

81. Your mother, O king, was full of misery and grief. Weeping and crying she placed the corpse of her husband on the funeral pyre.

82. She had become emaciated due to starvation and other miseries, over and above it, she was now agitated over the demise of her husband. Hence, she firmly resolved to immolate herself and to enter into the funeral.

83. On hearing about all these, Aurva, the great sage, himself came out of the hermitage. Restraining her from self-immolation he said thus :—

84. "You must not die now, O queen. There lies in your womb a son who will be the most excellent one among all Emperors".

85-86. On hearing these words of his, your mother of great fortitude, abstained from death. The sage took her to his hermitage. Desirous of seeing your lotus-like face, she curbed her miseries and stayed comfortably within the bounds of his hermitage. At the proper time, she gave birth to you in the hermitage of Aurva.

87. That sage performed all the post-natal holy rites for you. You have been brought up in the hermitage of Aurva. He took pity on you.

88-89. The story beyond this is already known to you. O suppressor of enemies.

King Kārttavīrya of such potentiality and power ruled over this Earth. Due to the power of observance of this holy vow, he became famous in all the worlds. Your father was defeated by his descendants and he fled to the forest.

90. All details connected with him have been recounted to you by me.

This holy rite too which is the most excellent one among all holy rites, has been fully recounted to you.

91-92. This holy rite has been recounted along with its Mantras and Tantras. It yields the benefit of all the worlds. To a person who performs this holy rite, O king, there is no desire among the fourfold aims of a man that is difficult of accomplishment in all the three worlds.

The holy rite of king Haihaya and the story of sage Jāmadagnya has been succinctly recounted by me. What else shall I tell you ?"

Jaimini said :

93-94. "Thereupon, king Sagara said to the sage with palms joined in reverence—"O holy lord, I wish to perform this holy rite. Instruct me well in this connection and grant me permission for undertaking the same.

95-97a. By means of this holy rite, O Brahmanical sage, I shall undoubtedly be blessed."

On being requested thus by the king, the great sage said "So be it". He initiated the king along the path mentioned in scriptural texts.

On being initiated by Vasiṣṭha, Sagara, the excellent king, gathered together all the materials and duly performed the splendid holy rite.

97b-100. Following those injunctions, the king worshipped the lord of the Universe. Getting the permission of the preceptor, he concluded the same in a befitting manner.

The king of great intellect then took the vow—"I shall perform this excellent holy rite strenuously for the whole of my life."

After taking leave of the king and making him return when he followed, the holy sage Vasiṣṭha went back to his hermitage.

CHAPTER FORTYEIGHT

Sagara keeps his vow

Jaimini said :

1. After the departure of that excellent sage, Sagara the best of the kings, resided in Ayodhyā and ruled over the earth.

2. He was equipped with all types of wealth and assets. He was conversant with the principles of *Dharma* and *Artha* (politics and economics). He was a boy only in years but in his activities he earned the appreciation of all elderly persons.

3. But he was always dejected in his heart. He neither took food during the day nor did he sleep during the night. Recollecting something, he used to heave deep hot sighs.

4. On hearing that his kingdom had been annexed by the enemies after vanquishing his father, that he had fled to the dense forest along with his (king Sagara's) mother and that he had passed away in the same forest, the king became grief-stricken. Habitually, true to his promise, he angrily took the vow of exterminating the entire race of his enemies. A king belonging to the family of Ikṣvāku is unable to bear the fire of discomfiture.

5. Once, the king, having celebrated a solemn ceremony, resolved to defeat his enemy and to conquer all the quarters in due order.

6. Surrounded on all sides by many thousands of chariots and elephants, horses, chariots,* and foot-soldiers, the king set out from his excellent city.

*Repeated in the SK. Text.

7. In order to destroy his enemies he started with his combined force consisting of six *Aṅgas*[1] (Parts, Units), which appeared like the ocean that is agitated due to different kinds of animals and series of waves, on account of the galloping horses; he appeared to be moving along with the entire world consisting of the groups of *Kulagiris*[2] on account of the herds of elephants in rut; he appeared to be moving along with the firmament brightened by the good (i.e. white) rays of the moon, on account of the stream of white umbrellas and banners (of the army on march).

8. As the king proceeded ahead in his campaign, the low lying areas (depressions) of the earth were filled up with the dust particles of the mountain ranges pounded by the feet of the armies of the front ranks. The ground thus raised there, always became a fence like hedge, due to the dust particles raised severally by the armies consisting of the four units.

9. He killed many haughty warriors confronting the arrays of elephants, horses, and chariots. He wore the splendour of the moon-crested lord (Śiva) who killed the armies of the hordes of Asuras; during the periods of encircling and attacking the cities of the enemies, he used to proclaim from a distance, the duties (of the enemy soldiers) in the case of defeat and mortification; he used to give them sufficient time to move away quickly and he used to assure them of no harm or loss to their lives (he made them confident of the safety to their lives).

10-13a. The king was desirous of conquering the quarters (the entire world). That king whose realm he attacked, immediately bowed down to him. After defeating all the kings he made them followers of his footsteps. He let some go on some conditions indicated and returned their kingdom to them.

---

1. The six units of the army are : four usual units of elephants, chariots, cavalry and infantry as well as the unit in charge of food for animals and human beings and the unit in charge of entertainment such as dancing girls, musicians, those who play on instruments etc.)

2. Seven principal mountains such as Mahendra, Malaya, Sahyādri and others.

Thus, he went to various directions. When he went to the South, he remembered the previous enmity and marched against the Haihayas.

13b-14a. A great battle causing hairs to stand on ends, took place between him and the Haihaya kings who had full complement of chariots and elephants and who were great warriors.

14b-17a. In that great battle, the powerful and infuriated lord of the Kosalas killed thousands of kings and their armies.

The king who wanted to put an end to the enmity (by taking revenge) defeated the Haihaya kings, shattered and burnt their city and entirely reduced it to ruins.

Sweeping the whole of the land and crushing it down with his entire army, he reduced the kingdom of the Haihayas to dust.

17b-18a. Leaving off the city and the kingdom those kings who survived fled everywhere with all their riches and glory gone, and their lustre faded.

18b-19a. The king rushed against those fleeing kings and killed them along with their followers like the frantic, infuriated god of death killing the subjects.

19b. Sagara whose anger had been roused and who slew his enemies in battle discharged against them the extremely terrible Bhārgava[1] missile that struck terror among the enemies.

20. The kings were rendered helpless with their bodies being burned by the flames of the Bhārgava missile which was discharged by him. The missile which was extremely terrific and which made the three worlds frightened shone brilliantly. Immediately they were rendered blind by the darkness due to the columns of smoke made to whirl round by the Vāyu missile (one whose deity is the wind god). They wandered here and

1. As Sagara received his military training under Aurva and had no contact with Paraśurāma, this Bhārgava missile might be the fire-missile developed by Aurva who was advised by his *pitṛs* not to finalise it.

there and rolled about on the ground where for a short while their limbs were hidden beneath a great deal of dust particles.

21. The movement of the kings was hindered by the brilliant glow of the Āgneya missile. They could not see their way around. They became separated from one another belonging to their group. They became helpless in their bodies. Their minds became agitated and confused. They were frightened. They abandoned their clothes, weapons, coats of mail, ornaments etc. With their hairs let loose and dishevelled, they exhibited various caprices of insane persons in front of their enemies.

22. After defeating all the Haihayas in battle, Sagara the powerful King, had the features of an agitated ocean. He moved against the Kāmbojas.

23. Kāmbojas,[1] Tālajaṅghas, Śakas, Yavanas, Kirātas and others—his enemies who had offended him formerly, became utterly confounded as they lost courage on hearing the sounds of the wardrums and various other musical instruments (of Sagara's army). They immediately abandoned their kingdoms, armies, cities and ladies of their harems. They wandered here and there to various directions due to their fear (of a fresh discharge) of his arrows and missiles.

24. The enemies of that king were frightened. Their vision became blinded by the flames of the fire of his valour. They abandoned their homes, realms etc. along with their sons and others. Being attacked and chased by the armies of their enemies, they fled to the forest region where also they were stunned and stupefied by another enemy who got up from his sleep in the caves of the mountain.

25. After exterminating the Tālajaṅghas along with their armies and vehicles, that king, the suppressor of enemies, gradually destroyed their kingdom.

1. Kāmbojas were a people in northern Afghanistan. The Shiaposh tribe which now resides on the Hindukush is said to have been descendants of ancient Kambojas—(*De* 87). Kāmbojas, Śakas, Yavanas were people in the north-west Frontier. But they are blubbed together with Kirātas (tribe from North-eastern India, Tipārā, Sikkim (West) and Eastern Nepal and Tālajaṅghas from the Narmadā valley.

26. Extremely infuriated he slew many of the Yavanas, Kāmbojas, Kirātas and others as well as Palhavas[1] and Pāradas.

27. On being struck down by him in battle, those kings became frightened. Those who survived the slaughter fled all round in groups.

28. "I am the son of that king whose kingdom was taken away by many of you. I am desirous of wreaking revenge. I have come here purposely as I have taken a vow of killing you all forcibly." Thus the king Sagara who had the virility of elephants and the splendour destructive of Kṣatriya heroes, made his enemy kings hear his life story. He thus reminded the other kings (of his previous history).

29-30. On seeing that the excellent king had taken the vow of annihilating the races of all his enemies, seven of the enemies of the excellent king, viz. Pāradas, Palhavas and others who were born of royal families and who were very famous, became frightened. In order to save their own lives they sought refuge in Vasiṣṭha the family preceptor of the Ikṣvākus along with their womenfolk and children.

31. "Be our refuge, O Brāhmaṇa. We are distressed and we desire freedom from fear. Our bodies are being burnt by the fire of Sagara's missiles. We are about to die.

32. Determined in wreaking vengeance, he kills all of us without exception. We are desirous of preserving our lives by coming out of that danger.

33. Our kingdoms have been split. Our pleasures and prosperity have been ruined. Our wives, children and relatives have been separated from us. It is only for saving our life that we are seeking refuge in you.

34. There is no other person in the world who, by friendly persuasion or by the application of force, can turn him back and protect us from this great danger.

---

1. The Purāṇa distinguishes between Palhavas and Pāradas. Pāradas were Parthians (probably Pṛthus in ṚV). But De opines that Pāradas dwelt in northern Beluchistan (*De* 148) Palhavas were a tribe in Media (Mada)—a part of the Parthian (ancient Persian) empire. Their country was famous for horses (De. 143)

35. You had been chosen as the family preceptor of the kings born of the solar race by the kings, his predecessors in the family. Your power and influence is such.

36. Therefore, restrained by the respect for the greatness of his preceptor, he shall not transgress your behest like the great ocean that does not trespass the boundary of the sea-shore.

37. O holy lord, you are our friend, father and mother, You are preceptor of all the people. Hence, O highly fortunate one, it behoves you to save us from this difficult situation".

Jaimini said :

38. On hearing these words of theirs, the holy lordly saint Vasiṣṭha slowly surveyed those who sought refuge in him.

39. On seeing those persons who were born of royal families, who had survived the general massacre and most of whom were old men, women and children the holy lord who was merciful towards all living beings, became distressed.

40. After looking at them with due honour, and mentally pondering for a long time, the highly intelligent sage revived their lives with the slowly uttered words—"Do not be afraid".

41. The highly fortunate one, indued with great sympathy, spoke to them kindly and made those persons who sought their lives to agree to the conditions of the king.

42. In order to fulfil the vow of the king, Vasiṣṭha stipulated the condition that those persons who had been burned by the anger of the king should be denied all those holy rites laid down for persons of royal families. He went to the excellent king himself. He pacified him slowly in fitting manner. He then requested him for permission to the surviving enemies to go away for good.

43. Though the king was still angry, he respected the words of his preceptor. Those enemies were compelled to eschew the holy rites laid down for their families as well as their mode of dress. He made them accept rites different from what are laid down in Śrutis and Smṛtis. They were forsaken b t

maṇas. He let off each and everyone of those kings alive but no better than dead.

44. He made the Śakas shave off half of their heads, he made the Palhavas grow moustache (and beard). He made the Yavanas devoid of the moustache. He made the Kāmbojas to retain the chin (i.e. the beard).[1]

45. In this manner he made others also born of royal families, very ugly. They were denied the right of performing the holy rites mentioned in the Vedas. They were forsaken by the Brāhmaṇas.

46-48. After forcing them to accept these stipulations, he left them alive. Those enemies abandoned their characteristic features and mode of conduct. They became outcastes. They were censured by the people of all castes. All of them were slighted and insulted. They became ruthless, shameless Mleccha barbarian tribes. They roamed about in the world in groups.

49. Released by that king these Śakas, Yavanas, Kirātas and others, immediately abandoned their modes of dress and conduct of life. Their only resorts were mountains, forests, caves and such other places. Even today they are censured by good people. These tribes maintain themselves by evil activities and wicked pursuits. But they keep up the vow of the king and prevent it from being broken."

CHAPTER FORTYNINE

Conquest of the World by Sagara

Jaimini said:

1. "Then taking permission of Vasiṣṭha, the excellent sage, Sagara accompanied by a great army, marched against the Vidarbhas.

---

1. These were probably the fashions of hairstyles among those tribes which are attributed to king Sagara's orders of punishment.

2. Then with great pleasure the king of the Vidarbhas offered to him his daughter whose name was Keśinī. She was unparalleled in beauty etc., and therefore was suitable to him in every respect.

3. In an auspicious hour, that ruler of the earth, a tiger among kings duly took the hand of Keśinī, in marriage, with the fire god as witness.

4. Honoured extremely well by the king of Vidarbhas, he stayed in his palace for a few days and taking leave of him, he set off from that place.

5. (He set off from that place) on being permitted by him. Then he was welcomed by the Pāribarhas. Coming out of their city, the king approached the Śūrasenas.

6. Then he was honoured by the Yādavas, his maternal uncles. After being propitiated by them with plenty of wealth, he started from Madhurā (Pkt. form of Mathurā).

7. Thus by conquering the whole of the earth he made all the kings his vassals (literally. "moving at his hint") paying revenues and tributes.

8. Thereafter, he permitted the kings to go back to their kingdoms along with their armies. The king then allowed his followers to return.

9. Accompanied by a great army and his royal retinue and camp-followers, he reached his kingdom slowly without afflicting the realms in between.

10. He was honoured by the people of the villages and outlying districts with many gifts and presents. Then, he quickly reached Ayodhyā.

11. On coming to know about his arrival, the citizens became enthusiastic over the great festivities and therefore adorned the city.

12-16. The entire city prepared itself for a great festival. The surface of the ground was sprinkled with water and swept clean. It had hundreds of pots filled with water (signifying auspiciousness). Hundreds of tall flagstaffs were raised. The city was decorated with banners and emblems, fumes of agallochum spread everywhere. The city became bright and resplendent with many flowers of different colours. It was embellished with gem-studded ornamental gateways, lofty towngates, tall minarets and palaces. Its highways were beautified by means of showers of flowers and fried rice. Every house in the city was prepared for the great festivity. The city had rows of houses where all the deities presiding over the sites of buildings had been worshipped. It was rendered beautiful all round by the delighted citizens and villagers eager to see the king who had conquered all the quarters.

17-20. Then the ministers, counsellors as well as the residents of the harem came there, surrounded by groups of courtezans and ladies of the city. All the citizens assembled there. The king met them and receive d honour, welcome and blessings from them. There were a lot of deafening cheers of 'Victory' reverberating in all the quarters. The sweet sounds of different kinds of musical instruments got mixed with them. The king loudly greeted them. Accompanied by those joyous people and delighting his subjects, he entered the excellent city.

21-24. He was greeted and lovingly honoured by the Brāhmaṇas through sweet chants of the Vedic Mantras. He was warmly and highly eulogised by heralds, bards and panegyrists.

The residents of the outlying districts and countries uttered cries of Victory all round. The songsters and musicians began singing to the accompaniment of the sweet notes of the *Viṇās* (lutes) and *Veṇus* (flutes) as well as the sound produced by beating the time. The harlots followed him dancing. A graceful white umbrella was spread over him. Showers of fried rice and flowers greeted him allround. Thus he entered the city of Ayodhyā like Indra entering his city.

25. Through a path that was *Dṛṣṭipūta* (i.e. protected from impurity by sight by disallowing people of wicked vision and keeping it spotlessly clean), that was rendered fragrant through scents and that was traversed first by the Brāhmaṇas, he walked upto a magnificently decorated mansion in the middle of the city.

26. Accompanied by both of his wives, he got down from the vehicle and joyously entered the house of his mother, where the people were delighted and well nourished.

27. With humility, he approached his mother who was seated in a couch. Touching her feet with his head, he made obeisance to her.

28. After congratulating him with blessings in words choked with delight, she got up with great excitement and embraced her son.

29. With great pleasure, she blessed and congratulated both the daughters-in-law. The king honoured her with many a narrative and stayed there for a long time.

30-32. Then, after being permitted by her, he set out trom her abode. Thereafter, accompanied by his followers, and fanned with white chowries, the glorious king slowly entered the assembly-hall like the king of the Suras. After entering the highly splendid assembly-hall resorted to by many kings, he bowed down to all elderly persons. He was blessed by them. Then the lord of men sat on a magnificent and splendid throne.

33-34a. He was attended upon by his vassal kings, the rulers of the various outlying territories. Recounting various tales the excellent king stayed there delightedly along with his kinsmen.

34b-35a. By conquering the territories of the various quarters, he kept up his vow. Thereupon, the liberal-minded king duly maintained the three *Arthas* (the three aims of worldly life viz. wealth, love and righteousness).

35b-38a. He conquered his enemies by means of his own prowess. He became the overlord of all the quarters. Like Viṣṇu, he ruled over the earth under his single Royal umbrella. He fulfilled duly the vow that he had made on being infuriated by the discomfiture of his deceased father. After vanquishing all his enemies, he protected the earth consisting of seven continents, seven oceans, many cities and villages and rows and rows of houses.

38b-39a. As time passed on thus, Vasiṣṭha, the lordly sage came there desirous of seeing the king once again.

39b-40a. On seeing the excellent sage come, the king got up excited. Accompanied by those vassal kings and with the materials of worship in his hands, he greeted the sage.

40b-41a. The highly intelligent king, fully endued with devotion to his preceptor, worshipped the sage duly with articles of worship, water for washing feet (*Arghya*, *Pādya*) and other things and bowed down to him.

41b-44a. After blessing Sagara, Vasiṣṭha said—"Be seated". The king sat in his excellent golden seat alongwith all those vassal kings and his wives, after being permitted by the sage. Āpava Vasiṣṭha slowly uttered these gentle words to the excellent king who seated near him, even as the other kings were listening.

Vasiṣṭha said :

44b-49a. —"O king, I hope that your kingdom is well-secured internally and externally; that your ministers and groups of counsellors and the people in the entire kingdom are quite well. Fortunately all the enemies along with their entire armies and vehicles have been conquered by you without much effort, in your battles. Having taken a pledge but respecting my words, you made the enemies cast off their old rites and let them go alive. I heard that after defeating them you went, alongwith your vehicles and armies with a desire for the conquest of the quarters, in order to vanquish others. Having heard now that you have once again conquered the quarters and come back to the city, O excellent king, I have now come to see you out of love."

Jaimini said :

49b-50a. On being told thus by Vasiṣṭha, Sagara, the conqueror of Tālajaṅgha, replied to the great sage with palms joined in reverence.

Sagara said :

50b-56a. "Indeed we are quite well in every respect, O great sage. There is no doubt about it. All the deities are always favourable to us, O sage. How can miseries and calamities befall me since your holiness always mentally wishes for my welfare.

I have been blessed by your holiness. I have been made delighted with all my task fulfilled since, O preceptor, you yourself have come here to see me. Since you have mentioned my conquest over the enemies and similar things, let me say that it has been carried out entirely due to your blessings.

I think that everything is obtained by the kings due to your favour. Otherwise, what power do I have to kill enemies of such types.

Even my little effort and endeavour is rendered big by you.

Even a small quantity of fruits gives pleasure to the person who planted the tree."

Jaimini said :

56b-57a. Honoured thus very well by Sagara, Vasiṣṭha, the great sage, took leave of him once again and went to his hermitage.

57b-58a. After Vasiṣṭha, had gone back, king Sagara, lived in Ayodhyā with great delight in his mind and ruled over the entire world.

58b-59a. He had two wives endowed with beauty, nice behaviour and good qualities. With them he enjoyed worldly pleasures conducive to his happiness, in a manner befitting his desire.

59b-61a. The two wives named Sumati and Keśinī were equally beautiful with blooming lotus-like faces. They were endowed with beauty, liberal-mindedness and various other good qualities. Their breasts were plump and round. They had bluish curly tresses and they were adorned with all types of ornaments. They were richly endowed with all good characteristic features. They were in their prime of youth. They were very dear to him. They were always near him. They were always engaged in what is pleasing to him and what is conducive to his welfare.

61b-64a. They always captivated his mind by means of their good conduct and graceful activities.

Delighted in his mind as the administration reached the pinnacle of perfection, the king sported with them as he desired and lived in the city.

The appellation *'Rājā'* (one who delights and pleases) did not suit other kings based on their qualities but it fitted well with the noble-minded Sagara.

64b-66. Even a small quantity of *Dharma* becomes large, but to that king wealth and love did not become large in that manner (?). He was not greedy in his mind. Hence, he enjoyed wealth without affecting Dharma adversely. For the same purpose, O leading king, he enjoyed love without affecting the other two (i.e. wealth and Dharma).

CHAPTER FIFTY

Sagara's Visit to Aurva's Hermitage

Jaimini continued :

1. "Thus that king duly protected the earth consisting of seven continents very well, like another Dharma (God of Righteousness).

2. He duly established the Brāhmaṇas and other castes in their respective duties separately. He protected them without getting his sense-organs affected adversely.

3. The subjects belonging to all the different castes behaved with due deference to the most excellent among them (the less distinguished among them followed and obeyed the more distinguished ones). The castes followed the due order of seniority and excellence. They enjoyed the objects of pleasures in due order.

4. When that king was ruling, death never approached a young child while an old man was alive. This was true of all castes.

5. Then the entire nation flourished with all hindrances removed. There were many outlying countries and districts fully inhabited by the people of the four castes.

6. While that king reigned, the whole realm consisted of many hundreds of houses and villages divided into various zones and had many residential apartments.

7. At that time no Brāhmaṇa on the earth was *Anāśramin* (one who does not follow the rigorous disciplines of the four stages in life). All the enterprises of all the subjects became fruitful.

8. Men began only those activities which befitted them. Then the activities of the men were in consonance with the four aims of men in life (i.e. virtue, wealth, love and salvation).

9. People inhabiting the groups of cities and villages were always engaged in great festivities. They were endowed with devotion and loyalty to the king as well as were desirous of the welfare of one another.

10. No one among the subjects was despicable, accursed, impoverished, sickly, greedy or miserly.

11. People were delighted with other's merits. They were eager to have contacts with good people. They bowed down to elderly people and always indulged in learning good things.

12. They were afraid of slanderous remarks of others. They were always delighted in the amorous sports with only their own wives. By nature they desisted from associating with wicked people. They adhered to righteous activities.

13. When that Kṣatriya king was governing the subjects and the earth acquired by his own valour, the people everywhere were theists (or believers in Vedas).

14-15. When that mighty king was ruling over the realms, O highly fortunate one, the seasons had the regular normal timings. The whole of the earth yielded plenty of paddy and other plants.

16. His assembly-hall brilliantly illuminated by plenty of gems and jewels shone like that of Śakra (Indra) in heaven. As Indra's assembly was occupied by the Devas on seats decorated with precious stones, so his hall was occupied by hundreds of kings and the overlords of eighteen *Maṇḍalas* (zones or political divisions). They used to visit him in order

to serve him. They were well-renowned on account of their excessive valour and exploits. Those coronated kings were seated separately in seats studded with gems.

17. His vassal kings occupying different territories used to visit him with presents. During those occasions, they used to keep the camps of their armies all round the city separately. They were desirous of seeing the king along with their sons. But frequently they had to send the information through the gatekeepers to the king, as he tarried in the harem for a long time.

18. Due to excessive friction of the series of crowns of kings who were bowing at his feet, the feet of that king appeared to have got scarred thereby.

19. His assembly hall shone like the cave of Sumeru, due to the precious gems and jewels scattered all round, by the groups of leading kings who had to attend on him.

20. Thus righteously ruled that king, the crest-jewel of the solar race, the suppressor of his enemies. He ruled over the earth with no one else to rule it (except king Sagara).

21. Though king Sagara protected the earth thus, he never had the pleasure that usually results on looking at one's own son.

22-25. Without that pleasure he was extremely distressed and many times he began to ponder. "Alas, I am devoid of a son. Certainly, on account of this, our forefathers in this family will face the loss of their balls of rice. When a good son is born, it is said, the forefathers delightedly hasten to his house even from the hell, because they are enthusiastic over the post-natal holy rites.

A man may reach heaven, due to a great deal of religious merits. Even then, if he has no son, the immortal beings in the heaven, do not keep the gates of heaven open to him.

When a good son is born, the father wins both the worlds (i.e. attains pleasure in this world and in the next) and his grandfathers in both the families attain heavenly world.

26-29. I will not attain that good which belongs to those blessed with sons. Due to the fact that I am issueless, certainly that goal is extremely inaccessible to me.

My prosperous and undivided kingdom is, it is said, not at all different from Indra's realm. Since I have no religious merit even that kingdom is of no benefit to me.

This throne occupied by my ancestors as well as this kingdom will become subservient to others on account of the fact that I am issueless.

30a. Hence, I shall go to the hermitage of Aurva accompanied by both of my wives. I shall propitiate that leading sage for obtaining a son.

30b-33a. I shall go there and intimate to that noble-souled sage the fact that I have no issue. Undoubtedly, I will carry out whatever he says."

After thinking like this, O king, the excellent king Sagara, who was aware of his duties, decided to go to the hermitage of Aurva.

After entrusting the excellent minister with the charge of administration of the kingdom, he joyously went to the forest riding his chariot, accompanied by both of his wives.

33b-35. He proceeded ahead and due to the rumbling-sound of the chariot he was observed with motionless eyes by the peacocks on either side of the pathway (i.e. the peacocks thought, on hearing the rumbling sound of the chariot, that it was the rumbling sound of the cloud). O king, he pointed out to his wives the deer that stood motionless for a moment, lifted up their faces, and then got ready to run away. He became delighted on seeing the trees richly laden with flowers and fruits.

36. The king entered the penance-grove. All around it consisted of many trees where the blossoms had not faded, the fruits of which were tasty, that had a grassy grounds all round and which had plenty of tender sprouts and cool shades.

37. All around, in every quarter, the cuckoos cooed loudly and sweetly, as their throats became clear due to their having tasted the tender sprouts at the tips of the mango trees.

38. It was endowed with the flowers of all the seasons. It was embellished by the hovering bees. It contained many

trees round which turned the creepers, stooping down with bunches of flowers.

39. It was covered with hundreds of trees occupied by herds of monkeys. It contained multitudes of chirping birds such as the extremely delighted peacocks, *Sāraṅga* birds and others.

40. It was very fascinating, due to the songs of singing Vidyādhara maidens. It had many sylvan caves where couples of Kinnaras used to wander about, making them shine brilliantly.

41. It was surrounded by lakes, the banks of which were occupied by many birds of sweet notes, such as the swan, the ruddy goose, the parrots, the *Kāraṇḍavas* (a sort of duck) and the *Sārasas* (a variety of crane).

42. The quarters were filled with gentle breezes wafting slowly over the lakes abounding in lotuses and lilies of various sorts.

43. Proceeding ahead thus in his chariot along the penance grove that had the qualities described above, the king attained the greatest delight.

44. Having reached the precincts of the hermitage, his mind attained calmness. The glorious king then got down accompanied by his wives.

45. "Let the horses rest"—so said the king to the charioteer. Then he came to the outskirts of the hermitage of the great sage of sanctified soul.

46. From the disciples of the sage, he heard that the sage had concluded his daily routine of holy rites. In order to see the sage, he then entered the hermitage with an humble attitude.

47. Accompanied by his wives, the king delightfully bowed down his head to the great sage seated in the middle of the sages and accompanied by groups of ascetics.

48. Sage Aurva of great power and potentiality, directed the king who bowed down to him along with them (i.e. the two queens) to take his seat saying lovingly—"Sit down".

49. After honouring him very well by means of *Arghya*, *Pādya* etc. the great sage pleased him along with his wives by

according him a hospitable reception befitting the sylvan environment [i.e. with the products of the forest such as roots, fruits and the like].

50. After the hospitable reception, the king took rest for a while. Thereupon, he bowed to him and sat in front of him. Aurva then addressed the following gentle words to the king.

51. "I hope that your kingdom is all right externally and internally. I hope that you protect all your subjects righteously.

52. I hope that you yearn properly to win over the *trivarga* (three aims in life viz. *Dharma*, *Artha* and *Kāma*) by means of proper expedients. I hope all the expedients in politic (such as alliance, war, diplomacy and others) are well practised by you and they yield proper results to you.

53. Fortunately, O excellent king, all the enemies have been conquered by you. How glad I am that the entire kingdom is righteously protected by you.

54. There is no loss or destruction to those who strictly abide by Dharma. Does not Dharma save that person by whom it has been kept up and sustained ?

55. I have already heard that you have arrived at your capital along with your army after conquering the whole of the earth and that you have married.

56-58. The proper protection of the subjects is the most excellent duty of kings. They become happy here and hereafter only on that account.

Then why, O king, have you abandoned the duty of administration of the kingdom and approached me along with your wives ? Tell me".

Jaimini said :

On being asked thus by the sage, the excellent king Sagara joined his palms in reverence and spoke these sweet words.

CHAPTER FIFTYONE

The Banishment of Asamañjasa

Sagara said :

1. O great sage, there is no doubt in this that I am quite well in every respect, since your holiness, the most excellent among the descendants of Bhṛgu, has solicitude for my peace.

2. How can I, who have been formerly trained in such a manner in wielding missiles and weapons by you, be incapable of restraining all the enemies now?

3. You are my preceptor, friend, and well-wisher, deity and kinsman. Nor do I know anyone else as my father except you.

4. All the kings were defeated by me through the missiles, the use of which has been taught by you. It is the power of your penance, remembering which, all of them had been defeated by me.

5. By means of your penance, you sanctify and protect the entire universe. Undoubtedly you are capable of creating and annihilating it also.

6. The potentiality of your penance is great. It is not common to anyone else. Here, even a part of it, if seen, causes wonder.

7. O holy lord, in your penance-grove, ever since its infancy the fawn, slowly but unhesitatingly approaches the seat of the lion and drinks water.

8. Here, due to full confidence, even a slim delicate hind offers her udder to her young one. The Ruru deer removes the itching sensation of its cheek at the tip of the horns of the black deer.

9. In order to sustain itself, a tigress killed a hind which had recently given birth to its fawn, in another forest. But the same tigress nurtures the young ones of that hind in your penance grove.

10. It is because of your penance that in the outer jungle a lion was chasing a fleeing elephant. But as soon as

they entered this penance grove, they had stopped running. They stand in the same place, afraid of you.

11-12. The mongoose, rats, cats, peacocks, rabbits, serpents, wolves, boars, tigers, the fabulous eight-footed Śarabhas, bears, monkeys, jackals, *Gavayas* (mountain-ox), the cows, the deer and the buffaloes abandon their natural enmity and become friendly.

13. A power of penance like this, striking the world with surprise, is not seen anywhere. O Brāhmaṇa, excepting in your case, it is difficult to be found elsewhere in the world.

14. Due to your blessings, I have conquered this earth, O Brāhmaṇa sage, and have come back to my own realm alongwith my captive enemies.

15. I have all ministers under my control. I have shown sufficient and suitable care and application to the three *Vargas* (viz. virtue, wealth and love). I have protected the kingdom very well along the path advised by you.

16. As I continued my activities thus and stayed on the kingdom, O leading scion of the family of Bhṛgu, there arose in me a desire to see your holiness and that too with a purpose.

17. Will the protection of the Earth alongwith the offerings of balls of rice be restricted to me ? (Will it stop with me ?) Will it be so due to the fact that I have no issue ?

18. This is the excessive misery in my mind and it cannot be remedied. I have approached you, thinking that, in this world there cannot be anyone else who will be able to remove it."

19. On being told thus by Sagara, the holy lord Aurva remained silent for a moment thinking within himself, and spoke these words alongwith his directions.

20. "Observing restraints, you stay on here for sometime along with your wives; thereby you will obtain your desire. No doubt need be entertained about this".

21. The righteous-souled king stayed there along with his wives. He was delighted and endowed with devotion. He was eagerly engaged in serving him (Aurva) for a long time.

22. By means of their humility, good conduct and devotion, the wives of the king accorded great satisfaction to the sage. They were always alert.

23. The great sage was satisfied with their devotion and sincere service. He called the queens and said these words :

24. "O gentle ladies, let any boon be chosen from us; whatever you desire. I shall grant it even if it is very difficult to get. There is no doubt about it".

25. Then both of them bowed down their heads and respectfully spoke to the great sage—"O holy Lord, we desire sons".

26. Then the saint said to them : "Desirous of doing what is pleasing to you both and to the king, this desired boon has been given by me.

27. Due to my blessings, both of you shall be fortunate enough to have sons, certainly. Let these further words of mine also be heard.

28. One of you will bear a single son. He will not be very virtuous. Still he will be alive till the end of Kalpa.

29. The other will give birth to sixty thousand sons. Ere long, all of them will meet with destruction without fulfilling their assigned work.

30. These two boons with such characteristic features have been given to you both. Whatever is desired by either of you, may voluntarily be recounted."

31. When this was spoken by the sage, the daughter of the Vidarbha king chose a son who would perpetuate the line. The other queen chose the other boon of begetting many sons.

32. After granting this boon to king Sagara and honouring him along with his wives in a suitable manner, the great sage sent him off towards the city.

33. Permitted by the sage, the ruler of the Earth who was satisfied because his desire had been fulfilled, got into the chariot along with his beloved ones and went to the city quickly.

34. After entering the beautiful city fully inhabited by delighted and well-nourished people, he stayed there with great joy alongwith the people of the city.

35. At the same time, O king, the two queens intimated to the king with great joy the fact that they had conceived.

36. The foetus of the queens developed day by day like the moon in the bright half of the lunar month, alongwith the wealth of pleasure and contentment of the parents and the citizens.

37. When the time was complete, Keśinī gave birth, in an auspicious hour, to a son of unmeasured lustre and resplendent like the fiery sun-stone.

38. After the due performance of Jātakarman (post-natal holy rite) etc., the king named him Asamañjasa.

39. At that time, Sumati too gave birth to a pot-gourd-like foetus. On seeing it being given birth to, the king wished to throw it away.

40. On coming to know of it, the holy sage Aurva came there as though by chance. Welcomed and honoured perfectly by the king, he hurriedly spoke to him thus.

41. "This foetus in the form of a pot-gourd, O king, should not be thrown away. It does not desrve to be abandoned because it contains the nucleus of your sixty thousand sons.

42. Hence, let it be cut into small pieces and be preserved carefully in pots of ghee covered with lids. The pieces should be kept in separate pots.

43. If this is done properly, O king, you will have sons as are mentioned before, due to my grace. There is no doubt about it.

44. When the time is complete, they will break open the pots and come out separately. Thus, O king, sixty thousand sons will be born unto you".

45. After saying thus, the saintly lord Aurva vanished there.

The King carried out everything in the manner mentioned by Aurva.

46. After a year was completed, children were born every day out of the pots of ghee, after breaking them open one by one.

47. In this manner the sons of the king were born and brought up in groups, O king, making up the total of sixty thousand.

48. They had great strength and valour. They did not perform any rite separately. (They worked collectively in every respect). They were unassailable and ruthless in particular.

49. The king, the most excellent among the intelligent ones, was not very much pleased with them. But he considered the holy son of Keśinī as his beloved son. He honoured him much.

50. The king duly celebrated his marriage. He too delighted his friends by means of his good qualities.

51. A glorious son well-known by the name of Aṁśumān was born to that son of Keśinī.

52. Even in his infancy, he was extremely intelligent. By means of his exalted and noble qualities, he extremely delighted his friends and grand-father.

53. In the meantime that son of the king, Asamañjasa, was possessed by a certain *Piśāca* (ghost). He became devoid of all good pursuits and activities.

54. In his former birth, he was a Vaiśya in the realm of a certain king. He was conversant with Dharma. He possessed plenty of wealth and food-grains.

55. Once, as he was wandering about in the forest, he saw an excellent treasure-trove. Overwhelmed by the habitual greed of a *Vaṇik* (merchant), he bagan to take possession of the same.

56. Then the piśāca who was keeping watch over that treasure-trove approached him and said :—

"I have been hungry for a long time staying here and keeping watch over this treasure-trove.

57. Hence, in order to alleviate it, give me beef and at my behest take away this treasure as you please".

58. He promised the same to him saying—"I shall give you beef". Encouraged by the Piśāca, he took possession of the treasure-trove.

59. On account of his foolishness, he did not give the ghost what had been promised. He did not take note of the

anger of the ghost arising from his failure to give what had been promised, O king.

60. After waiting for a long time with a desire for food, the ghost from whom the wealth had been taken away became distressed due to hunger and died.

61. The Vaiśya attained death at the proper time and was born again as the son and perpetuator of the line of Sagara and Keśinī.

62. Recollecting the previous enmity, the bodiless one assumed the form of wind, O King, and entered the body of the prince.

63-65a. On being possessed by the ghost the prince became cruel-hearted. His mental balance was upset on being forcibly attacked by the ghost. Like a merciless fellow, he began to work havoc in the city without any propriety or justice. The wicked fellow began to kill boys, young men, old men and women. After killing them, the merciless one threw their bodies in the Sarayū.[1]

65b-69. On being harassed by him many times and observing his ignoble activities, the citizens went to the king and appealed to him.

On hearing it, the king was overwhelmed with grief. He called the prince to him and conscientiously forbade him on various occasions. Although he was prevented by that noble-souled father many times, there was no positive result. (All his advices) became like burnt barley grains put in hot water (i.e. became fruitless). When he was not able to make him desist from his sinful activity, the king banished him from his realm because he was afraid of the public outcry".

1. The Piśāca motif is adopted by the author of Bd.P. to justify the changed attitude of prince Asamañjasa. According to Bh.P. IX.8.15.19, prince Asamañjasa was a Yogī who outwardly behaved in a censurable manner (probably as prescribed for Pāśupatas). When banished, he returned all the children hale and hearty to their parents who believed that Asamañjasa killed them.

CHAPTER FIFTYTWO

The Sacrificial Horse is let loose

Jaimini Said :

1. "After banishing his son, the virtuous-souled Lord Sagara transferred his love for him to the child Aṁśumān whose conduct was righteous.

2. At the very same time, O king, the sons of Sumati grew up collectively. All of them were amiable, devoted and faithful to one another.

3. They had adamantine bodies. They were cruel, merciless and shameless. They were habitually evil in their activities. They had the same nature and characteristics.

4. They co-operated in doing simultaneously the same work. They were deluded in their minds. They were easily irritable. They could not be easily assailed by any living being. They regularly harassed the people.

5. They had no concern for humility, good conduct or the path of virtue. They harassed the entire world around as they pleased, like Asuras.

6. Attacked and tormented by them, the whole world became distressed and unhappy in particular with Yajñas and paths of virtue destroyed. The people could not have their regular self-study of the Vedas nor could they perform holy rites by uttering the *Vaṣaṭkāra mantra*.

7. When everything was being completely destroyed by the sons of Sagara who were haughty on account of the boons they had been granted, the Devas, Asuras and the great serpents became extremely agitated.

8. The earth overwhelmed by the ocean began to quake though its name is *Acalā* (immovable). There was a break and hindrance in the penance and abstract meditation of the ascetics.

9. Depr ved of the *Havya* and *Kavya* offerings, the Devas and the Pitṛs became oppressed by great sorrow. They went to the abode of Brahmā.

10. After going there, the Devas with Śarva* (prob. Śakra) at their head, duly reported to him the entire activities of the sons of Sagara.

---

*misprint for Śakra. Vide V. 34 below where Vāsava is mentioned.

11. On hearing their words, Brahmā, the grandfather of the worlds, became engrossed in thought for a short while. The most excellent one among the Suras then said :

12. —"O Devas, listen, attentively to my words. Welfare unto you. There is no doubt that the sons of Sagara will be destroyed ere long.

13. Wait for a short time. Everything is being controlled by time. Everything else is but an instrumental. That time alone is the master of all.

14. Hence, O excellent Suras, what I am going to say for your welfare should now be carried out by all of you without any slackness.

15. The holy lord Kapila, the most excellent among victorious ones, the most exalted among the leading Yogins, is born on the earth with a partial power of Viṣṇu, for the welfare of the universe.

16. He is now sitting, meditating in a lonely place somewhere in the ocean, the water of which had been sucked up by Agastya. This meditation has been going on for the last hundred years according to the reckoning of heaven-dwellers.

17. At my behest, all of you go to the leading sage Kapila. Stand near him wishing for the conclusion of his meditation.

18. At the close of his abstract meditation, you will bow down to him and tell him your purpose in full. He will do what is conducive to your welfare.

19. O excellent Devas, do something whereby a break in the abstract meditation of the sage can be caused through the sons of Sagara".

Jaimini Said :

20. On being told thus by him, the Devas bowed down to Brahmā and went to Kapila, the most excellent among the Brāhmaṇas; with palms joined in reverence, they spoke to him :—

The Devas said :

21. "Be pleased with us, O excellent sage. We have

sought refuge in you. The whole of the universe, harassed by the sons of Sagara, is perishing.

22. It is well-known that you are the cause of the sustenance and annihilation of the worlds. With the partial power of Viṣṇu, you have incarnated on the earth and you stay here as the leading Yogin.

23. A physical body has been voluntarily assumed by you, only for the destruction of the great distress of men afflicted by the three types of agony. Indeed, you are the most excellent among those who perform austerities.

24. Undoubtedly, O Brāhmaṇa, you are capable, at your will, to mentally, create the entire universe, sustain it and annihilate it.

25. You are our creator and dispenser of our destiny. You are our preceptor. You are our greatest resort. You are our protector. Put an end to our adversity.

26. O leading Brāhmaṇa, be the resort and refuge of the leading Brāhmaṇas in particular, who reside in the three worlds and who are being persecuted by the sons of Sagara.

27. Indeed, the activities of people like you will be of *Sattva* (very good) nature. Hence, O sage of good holy rites, it behoves you to save us and all the world.

28-31a. If not, O holy saint, the entire universe will be destroyed prematurely."

Jaimini Said:

"On being told thus by all the Devas, Kapila slowly opened his eyes. Glancing at them, he spoke these pleasing words —"Utterly burned by their own actions, the sons of Sagara will surely perish when the proper time arrives. Let that time be awaited by you all. For the achievement of your purpose, O excellent Suras, I shall become the cause of destruction of those evil-minded ones.

31b-33. Ere long, the sons of Sagara, whose minds are inclined towards sinful activities and whose intellects have been adversely affected by Kāla (Time, God of Death) will be burned by the fire of my anger. Hence, O Devas all the worlds shall be rid of distress. They will have fear from nowhere. Let them (sons of Sagara) be wicked in their actions. They will quickly meet with their annihilation. So be free from fear and go back to your own city. Wait for some time. Thereafter, you will realise what you desire."

34-38. On being told thus by Kapila, all those Devas including Indra, became delighted. After bowing down to him they went towards heaven.

In the meantime, king Sagara, the Lord of the Earth desired to perform *Vājimedha* (Horse-Sacrifice), the great Yajña. With the permission of Vasiṣṭha, he gathered together all the necessary requisites. Accompanied by Aurva and other Brāhmaṇas he duly took the initiation for the performance of sacrifice.

For the purpose of letting the horse roam about, the king of great renown called all his sons and commanded them thus :

"O my sons, make the horse roam about all round the earth. It behoves you to do this immediately and bring it back to me."

Jaimini Said :

39-43. "At the behest of their father they took the horse and made it wander over the entire earth.

It was only because of the directive of the Vedic injunction that the horse was made to go round the earth and not for the conquest of the quarters nor for levying taxes and tributes as the whole of the earth had already been conquered by that king.

Kings had already been made payers of tributes by that king of exalted heroism in the battle-field.

Then those princes reached the lower ground surface of the salt ocean wherein there was no water. With great delight they encircled the horse and entered the interior of the earth.

CHAPTER FIFTYTHREE

The destruction of the sons of Sagara

Jaimini Said :

1. When they reached there, the wind-god who had been directed by Indra, carried away the horse to the nether-worlds within a moment.

2. Stealing the horse without being seen by any of them, O king, the windgod carried it away along that path to the vicinity of sage Kapila.

3-4. When the horse disappeared, all those princes became perplexed. Searching for the horse, they went round and round the earth. After searching the entire earth including the cities, mountains and forests, they attained great sorrow, because they were still unable to see the sacrificial animal.

5. Then they went back to Ayodhyā, surrounded by the sages, met their father, bowed down to him and intimated to him everything.

6. "The moment we entered the ocean after wandering over the whole of the earth, the horse was taken away by some one though it was being vigilantly guarded by us who were on the watch."

7-8. On being told thus by them the excellent king became infuriated and told them—"Go away hence, unrighteous ones, never to return again. How was it lost by you, while you were alive. You were indeed evil-minded ones. There is no question of your returning without the horse here".

9. Then all of them together set-off from that place and said to one another: "Even now the horse is not to be seen, what shall we do?"

10. The whole of the earth was searched by us, including the mountains, forests and parks. The horse is not seen anywhere nor its news is heard.

11. Hence, starting with the ocean and extending as far as the nether-worlds, we shall split the earth and dig it. We shall enter the netherworlds and search for the horse'.

12. Having decided thus, all those sons of Sagara, of cruel resolve, dug the earth everywhere beginning with the sea-shore.

13. Being dug by them, the earth became greatly excited and cried aloud. On seeing their activity, all living beings cried in distress.

14. After digging the Bhārata sub-continent and casting it off on the ground, they united a thousand Yojanas of the earth to the ocean.

15. Digging the earth upto the netherworlds, the sons of the king saw the horse grazing in the netherworlds.

16. Delighted very much they gathered together and laughed out of contentment. Some of them danced with great joy.

17-21. They saw the noble-souled Kalpa of brilliant lustre who was very old; who was seated in the lotus-posture, with his eyes fixed at the tip of his nose, who had kept the head and neck straight and long; who had kept the chest projecting forward, who was shining with his own splĕndour radiating all round in full like a lamp placed in a windless spot; whose body was full of perfect knowledge shining within himself; whose mind was engaged in abstract meditation; who appeared like the motionless ocean; who was duly engaged in the yogic exercise; whose mind was engrossed in what should be meditated upon; who was the most excellent among leading Yogins and who looked like the fire with its clusters of flames extinguished.

On seeing him staying there, they consulted one another about him for a short while. For a short while, they underwent excessive agitation.

22-23. Thinking that it was he who stole the horse, the evil-minded sons of Sagara, induced by the God of death, surrounded Kapila, the excellent sage. Encircling him they said, "This is the thief. There is no doubt about it. This evil-minded robber of the horse deserves to be killed by us".

Jamini said :

24-27a. "All those Sagaras whose intellect had become

deluded and whose death was imminent, suddenly molested the sage who was sitting like an ordinary person.

Then sage Kapila who had never been dejected in mind, was overwhelmed with wrath, because he had been upset due to the break in his abstract meditation. He was agitated. Assailed by those evil-minded ones, the unassailable sage Kapila became agitated. He assumed a huge size like the fire that increases in size at the end of the Kalpa on account of the gusts of wind.

27b-30a. The fire of anger arising out of his body as vast and majestic as the ocean, burst forth like the Saṁkarṣaṇa fire issuing from the poison of Śeṣa out to burn down the nether-worlds. His anger was further kindled by the recollection of attack. The sage who had a lustre similar to that of a wheel of fire (i.e. whirling fire) opened his eyes. Then for a moment, O king, his eyes became extremely red and shone like the Sun and the Moon simultaneously appearing in the sky at dawn.

30b-35. He looked at the princes with rolling eyes gravely, like the God of annihilation at the close of (Kalpa) period. Sparks and flames of fire suddenly emerged from the eyes of that infuriated sage and spread all round in various directions continuously, like the sparks of *Kālāgni* (destructive fire at the time of final annihilation). The sparks of fire of the Sage's anger pervaded the quarters all round, with columns of smoke projecting forward and emitting floods of sparks frequently.

The sparks emanating from his eyes like the poisonous flames with the cavity of the belly of a python, shone like the flames of the Vaḍavā-fire (submarine fire) of the violent ocean.

The fire of anger, O great king, that pervaded the spaces in the quarters by means of its flames, enveloped the firmament and burned the sons of Sagara.

36. The world became enveloped by the clusters of flames of fire and smoke whirling round and round on account of the angry (i.e. violent) blasts of wind that blew with a loud report. It became filled with the dusts of the earth too, that were blown up excessively. Hence, the world became too much afflicted.

37. All round, the fire appeared to be scraping the firmament by means of its flames struck by the velocity of wind.

It immediately burned down completely the sons of the king who were the enemies of the Suras.

38. Even as all the worlds were watching, the fire of Kapila's anger reduced the Sagaras to ashes completely, sparing only the horse.

39. Thus the sons of Sagara, of sinful mind, were burned suddenly on account of that fire of anger like the dry trees that get consumed in the forest conflagration.

40. On seeing the annihilation of those evil-minded Sagaras, the Devas spoke to one another in wonder, along with the Sages.

41-42. "O the ultimate bad result of those persons who have committed terrible sins has not been delayed. Indeed, in this world, men of wicked souls have to meet with a bad end. These wicked and cruel-minded persons, huge in size like mountains, have suddenly and forcibly perished like dry grass in fire.

43. They had caused anxiety and torture to all living beings. They were extremely censured by good men throughout their lives. Fortunately, they have met with their destruction.

44. Which man can attain happiness in this world after committing an inauspicious action that is censured by the worlds and that causes harassment to others?

45. These sinners had made all living beings cry aloud. They have now been struck dead by means of Brahmadaṇḍa (the punishing rod of a Brāhmaṇa). Hence, on account of their own evil actions, they have gone to hell where they will be spending many many years.

46. Hence, only good actions should be performed by intelligent persons. The other type of actions censured by the world should be cast off far away (i.e. completely avoided).

47. As long as one is alive, one should strive for the attainment of final beatitude. This should be done by one who knows what is good for him. One should not harm or injure any one, as life is transitory.

48. This body is non-permanent. Riches are extremely fickle. The entire worldly existence is utterly worthless. How may the learned one believe it (otherwise)?"

49. Even as the leading Suras and sages were telling one another thus, the sons of Sagara perished after becoming the fuel to the fire of the anger of the sage.

50. The sons of Sagara whose bodies were burnt down suddenly, (as if) paralysed the earth with their ashes and instantaneously fell into hell due to their sinful deeds.

51. After burning those sons of Sagara entirely, the fire arising from his anger was on the point of burning all the worlds suddenly in a moment.

52. The Devas who became frightened gathered together and stood by in the firmament. Being desirous of suppressing the fire of anger, they eulogised the noble-souled sage."

CHAPTER FIFTYFOUR

Recovery of the Sacrificial Horse

*Jaimini Reported** :

1. "It behoves you, O Leading Brāhmaṇa to restrain immediately this fire of anger. If not, the entire universe is likely to be burnt by it untimely.

2. Your greatness has been seen. The whole world including the mobile and the immobile beings has been pervaded by this fire of your anger. Forbear, please restrain this anger, O leading Brāhmaṇa. Obeisance to you."

3. On being eulogised thus, the saintly lord Kapila, immediately controlled the extremely terrible fire of anger.

4. Thereupon, the entire universe including the mobile and the immobile beings became calm. Devas and the ascetics became free from distress.

*This is not correct. It is the gods who are praying Kapila. Hence it should be : Gods prayed :—

5. In the meantime, the saintly lord Nārada, O King, casually went to Ayodhyā from the Devaloka (the world of the Devas).

6. On seeing that Nārada had arrived, Sagara worshipped him perfectly in accordance with the injunctions of the scriptures, with *Arghya*, *Pādya* and other materials of worship.

7. Accepting that honour and worship, Nārada sat on the exalted seat and spoke these words, O King, to Sagara the tiger among kings.

Nārada said :

8. "Your sons who had gone to take horse around the world, O excellent king, have been struck down by the curse of a Brāhmaṇa. All of them have perished.

9. Your sacrificial horse, O King, that was being guarded by all of them was taken somewhere in the heaven without being noticed by anyone, as ordained by fate.

10. They began to search for the lost horse all over the earth. For a long time, O king, they did not get any information of its whereabouts.

11. Thereupon, they decided to search for the horse underneath the earth. Beginning earnestly, those Sagaras dug up the surface of the earth.

12. While digging the earth, O King, they saw the horse in Pātāla (Netherworlds) and near it they saw the great sage Kapila, the leading Yogin.

13. On seeing him, they committed a sinful deed. All of them being urged by Kāla (God of death), saying—"This is the robber of the horse", they made Kapila sufficiently infuriated.

14. Thereupon, your sons perished with their bodies as fuel to the fire emanating from his eyes and caused by his anger, the fire that burned the quarters.

15. You need not grieve over them. It does not behove you to grieve over them, O leading King, because they were cruel, of sinful conduct and were creating troubles and impediments to all people.

16. Retain your courage as your asset, as the occurrence

of everything concerning you was inevitable. Learned men do not bewail over what is lost, what is dead and what has passed by.

17. Hence, O excellent king, entrust this boy Aṁśumān, your grandson of great intellect, with the mission of fetching the horse back."

18. After saying this to Sagara, the tiger among kings who was accompanied by the members of the holy assembly and the sacrificial priests, sage Nārada vanished in a trice even as they were watching.

19. On hearing those words of Nārada, the excellent king of exalted intellect became afflicted with misery and grief. He remained engrossed in thought for a long time.

20. As he sat in the assembly, pondering over his fate, with his head bent down, Vasiṣtha who was conversant with what should be done at the proper time and place, said to the king consoling him.

21. "What is this ? If grief were to find place in the heart of courageous people like you, its benefit has not been attained by courage (i.e. courage has become futile).

22. Give up dejection in your mind. Consider that every thing follows the dictates of destiny. Thus it undoubtedly behoves you to carry out the subsequent duties."

23. On being advised thus by Vasiṣṭha, the king who knew the true essential nature of objectives and duties on hand, regained his inherent vitality and fortitude. And he replied— "So be it".

24. He called his grandson Aṁśumān who had been habitually modest and slowly spoke to him thus, in the assembly of Brāhmaṇas and Kṣattriyas.

25. "Dear child, all of your uncles have been struck down by the curse of a Brāhmaṇa. Having committed sinful deeds, they have fallen into hell to remain there for many many years.

26. You alone are the child, a perpetuator of my line. You alone are the protector of this kingdom. My welfare both here and hereafter is solely and wholly dependent upon you.

27. Hence, you go, at my behest, to the proximity of Kapila at Pātāla. Take up the great responsibility of fetching back the sacrificial horse. Try strenuously for the same.

28. Request him duly. Particularly, take great care to make him pleased. It behoves you, dear one, to return quickly, taking the horse with you".

Jaimini said :

29. "On being instructed thus by him, Aṁśumān bowed down to the father of his father and said—"So be it." The highly intelligent boy set off to the proximity of Kapila.

30. He approached the sage duly. He bowed down to him in accordance with the injunctions of the Śāstras as well as his own mind. Bending down in humility, he spoke thus slowly :

31. "Be pleased, O great among Brāhmaṇas. I seek refuge in you. Restrain immediately your anger that has caused destruction of the worlds.

32. If you are furious, the entire universe will meet with destruction. Be pleased to calm down quickly. Let all the worlds be rid of pain and misery.

33. Be pleased with us, O highly fortunate and exalted one. Look at us with gentle eyes. Know me to be the child in the family of those who have been completely burned down by the fire of your anger.

34-35a. My name is Aṁśumān and I am the grandson of king Sagara. I have come here at his behest as well as with a desire to gain your favour, and also to take back the horse if you are pleased to return it."

35b-36a. On hearing these words of his, the sage, the leading Yogin, became pleased. Glancing at Aṁśumān he spoke thus—

36b-39. "Welcome to you, O dear one. How glad am I that you have come. Hurry up. This horse may be taken back to Sagara. Let his sacrifice that had been held up in the middle, function well. Any boon that you may have in your mind can be chosen from me. Satisfied with your devotion, I shall grant it to you even if it be very difficult to obtain. Go and tell your grand-father about the destruction of these Sagaras and that it does not behove him to lament over the death of these sinners".

40-41a. Then, bowing down to the leading Yogin, Aṁśumān spoke thus. "If you wish to grant me a boon, O great Sage, I shall request you thus. If I deserve a boon from you, be pleased to grant this one.

41b-42. All of my uncles have been burned down by the fire of your anger. They are sure to fall into hell, O Brāhmaṇa, and remain there for many long years. No offering of the balls of rice or water libations can save those who are struck down by the curse of a Brāhmaṇa.

43-44. Those who are devoid of balls of rice and water libation in this world, O great sage, cannot expect the attainment of the world of ancestors (*Pitṛs*) as laid down in the Śrutis. But due to your blessings let them have an everlasting stay in heaven. O holy Lord, I shall be contented with this boon.

45. Hence, be pleased to tell me the means of getting them a place in heaven. Please tell me the ways and means whereby they can be redeemed from the adverse effects of the fire of your anger."

46-47. Thereupon, the leading Yogin told him with great delight in his mind—"Their redemption from hell, O dear one, cannot be carried out by you. Those persons of sinful activities must necessarily stay in hell. Let proper time be waited for, when a grandson will be born to you.

48. At the end of that period, O dear one, a highly intelligent grandson will be born to you. He will be known by the name of king Bhagīratha. He will be conversant with the principles of Dharma and Artha.

49. Prompted by his reverence to his ancestors, he will put forth great efforts. He will perform a great steady penance and bring Gaṅgā from heaven.

50. All your ancestors will attain heavenly goal, when the ashes of their limbs and bones are sanctified by its waters.

51. Such is the greatness of Gaṅgā, O prince, she will become well-known in this world as 'Bhāgīrathī'.

52. If the ashes of bones, hairs and nails of any embodied being are flooded with its waters, it will go to the heavenly world from even hell and remain there permanently.

53. Hence, you go. Welfare unto you. You do not deserve to grieve over any thing. Give this horse to your grand-father".

Jaimini said :

54-56. "The highly intelligent Aṁśumān said, "So be it", and bowed down to him devoutly. Permitted by the sage, he went back to the city of Sāketa (Ayodhyā).

He approached Sagara and bowed down to him duly. He then reported the details about himself, the sage and those uncles.

He gave him the horse that he had brought back with great effort. Finally he said to him—"What is to be done by me hereafter ?"

CHAPTER FIFTYFIVE

Aṁśumān installed as Crown Prince

Jaimini said :

1. Then Sagara was beside himself with excessive affection. He embraced his grandson, blessed him, fondled him very much and praised him.

2. Then accompanied by the *Ṛtviks* (sacrificial priests) and the *sadasyas* (members of the holy assembly) who had mastered the Vedas, the excellent king resumed the Yajña in accordance with the prescribed injunctions.

3. Then the sacrifice endowed with the equipments and articles of good quality, and conducted very well by Vasiṣṭha, Aurva and other sages, began to be celebrated.

4. The altar was made of gold. There were big and small vessels in full complement. In that sacrifice everything was luxuriously plentiful and in accordance with the dictates of the scriptures.

5. All the Ṛtviks with the Yajamāna (the performer of sacrifice) at the head, in due order of procedure, concluded sacrifice that began thus.

6. After concluding the sacrifice, the king, who was the most excellent among those who were conversant with the injunctions of scriptures, offered due Dakṣiṇās (monetary gifts) to the Ṛtviks.

7. Then he distributed money to every one of them more than what he (the receiver of Dakṣiṇā) expected, to the Ṛtviks, to the sadasyas and to the Brāhmaṇas who came as suppliants.

8. After propitiating the Brāhmaṇas and others thus, in due order, by means of monetary gifts, he fell at the feet of preceptors and Sadasyas and sought their forgiveness (for his acts of omissions and commissions).

9-12a. Then, accompanied by his followers and kinsmen, he went to Sarayū and performed the concluding holy bath called *Avabhṛtha*. He was accompanied by the Brāhmaṇas and people of other castes and Ṛtviks. He was followed by groups of courtesans, heralds, bards and panegyrists. The ladies (of the harem) were with him. He had all the royal paraphernalia like the white umbrella, chowries and furry fans shaken to and fro. He shone well with all these accompaniments. The sounds of the different kinds of musical instruments deafened (as it were) the various quarters. He joyously performed the holy valedictory ablution (i.e. *Avabhṛtha*) in accordance with the injunction in the scriptures as well as conventional practice.

12b-14. After the holy bath, accompanied by his wives, friends and the Brāhmaṇas, he re-entered the beautiful city, where there were thousands of delighted and well-nourished persons. There were the sweet notes of *Vīṇā* (Lute), *Veṇu* (Flute), *Mṛdaṅga* (a kind of tabor) and different kinds of other musical instruments. There were loud sounds of auspicious chanting of the Vedic Mantras sung by the Brāhmaṇa folk. He was being panegyrised by the heralds, Sūtas, bards and other panegyrists standing all round him.

15. There were white fans, good umbrellas and colourful banners, flags and festoons displayed in the city. The grounds, bazaars and other places had been swept and sprinkled clean with water and they appeared very splendid.

16. The city shone splendidly on account of the rows of mansions, lofty and brilliant like the Kailāsa mountain. The quarters were rendered fragrant by means of the sweet scent arising from fumes of Aguru.

17-18. Heaps of fried rice were showered on him frequently by the womenfolk of the city all round. He was delightedly viewed by the citizens. He was honoured at various places by the merchant community with many kinds of presents. Thus he went into the city slowly.

19. After entering his beautiful abode that had been embellished with all kinds of ornamental fittings, he honoured well, all his friends and Brāhmaṇas too.

20. Being served and attended upon by the kings, the rulers of different countries, Sagara the tiger among kings stayed in there like another Indra.

21. Having fulfilled his desire thus in the company of his friends and allies, Sagara the most excellent among kings rejoiced there accompanied by his two wives.

22. With approval of Vasiṣṭha, the king gladly crowned Aṁśumān, his grandson, who was humble and modest, by disposition as the heir-apparent.

23. On account of his exalted liberal qualities, he became a great favourite with friends, kinsmen and the residents of the city as well as the outlying districts and rural territories, O king.

24. The subjects were delighted with him and they loved him because, though he was a boy, he had unmeasured valour and prowess, just as one loves the fresh crescent of the moon that has risen just at the beginning of the bright half of the lunar month.

25. Accompanied by him, his friends and allies as well as the two wives who suited him in every respect, the glorious king rejoiced and lived for a long time.

26. The mighty king, Sagara, who was like another Dharma himself, protected the earth including the mountains, forests and parks, as though he was young.

27. Thus the great lord of the Northern Kosalas whose person shone like a precious gem in the crown of kings of the solar race, delighted the minds of all the worlds like the full moon. Along with all his subjects he rejoiced very well.

CHAPTER FIFTYSIX

The Descent of Gaṅgā

Jaimini Said :

1. "The life story of the noble-souled Sagara has been recounted to you in full, elaborately as well as succinctly. This story is conducive to the destruction of sin.

2. This subcontinent named Bhārata lies extensively from South to North. Its expanse is nine thousand Yojanas (?).

3. A thousand Yojanas were dug up by the sons of the king Sagara who were in search of the horse. The remaining eight thousand Yojanas were made to fall(?)

4. Since the abode of sharks (i.e. ocean) was dug up and developed by the sons of Sagara, it obtained the name Sāgara in the worlds since then.

5. The ocean splashed its waters all round and flooded the earth including the holy centres, fields and forests upto Brahmapāda (the foot of Brahmā).

6. Then, all the Devas, Asuras and human beings living there were scattered here and there. They became afflicted with great sorrow.

7. There is a well-known holy place named Gokarṇa[1] which is worshipped by all the Suras. It is situated on the shore of the Western ocean. It extends to one and a half Yojanas.

8. There are innumerable holy spots there. There are abodes of sages and Devas. Many groups of siddhas have been living in that holy centre from the earliest times, O king.

9. That holy spot is famous throughout the world. It is splendid and it destroys sins. That holy spot lay in the South-Western portion of the sea.

10. It is the place where the sages of well praised holy rites performed penance and attained the highest liberation from which there is no coming back again (in *saṁsāra*).

11. Due to the potentiality of that holy place, god Śaṅkara stays there forever with great delight along with the goddess, the groups of goblins and Devas.

12. If people decide to go on pilgrimage to that holy spot, and make the proposed journey, their sins perish like a dry leaf in a stormy wind.

13. A desire to resort to that holy spot never occurs to the evil-minded ones who may even reside very near it.

14. Only, through great religious merit can men have the desire and pleasure of making a holy pilgrimage to that sacred holy spot. Never otherwise, O king.

15. If, out of compulsion, the mobile and the immobile living beings die there, O king, they attain permanent abode in heaven immediately.

---

1. Gokarṇa—a holy place in north Kanara, Karwar Dist. of Karnatak. It is 30 miles from Goa between Karwar and Kumta. It contains the temple of Mahādeva called Mahābaleśvara, established by Rāvaṇa. The legend goes that Rāvaṇa was taking god Śiva's *Ātma-liṅga* to Laṅkā. Due to urgency of easing, he had to entrust it to a bystander who was god Gaṇesa in disguise. He did not want that the Ātmaliṅga should be with a demon. He placed it on the ground. When Rāvaṇa returned, he tried to wring it out of the earth. But in vain. He went away disappointed. But due to physical wringing by Rāvaṇa, it got the shape somewhat resembling a cow's ear. The legend tries to explain the peculiar shape of this Śiva-liṅga.

16. It is the most excellent holy spot among all sacred centres; by recalling it (mentally) a man becomes rid of all sins. It is the abode of all sacred Tīrthas (holy waters).

17. Some sages desirous of spiritual achievement used to live there, taking their holy bath in all these Tīrthas and always worshipping Śiva.

18. Those who are devoid of lust and anger, who live in them without rivalry, attain that Siddhi ere long.

19. Those who stay there engaged in Japa, and Homa will attain the desired Siddhi. They must be quiescent, self-restrained and observe the vow of celibacy.

20. If holy rites such as the worship of the Pitṛs, Devas and Brāhmaṇas, charitable gifts, Homas, Japas etc. are performed in this holy spot, O King, the fruit there-of will be ten million times more than that (performance of these acts) in the other holy spots.

21-23a. When that extremely sacred holy spot became submerged in the waters of the sea, the sages endowed with great penance, who lived there climbed on to the Sahya, the excellent mountain, for the sake of a residing place. Staying there, all of them consulted one another and got ready to go to Rāma who was performing penance on the mountain Mahendra.

The King enquired :

23b-26. After the waters of the ocean had been drunk by Agastya, when the holy spot including holy sacred waters, hermitages and forests had been made to fall down, when the king's sons (i.e. Sāgaras) dug up all round, when the other parts of the earth such as cities, villages, mines etc. and the countries lying near the ocean were destroyed, O excellent sage, what the persons with their abodes there, do? Did they reside there alone with every great difficulty or did they go elsewhere? What was the duration of the period in which the ocean became filled with water once again? By what means (did it become full)? O Brāhmaṇa, mention this to me."

Jaimini replied :

27-29. When the marshy places lying near the ocean

were destroyed by those evil-minded ones, persons having their abode therein went here and there. Some of the persons residing in the holy spots continued to live there with great difficulty.

At the same time, O king, a son was born to Aṁśumān who became wellknown on the earth as Dilīpa. He was a righteous soul.

30. The highly intelligent king Aṁśumān had perfectly enjoyed the worldly pleasures, crowned Dilīpa (as the ruler) of the kingdom and went to the forest with a decision in his mind to perform penance.

31. Then the glorious Dilīpa protected the entire earth righteously after defeating all the enemies.

32. His son named Bhagīratha became very famous throughout the world. He was clever in comprehending all the topics concerning holy rites and virtue. He was resplendent and his valour and exploits were unmeasured.

33-35. After celebrating his (Bhagīratha's) coronation in the realm, King Dilīpa too went to the forest. Bhagīratha protected the earth very well after exterminating all thorns (i.e. enemies within and without). He rejoiced enjoying different kinds of worldly pleasures like the lord of Devas in heaven. That king heard about the fact that formerly his ancestors had to fall into terrible hell as a result of the fury of a Brāhmaṇa. On hearing that all his ancestors were struck down by the curse of a Brāhmaṇa, he became extremely sad and dejected.

36-38a. He became frustrated and extremely disinterested in the kingdom, his kinsmen and the enjoyments of all worldly pleasures. He entrusted the kingdom to the care of his excellent minister. The excellent king was desirous of taking his ancestors to heaven and so went to the forest for performing penance. At the outset he propitiated the lotus-born lord Brahmā by means of great penance for securing longevity. From him he got as long a life as he desired.

38b-39. Thereafter, O great king, he propitiated Gaṅgā and made her pleased. From her he got the boon that she would come down to the earth from heaven. Afterwards he propitiated Śiva by means of penance in order to hold her by means of his head.

40-45a. The lord who favours his devotees granted that boon to him. As Gaṅgā fell down from the top of Meru along with crocodiles, alligators and sharks, the lord of the worlds (i.e. Śiva) caught her by means of his head. Although she was flowing with great rapidity, she got merged deep into his resplendent matted hair after reaching his head. By seeing her disappear in the head of the lord Śambhu like water within the cupped palm of the hand, he once again propitiated Hara to get her released.

45b-46a. By the favour of Śarva, he got back Gaṅgā once again. As she reached the earth, Bhagīratha took her towards that spot where the sons of Sagara had been burned. Following the king she flooded the entire sacrificial premises of a saintly king (Jahnu) who was performing sacrifice on the way. When the entire sacrificial chamber and installation got submerged, the saintly king became angry. He drank the entire river, as though it had been mouthful of water.[1]

46b-48a. With great efforts Bhagīratha rendered service to that noble-souled saintly king for a hundred years. When he became pleased, the king got back Gaṅgā once again.

Since Gaṅgā remained within the belly (of Jahnu) for a long time and emerged thereafter from it, her other name Jahnavī became famous on the earth.

48b-51a. The celestial river followed Bhagīratha and with her own waters she splashed the ashes of the bones of all

---

1. Two places claim to be the spots of jahnu's sacrificial place where Gaṅgā was 'drunk' up by Jahnu (1) Bhairava ghāṭi below Gangotri in Garhwal (U.P.) at the junction of Bhāgīrathī and Jāhnavī.

(2) Sultanganj, to the west of Bhāgalpur (Bihar); the temple of Gaibinath Mahādeva there which is supposed to be on the site of Jahnu's hermitage is on rock which comes out of the bed of Gaṅgā in front of Sultanganj.

If the legend of the Gaṅgā being brought by efforts of 3-4 generations of the kings of the solar race be correct, it must have been a sort of an ancient canal constructed by those kings to bring waters from the Himalayas to the parched plains of north India. In that case obstruction to the canal at Bhairavaghāṭi by Jahnu is feasible and not at Sultanganj.

his ancestors. When the ashes of the bones were splashed with its waters, the sons of Sagara became rid of their sins at the very same moment. They went to heaven from hell.

51b. After having led all the Sagaras to the heaven, thus, the great river went to the Eastern ocean by the same path. The celestial river had flowed towards the four quarters from the top of Meru after being split into four channels.

52. Gaṅgā received four names due to these four different channels viz. Sītā, Alakanandā, Sucakṣus and Bhadrāvatī.[1]

53. Though their waters had been dried up when Agastya drank up the waters, the four oceans became full with the waters of Gaṅgā, once again.

54. When the ocean extended by the sons of Sagara became filled up, many countries lying nearby became sub-merged.

55-57. The holy spots too lying at the outskirts of the ocean all round became sub-merged. The people who had their abodes therein went here and there. The holy spot Gokarṇa about which I have told you, became submerged in the ocean, as it was near the ocean. Therefore, all those persons who had their abodes therein desired to uplift it, O King. They were desirous of meeting the mighty scion of the family of Bhṛgu and so started from the Sahya mountain.

1. M.Ali identifies the rivers as follows:
Sītā = Yarkand-Tarim-Hwang-Ho
Alakanandā = Gaṅgā
Su-Cakṣus = The Oxus
Bhadrāvatī or Bhadrasomā—Syrdaria (*Geog. of Purāṇas*, p. 201)

CHAPTER FIFTYSEVEN

Varuṇa visits Bhārgava

Jaimini continued :

1. "Thereafter, Śuṣka, Sumitra, and other sages of praiseworthy holy vows and rites, went towards the mountain Mahendra with a desire to see Bhārgava Rāma.

2. Passing through very many countries, forests, rivers etc., those leading sages gradually reached the excellent mountain.

3-5. After climbing it slowly, they reached his well-renowned hermitage and its precincts. All the cruel beasts of prey therein had become quiescent. The splendid penance grove the middle, was very fascinating on account of groves of trees laden with the fruits and flowers of all seasons. The shade was lovingly cool and pleasing. It was one without anything to be compared with. The wind was very fragrant and pleasant. It was echoing with the sounds of the chanting of the Vedic Mantras. With their faces very much delighted, they entered the hermitage with the elderly ones at the head, in the order of seniority in age.

6. Those ascetics saw Rāma who was comfortably seated on a *Brahmāsana* (mat made of the Darbhagrass) with a soft deerskin placed over it. He was very calm and was surrounded by his disciples.

7. He appeared like a person engaged in penance for the extenuation of the defect (sin) of burning the three worlds deliberately at the outset, like the *Kālāgni* (fire at end of a Kalpa).

8. After approaching the excellent scion of the family of Bhṛgu who was engaged in the great vow of sagehood, those sages who were by nature humble in their conduct, saluted him with their heads bowing down, due to devotion.

9. On seeing those sages come, the leading member of the family of Bhṛgu, respectfully worshipped them very well, with the materials of worship such as *Argha*, *Pādya* etc.

10. When the hospitable reception was over and the sages who had come from other countries were seated comfortably, Rāma the bravest among the members of the family of Bhṛgu, spoke to them these words smilingly.

11. "Welcome unto you all, O highly exalted ones of great fortune, you have come here. Tell me without hesitation what should be done by us."

12. After bowing down to Rāma, those sages said thus:—"O excellent sage, understand that we are the sages who had our homes in Gokarṇa.

13. That great holy place along with the sacred ponds etc. was caused to fall into the waters of the ocean by the sons of Sagara who were digging up Earth for some other reason.

14. Undoubtedly, we desire and expect from you to regain that holy spot that sanctifies everyone, after causing the waters of the ocean to recede.

15. It is well known that you were born in the family of Bhṛgu, with the potentiality of a part of Viṣṇu. Therefore, there is nothing in the three worlds which cannot be carried out by you.

16. We have heard that you alone are the person capable of presenting this desired object in the whole world. It was to request you for this, O Rāma, that we have all come here.

17. It behoves you, O leading Brāhmaṇa, to grant that excellent holy spot now, after causing the waters of the ocean to recede, by your own prowess".

Rāma said :

18. "All these things are completely known to me, O ascetics. The task that you all have set could also be carried out by me. No doubt need be entertained about this.

19. But this task desired and expected by you is excessively terrible in the world. Even by me, it can be carried out only by taking up arms and not otherwise.

20. I have granted the boon of freedom from fear to everyone. I have laid down my weapons. I am quiescent now. According to an earlier behest of my father, I have taken up the vow to perform penance.

21-22. Formerly, I had taken this vow in the midst of good men—"I will never take up arms". After that, I have come here to perform a penance.

Since the object of your desire can be achieved only by taking up arms, my mind is in a dilemma. It is vacillating like a moving swing."

Śuṣka said :

23. "The taking up of arms for the protection of the good does not make any one go astray from truthfulness (to his vows) as mentioned by Brahmā formerly.

24. Hence, for the sake of our welfare, weapons should be taken up by you. Thereby a great righteous action shall be carried out by you."

Jaimini said :

25-26. On being earnestly requested by the sages thus, the intelligent scion of the family of Bhṛgu acceded to it, for the sake of Dharma only in his view. Alongwith them, the excellent sage proceeded towards the South-Western direction, O king, with a desire to see the lord of rivers (Varuṇa).

27. The leading scion of the family of Bhṛgu, the noble-minded sage Rāma descended from Sahya, the cxcellent mountain and reached the western shore of the lord of rivers.

28-30. Everywhere round him the highly fortunate sage saw thc ocean that was agitated by the wind; that was a mine of all precious gems; that was being filled with water continuously; the majesty, depth and vastness of which could never be understood, like that of the minds of great men; that was very difficult to be crossed by everyone; that contained different kinds of crocodiles; that could never be assailed in the world like Dhātṛ (the creator and dispenser of destiny).

31-34. That was like the soul in pervading everything; that had slighted everything and become haughty; that was a support to all living beings; that was the king of rivers; that had a chain of hundreds of extremely unsteady and lofty billows, that was rendered splendid and beautiful by the mass of foams of hundreds of waves which split and dispersed, due to their having dashed into the cavities within heaps of rocks at the sides, and that had a deep rumbling sound. He saw the ocean along with the groups of sages. It was as though he was served by the cool sparkling sprays from the waves. For a short while, O leading king, the powerful sage took rest on the shores of the lord of rivers. He was desirous of meeting Pracetas (Varuṇa).

35. Then Rāma got up and stood facing the south. He spoke these words to Varuṇa in deep resonant tone like the sound of rumbling cloud.

36. "I have come here along with the groups of sages with a desire to see you. Hence, take up your own form O Pracetas, and grant me your vision."

37. Even after hearing these words Varuṇa, the lord of aquatic beings, O king, did not move from his place. He became bolder.

38. Although he was repeatedly called by Rāma, the king of waters did not grant his vision nor did he give any reply.

39. His (Rāma's) intransgressable request was disregarded by Varuṇa. He treated it with indifference because he knew that Rāma was very much a suppliant.

40. Thinking that his request had been disregarded by Varuṇa, Rāma, the most excellent one among the wielders of weapons, looked at him angrily.

41. Being much infuriated, he assumed a form similar to that of agitated ocean and wished to make the ocean devoid of waters by resorting to his own inherent power.

42-44. Then he sat near his bow 'Vijaya' and sipped the water ceremoniously. Rāma bowed down mentally to Śarva and took up the great bow. With eyes turned red due to anger, he drew the bow. Stroking the excellent bow along with its string, the excellent member of the family of Bhṛgu made a twanging sound with the string, even as all the living beings were watching. The loud report of the bow string was heard touching the vaults of heaven with great harshness.

45-47. The entire Earth consisting of seven continents and oceans shook thereby.

Then with great force, Rāma fixed to the bow an arrow with golden feather heads, an excellent arrow comparable to the *Kālānala* (fire at the end of the world). He joined to it a very terrible missile, belonging to Bhṛgu and having the fire-god for its deity. The bravest among the descendants of Bhṛgu joined a missile for the charging of which and to discharge which he chanted the requisite Mantra. Thereupon, the Earth including the mountains, forests and parks quaked and trembled.

48-50. Devas, Asuras and the great serpents became extremely agitated. On seeing the excellent scion of the family of Bhṛgu who had joined the missile (to the bow) and whose eyes were extremely red due to anger, the mobile and the immobile beings became bewildered and perplexed in their minds. The quarters became covered up with layers and layers of clouds along with the burning of quarters. Rough gusts of winds blew, making loud reports and spreading dust particles. The sun's rays became dim and its disc became red.

51-53. There was a heavy down-pour of bloody-coloured rain water along with thunderbolt and the fall of meteors. Everyone became bewildered saying "What is this ?"

Rāma pulled out a great arrow that was terribly emitting smokes and fumes, and on which the divine missile was charged.

As Rāma was drawing the bow with an arrow at the tip of which there were shooting flames, the sages saw him resembling the final fire at the close of Kalpa.

54. His terrifying body seen standing within the circle made by the bow the string of which was drawn upto his ears, became unapproachable to all.

55. His terrible form as he drew the bow was like the halo-encircled disc of the sun, rising at the close of Kalpa.

56. As he shook with anger, his body, which was terrible with its flames like the fire at the end of Kalpa, appeared like the circular face of Viṣṇu's discus.

Rāma attained the excessively terrific form of Viṣṇu in the guise of Man-lion, when he was surrounded (as it were) by the brilliant flame of the fire of anger.

57-58. As he drew the bow, Rāma's body with the face with the eye-brows knitted, became like that of Śiva desirous of burning the Tripuras formerly.

On seeing him with blazing body, all the sages began to eulogise him suddenly due to fright saying—"O Rāma, be pleased : be victorious."

59-60. The entire harem of the ocean-god became (as if) engulfed as it was hidden under the layers of smoke emerging from the fire of the missile.

Struck by the heat of blazing fire of the missile, the waters of the ocean became stirred up and the tide began to flow.

61-62. The living beings in the deep waters such as big whales, small whales, alligators, crocodiles, fishes, snakes and tortoises became extremely distressed.

When the waves were tossed up as the various living beings jumped up, fell down and lay exhausted in it, the ocean became suddenly and extremely agitated.

63-64. Along with the water that flowed, the living beings moving about within the waters made a great up-roar due to fright. They were distressed and rendered exhausted due to the high tide.

Then flames and sparks emerged from that arrow terrifying to everyone with their hissing sound. This was observed that they spread in all directions.

65-67. Violent gusts of wind whirled all round. Since it was full of flames of fire, it appeared like a red canopy.

As the waters of the ocean agitated by the fire of the missile increased in quantity like those of the ocean at the time of deluge, the waves moved towards the shore.

The ocean appeared to deafen the quarters through the excessive rumbling sound of the waters hit and stirred up by the fire of missile.

68-69. The mountain Sahya was rendered obscure and darkish by the waters encircled by the flames of fire of the missile all round, as they resorted to the mountain suddenly.

On seeing Rāma with the bowstring drawn as far as his ears, the ocean became very sad and gloomy like a sinner at the sight of Yama, the god of Death.

70a. With all his limbs quaking with fear the lord of rivers gave up his natural courage and became a coward.

70b-73a. He assumed his real form. He was bedecked in his ornaments. Varuṇa waded through his own waters. Pracetas (i.e. Varuṇa) appeared near Bhārgava with palms of his hands joined in reverence. He came hurriedly near Bhārgava as though he was extremely afraid of the swift arrow.

73b-75. Having fallen at the lotus-like feet (of Rāma) who had drawn the bow, the extremely frightened (Varuṇa) spoke with words faltering due to excitement.

"Protect me, O bravest among the members of the family of Bhṛgu, protect me with sympathy. I have sought refuge in you. Forgive this offence of mine, O Rāma, committed by me in ignorance. I stand by biding your directive. Command me—What shall I do ?"

CHAPTER FIFTYEIGHT

Rāma reclaims land from the sea

Jaimini continued :

1. On seeing Varuṇa who said this and fell on the ground at his feet, the intelligent leading member of the family of Bhṛgu, withdrew the missile.

2. After withdrawing the missile, Rāma looked at Varuṇa standing in front of him. Anger having subsided, he said to him smilingly.

3. "These leading sages who had their homes in Gokarṇa had come to me before, O lord of rivers, while I was staying on the mountain Mahendra.

4. The holy spot Gokarna inhabited by the sages was caused to fall down into your waters formerly, by the sons of Sagara who were digging the Earth.

5. After having approached me, those sages, the residents of that holy place have rushed down here to regain once again that holy spot which is very dear to Śiva.

6. It was for the sake of these sages that I have come down from the excellent mountain Mahendra along with these leading sages, to see you.

7. Hence, for my sake, it behoves you to make your waters recede and restore to them that holy spot in the water as before."

Jaimini said :

8. On hearing these words of Rāma, Varuṇa the lord of aquatic beings considered everything in his mind and spoke these words to Rāma once again.

Varuṇa said :

9. "My waters cannot be made to recede by anyone. Such is the boon granted to me formerly by Viriñci (i.e. god Brahmā).

10. But on account of your brilliant splendour I have given up all my natural courage. I have become afraid, O Bhārgava, and have fallen under your control.

11. How can I fail to perform this task, O annihilator of the families of Kṣatriyas, after having been especially urged by you for the sake of these sages?

12. Hence, I shall hold back on the ground as much of my water as you may have intended in your mind."

13. On hearing his words, Bhārgava said "so be it". He broke his bow and threw away his arrow.

14. Then he mentally decided the boundary. Wishing to point it out, O king, he took up his *Sruvā* (the sacrificial ladle). The intelligent sage was desirous of throwing it in the ocean.

15-18. After making him (Rāma) delighted in his mind and devoid of anger towards himself (i.e. Varuṇa), the lord of rivers disappeared. When he had gone, Rāma stood facing the north. He whirled his *Sruvā* with great speed and hurled it into the briny sea. When it was hurled into the ocean, the *Sruvā* went two hundred Yojanas in the direction of the north-west, O king, and fell down. That place is the holy spot named Śūrpāraka (Sopārā, in Dist. Thana, Maharashtra). It is conducive to rid oneself of all sins. It is on the shore of the lord of rivers and well-known in the three worlds. The *Sruvā* (sacrificial ladle) slipping down from Rāma's hands fell, O great king between that holy spot (and the shore of the ocean), thereby indicating Rāma's exploit.

19-22. The place, O king, where the ground created by Rāma was established is the holy place Śūrpāraka, glorious and renowned in all the worlds. The ocean withdrew its waters so far. After granting the Earth to Rāma, O king, he stood aside.

Rāma (the leading member of Bhṛgu's family) who never transgressed the bounds of decency made him stand by this agreement accepted by himself (i.e. Varuṇa), knowing that it is the eastern (?) boundary on the Earth, the ocean yielded the ground.

23-25. All the gods were surprised to see the exploit of Rāma. (Defective Text) When the water of the ocean receded there on the Sahya mountain, there were here and there (at some places) some markings of boundaries of towns and villages as before (their submerging in the sea). These he observed there by chance, due to their lower level. Thereafter, the most excellent member of the family of Bhṛgu, lovingly gave their respective places as desired by them to the sages of purified souls.

26. Then all those sages became delighted very much. Fully contented, they worshipped Rāma aud expressed their good wishes for him.

27-30. Then, being permitted by them, Rāma who accomplished for them all desires, went away.

When the excellent sage Rāma had gone to his hermitage from that country, all those sages collected together and went to the shore of the sea. After circumambulating that place with great effort, O king, they saw the Earth situated within the ocean, since it was eternal and the place of abode of all the Devas, (the holy spot) did not become ruined utterly although the earth was dug up and it was caused to fall into the ocean, and although it was lost in the water under which it remained for a long time. This happened due to the power of Rudra.

31. The holy spot emerging from the waters regained its original state, O excellent king. This is the capacity of lord Śiva which cannot be adequately thought of.

32. Thus the Earth was reclaimed (lit. created) once again out of the ocean. From the south to the north, O king, it extends to four hundred Yojanas.

33. Even today the ocean does not transgress the boundary. His great bow was never drawn and kept ready by Rāma the great sage.

34-37. Such is the potential power of Rāma and the king Sagara whose sons caused the sub-continent of Bhārata to fall into the ocean extending it more by a thousand Yojanas and developed the great ocean. The land extending to six hundred Yojanas was created once again.

Since the abode of alligators (i.e. the sea) was extended by the sons of Sagara, it got the name Sāgara well-known in all the worlds ever since then.

38. Thus the story of great men viz. Rāma, Kārttavīrya and king Sagara has been well recounted to you by me.

CHAPTER FIFTYNINE

The Birth of Vaivasvata

Bṛhaspati said :

1. The sages who were told thus attained great delight. Thereafter, they further asked with a desire to hear more.

The Sages requested :

2. "Please narrate the details of the races of kings of unmeasured prowess, their life and their powers and majesty, to us as we ask in the proper order."

3-5. On being requested thus by them, Lomaharṣaṇa, an expert in narration of stories, well conversant with statements, spoke these words even as the sages were desirous of listening to the later narratives.

Sūta said :

"Just as the sage of great wisdom (viz. Vyāsa) narrated to me when I asked him, I too shall narrate in due order the details of the races of kings of unmeasured prowess, their lives, grandeur and efficacy. Understand them from me.

6. It is related that Varuṇa's wife, goddess Stutā (Sunā in *Vāyu* 84-6-8), was a celestial damsel of great beauty. Her sons were Kali and Vaidya.

7. Jaya and Vijaya were the sons of Kali. They were extremely valorous. Ghṛṇi and Muni were the sons of Vaidya. They were very powerful.

8. They used to devour girls given in marriage to them or those who loved them. They devoured one another. After devouring one another, they met with destruction.

9. Kali (this is evidently another one not the one mentioned in 7) should be known as Surā's (?) son. His son is remembered as Mada. Hiṁsā was the eldest wife of Kali. She is remembered as wicked and dishonest.

10. Four other sons were born to Kali. They were cannibals. They were Nāka, and Vighna who were very famous, as well as Bhadrama and Vidhama.

11. Vighna was so called because he had no head. Nāka had no body. Bhadrama had only one hand. Vidhama is remembered as single-legged.

12. Tāmasī and Pūtanā were the wives of Bhadrama (or Pūtanā of dark and foul nature was the wife of Bhadrama). Revatī was the wife of Vidhama. The sons of these two were thousands in number.

13. Śakuni was the wife of Nāka and Ayomukhī the wife of Vighna. Their sons were Rākṣasas of great vigour and vitality. They used to roam about during the twilight at dusk and dawn.

14. The sons of Revatī and Pūtanā are remembered as Nairṛtas by name. All those Rākṣasas are *Grahas* (Evil demons attacking children and making them suffer from convulsions) particularly in regard to children.

15-16. Lord Skanda is the overlord of all those Nairṛtas as allowed by Brahmā.

Bṛhaspati had a sister named Varastrī. She observed the vow of celibacy. She had achieved yogic powers. She then used to wander over the entire universe without any attachment. She ultimately became the wife of Prabhāsa who was the eighth among the Vasus.

17-20. (Partially defective text). Viśvakarman, a Deva was born of her. He is the Prajāpati (Creator) of artisans and craftsmen. He had evolved the forms of Virāṭ (the supreme being). Another name of this liberal-minded grandson of Dharma is Tvaṣṭṛ.

By means of his Yogic power, he had created thousands of artistic works for the Devas. It was he who created the aerial chariots of the Devas.

Human beings depend upon the artistic creations of this noble-souled one. (They imitate them).

Virocanā, famous as the daughter of Prahrāda was the wife of Tvaṣṭṛ. She was the sister of Virocana and the mother of Triśiras, the great and intelligent Viśvarūpa who was the preceptor of the Devas.

21. Maya is remembered as the son of Viśvakarman. He was himself Viśvakarman (capable of all creative work). His younger sister was well known as Sureṇu.

22-24. The daughter of Tvaṣṭṛ who became well-known as Saṁjñā and the wife of Savitṛ (the Sun) gave birth to Manu, the eldest son of great fortune and exalted dignity, of Vivasvān (the sun).

Then she gave birth to the twins viz. Yama and Yamunā (See vv 31-32 where Yama and Yamī are the names mentioned). She assumed the form of a mare and went to the Kurus.

That lady of great fortune gave birth to two sons, the Aśvins. They were the sons of the sun-god who had assumed the form of a horse. She gave birth to the sons through the nostrils in the atmosphere itself. The two sons Mārtaṇḍa were Nāsatya and Dasra."

The sages enquired :

25-26. "Why was Vivasvān called Mārtaṇḍa by scholars?

Why should that fair lady deliver through her nostrils ? We wish to understand this. Narrate it to us who ask you."

Sūta replied :

27-29. "Even for a long time after it had been produced, the egg (the foetus) remained unbroken. That egg was broken by Tvaṣṭṛ. Bewildered by the destruction of the egg (foetus) as he mistook it, Kaśyapa fled from there.

When the egg was split into two, Tvaṣṭṛ looked at it and said thus.

"This egg cannot be deficient, O sinless one, you be Mārtaṇḍa."

The father affectionately said—"Indeed he is not dead (*Na Mṛta*) though he is within the *Aṇḍa* (egg)." On hearing these words of his, they said that the name was true to its meaning.

30. When the egg was split into two, he was told—"Be Mārtaṇḍa" even as he was within the egg. So the sun is considered Mārtaṇḍa by those conversant with the Purāṇas.

31-32. Henceforth, I shall mention the progeny of Vivasvān known as Mārtaṇḍa. Saṁjñā, the wife of Savitṛ, gave birth to three sons (children) viz. Manu, Yamī and Yama. Chāyā (the shadow) gave birth to Tapatī and Śanaiścara (the Planet Saturn). These are remembered as the sons of Mārtaṇḍa.

33-34. Vivasvān (the sun-god) of great fame was born of Dākṣāyaṇī (i.e. daughter of Dakṣa) and Kaśyapa.

The gentle lady Saṁjñā, the daughter of Tvaṣṭṛ, became the wife of Vivasvān. Originally she was well-known as Sureṇu but later on she became famous as Saṁjñā. It was she who became the wife of lord Mārtaṇḍa of excessive brilliance.

35. "Indeed, he did not die inside the egg" said Kaśyapa fondly but unwittingly. Hence the sun is called Mārtaṇḍa.

36. The brilliance and splendour of Vivasvān is always very excessive. It is with that, that the son of Kaśyapa scorched the three worlds.

37-38. Ravi, the sun god, begot of Saṁjñā three children, two sons of great power and vigour and one daughter. It is known Manu was the eldest of the sons of Sun-god.

Thereafter (was born) Yama (otherwise known as) Śrāddhadeva. Manu was a Prajāpati. Then Yama and Yamī were born as twins.

39. On seeing that form of unbearable splendour of Vivasvān Saṁjñā could not brook it. She created her own Chāyā (shadow) of the same colour and complexion (*Savarṇā*) as hers.

40. That lady of great fortune, born out of her shadow, joined her palms in great reverence and purity of mind and spoke to Saṁjñā.

41-44. "Tell me. What work has to be carried out by me ?".

Saṁjñā said to her—"Welfare unto you. I am going to the abode of my own father. You alone must remain in my house without any hesitation. These two sons of mine and this daughter of excellent complexion should be brought up by you. This arrangement should not be disclosed to the lord (and my two sons) by you. Saṁjñā was then told (by Chāyā). These two are my sons too. So be it. (I shall do as you say)."

On being told thus, that lady of pitiable plight went near Tvaṣṭṛ as if greatly ashamed. On seeing her come back, the father became angry and spoke to Saṁjñā.

45-49. "Go to your husband". On being directed thus again and again, she assumed the form of a mare and concealed her real form. That praiseworthy, uncensured lady went to the Northern Kurus and grazed the grass.

Thinking the second Saṁjñā to be the real Saṁjñā, the sun procreated two sons having the same lustre as his. Those two lords were equal in comparison to Manu the eldest son. Of these two, Śrutaśravas will become Sāvarṇī Manu. Śrutakarman (the second one) should be known as the planet Śanaiścara (the Saturn). He who became Manu is called Sāvarṇi also.

50. Saṁjñā of earthly nature (i.e. the shadow) loved her own sons more than the elder sons.

51-52. Manu forgave all that but Yama did not. Highly distressed at her enmity because she was a co-wife (for his mother), he began to grumble much and on many occasions.

Due to his anger as well as the force of inevitable future, Yama, the son of Vivasvān, threatened Chāyā with his foot (i.e. kick).

Then out of anger that mother of Sāvarṇī cursed Yama.

53-57. "You are threatening with your foot, all on a sudden, the wife of great renown of your own father. Hence, this foot of yours will undoubtedly drop down. Yama became highly afflicted in his mind on account of that curse. Accompanied by Manu, the virtuous-souled one (Yama) intimated everything to his father :

"I have been vanquished (humiliated) by the statements of Saṁjñā. I have become distressed due to the fear of the curse. Of course, the foot was raised by me against her, but it was not allowed to fall on her body. Whether this was due to my childishness or out of delusion, it behoves you to forgive me.

O lord of the worlds, O most excellent one among those who blaze and scorch, I have been cursed by my step-mother. I have your blessing to protect us from this great danger.

58-61. On being told thus, lord Vivasvān said to Yama : "Undoubtedly, my son, there must be a great reason for this, since you became infuriated despite being conversant with Dharma and remaining truthful in speech. Nor can the words of your mother be falsified.

Worms will take your flesh and go to the Earth. Then, O highly intelligent one, your foot will attain happiness. Thus your mother's words will be made true. By the avoidance of the effects of the curse, you will also be saved."

62. The sun then spoke to Saṁjñā (i.e. to Chāyā mistaken by him to be Saṁjñā) "When all the sons are equal to us, how is it that one is loved by you more than the others."

63. Parrying that question, she did not mention the real situation to Vivasvān. Then he entered into meditation himself and found out the truth by means of his yogic power.

64. The lord became angry and wished to curse her with utter annihilation. Then she mentioned all the facts to Vivasvān.

65-70. On hearing it, Vivasvān became so furious that he rushed to Tvaṣṭṛ.

Tvaṣṭṛ duly honoured Vibhāvasu (Sun-god). As he was desirous of burning him furiously, Tvaṣṭṛ pacified him slowly—

"This form of yours endowed with excessive refulgence does not appear splendid. Unable to bear it, Saṁjñā is grazing the grass in the meadows in the forest. You shall see your wife of auspicious conduct today. You shall see her richly endowed with praiseworthy prime of youth, O lord of rays, by resorting to your yogic power. It shall be favourable to everyone if the following agreement is assented to. O suppressor of enemies, I shall change this excellent (excessively refulgent) form of yours that you are having from the beginning.

Originally the form of Vivasvān was so refulgent that the rays spread sideways as well as upwards and downwards. The gentle lady Saṁjñā was afflicted by that form of the lord of Firmament (i.e. the sun). Thereby your wonderful form shall have rays spreading even in circular direction.

71. Tvaṣṭṛ was allowed to change the form. Thereupon Tvaṣṭṛ undertook to change the form of Mārtaṇḍa Vivasvān (the sun-god).

72. He placed him on the (circular moving) wheel (i.e. a lathe) and pruned (the slices of the irregular superfluous part of) his brilliance—when his refulgence was taken away, the sun had his brilliance uprooted (i.e. reduced).

73. Prabhākara (the sun) of splendid appearance wished to see his wife. By resorting to his yogic power, he saw his wife in the form of a mare.

74. Though she was invisible to all living beings on account of her holy observance, and brilliance he saw her by means of his yogic power. In the form of a horse, Mārtaṇḍa had sexual intercourse with her through the mouth.

75. Relaxing at the end of the intercourse she had a suspicion that it was another person (not her husband). Hence, she expelled the Semen Virile of Vivasvān through her nostrils.

76-79. From it were born the Devas, the twin Aśvins, the most excellent physicians. Born of *Dvādaśamūrti* (the sun god) they are remembered as Nāsatya and Dasra. These were the sons of Mārtaṇḍa, the eight prajāpatis. Bhāskara (the sun) showed himself to her with his more pleasing form. On seeing his wife, he became delighted and contented. He told her thus—"Yama had become very much afflicted in his mind on account of that curse. He delighted others through his Dharma. Hence, he is called Dharmarāja. On account of that auspicious action, he obtained the greatest splendour—the overlordship of the Pitṛs (Manes) and *Lokapālatva* (the state of being the guardian of a quarter i.e. south)".

80-81. The eldest Manu was a Prajāpati. The other one Sāvarni of great renown shall become Manu in the future Manvantara called Sāvarnika.

The holy lord is performing a severe penance even today on the top of Meru.

82-84a. His brother Śanaiścara attained the state of a planet.

With that form (the prunings of the sun) Tvaṣṭṛ evolved the discus of Viṣṇu.[1] It had great splendour. It was never obstructed anywhere. It was a great defending weapon against Dānavas.

The younger sister of those two, Yamunā of great fame, became the excellent river Yamunā, the sanctifier of the worlds.

84b-86. The eldest among them was Manu of great splendour. It is his creation that we are having now.[2] I shall recount in detail the creation of Manu Vaivasvata (son of Sungod). If any one listens to or reads about this nativity of the Devas, the seven children of great prowess of Vaivasvata, he shall get released from the mishap in which he may find himself. He will attain great fame.

1. This creation of Sudarśana, the discus of Viṣṇu, from the pruned part of the sun-god is given in Vp.III.2.11.

2. The description of dynasties of kings is an integral part of a Purāṇa. Though here the accounts are scattered at different places, they are given here from the beginning of the birth of Vaivasvata Manu to the future Sāvarṇika Manus. The story of the sun-god and his wives Saṁjñā and Chāyā and his progeny from them, the pruning of the sungod and his approach to his mareformed wife and birth of Aśvin gods—these are traditional accounts found in the *Mbh. Ādi* 76, *Anuśāsana* 150, Vp. III.2 and other Purāṇas with slight variations.

The progeny of Vaivasvata Manu and other legendary dynastic accounts are probably a part of the ur-Purāṇa. Hence we find them common in all Purāṇas.

CHAPTER SIXTY

The Progeny of Vaivasvata Manu

Sūta continued :

1. Thereafter, when the Cākṣuṣa Manvantara elapsed alongwith the gods, he (Brahmā ?) allotted the overlordship of the Earth to Vaivasvata, the great one.

2-3. Ten sons were born of Vaivasvata Manu. They were equal to him. They were :— Ikṣvāku, Nṛga, Dhṛṣṭa, Śaryāti, Nariṣyanta, Prāṁśu, Nābhāga, Diṣṭa, Karūṣa and Pṛṣadhra. These ten are remembered as Mānavas.

4. Urged and instructed formerly by Brahmā, the king began to perform a horse-sacrifice according to his wish.

5-6. Desirous of getting a son, the Prajāpati performed a sacrifice. He dropped Āhuti (ghee-offering) in the fire at the spot allotted to Mitra and Varuṇa. It is mentioned in the Śruti that Ilā was born at that spot wearing divine robes, bedecked in divine ornaments and having divine physical body.

7-9. Manu, Daṇḍadhara (wielder of the sceptre) spoke to her—"O Ilā, follow me, welfare unto you" Ilā replied to him who was desirous of a son, these words consistent with and conveying Dharma—"O most excellent one among the eloquent ones, I am born in the spot allotted to Mitra and Varuṇa. I am going near them. Hence, let not Dharma kill after being itself destroyed". After saying this, the gentle lady went near them.

10-14. After going near them, the excellent lady spoke these words with palms joined in reverence—"O Devas, I am born in the part pertaining to you. What shall I do for you ? I have been told by Manu—'Follow me'. When the chaste lady Ilā spoke thus, the two Devas, Mitra and Varuṇa said these words—"O lady of excellent hips and very fair complexion, O lady conversant with Dharma, we are very much delighted with your modesty and control over your sense-organs as well as truthfulness. O daughter of exalted fortune, you will attain our fame and reputation. You will become a man well-renowned and honoured in the three worlds as Sudyumna. You will become a favourite of the whole universe, righteous by nature, and the perpetuator of the line of Manu".

15. That gentle lady went back towards her father (i.e. Manu) after obtaining the boon from Mitra and Varuṇa. Manu's son, lord Sudyumna again attained the form of a lady.*

16-17. Budha approached her later on and she was secretly entreated for a sexual intercourse by Budha. Pururavas, the son of Ilā, was thus born of Budha, the son of Soma, (Moon).

After giving birth to a son through Budha, she resumed the form of Sudyumna.

Sudyumna had three heirs and successors who were extremely virtuous.

18-20. They were Utkala, Vinata and Gaya. Utkala acquired the realm Utkala and Vinata got the western territory. Gaya, royal saint, acquired the city Gayā in the eastern direction. After creating the progeny, when Manu entered the sun (i.e. passed away), he divided the Earth into ten parts each under a Kṣatriya. (?) The heir Ikṣvāku got the tenth portion.

21-23. Since he had the state of a girl, Sudyumna did not get any share in the realm. At the instance of Vasiṣṭha, the highly lustrous prince was in Pratiṣṭhāna**. The establishment of the noble-souled virtuous king Sudyumna was in Pratiṣṭhāna. On hearing this, the sages asked Sūta :—

"How did Sudyumna, the son of Manu, attain the state of a woman ?"[1]

Sūta said :

24-26a. "Formerly, the eternal bachelors Sanaka and others came to Ilāvṛta in order to see Maheśvara. They saw the

---

*The former half of the printed verse must be really the latter half and vice versa.

**Jhusi (near Allahabad).

1. The strange story of bisexual Ilā-Sudyumna, child of Vaivasvata Manu, is found in *Mbh. Ādi* 75, *Anuśāsana* 147, Bh.P.IX.1

bull-emblemed lord indulging in amorous sports with Umā in a secluded spot. All of them turned back. Śiva then became ashamed. The beloved then said to her lover these words for the sake of her own pleasure :—

"O lord, the man who enters my hermitage will become a woman. That woman will be splendid and equal to celestial damsels."

26b-27a. All the living beings there, the Piśācas and the animals became females. They began to sport along with Rudra like the Apsaras (celestial damsels).

27b-28. That king Sudyumna, who had been out for hunting entered Umāvana (the park of Umā). When Rudra had assumed the state of a woman along with the Piśācas and Bhūtas (goblins), that king Sudyumna too acquired the form of a woman once again. Due to the favour of Mahādeva he regained manhood. (the state of being the son of Manu)."

CHAPTER SIXTYONE

A dissertation on Music

Sūta said :

1-3. Understand the genealogy of the sons of Manu in detail. Pṛṣadhra injured the cow of his preceptor at night. At the close of it, he incurred the curse of the noble-souled Cyavana and became a Śūdra.

The descendants of Karūṣa were (Kārūṣas) Kṣatriyas who could not be suppressed in battle (who were haughty due to their capacity for warfare).

The successors of Nābhāga were a thousand groups of Kṣatriyas who were valorous.

Bhalandana the son of Diṣṭa was a great scholar.

4. Bhalandana's son named Prāṁśu was very powerful. Prāṁśu had an only son who became equal to a Prajāpati.

5. He was taken to heaven by Saṁvarta along with friends and kinsmen. In this connection a great dispute arose between Saṁvarta and Bṛhaspati.

6-7. On seeing the magnificence of Yajña, Bṛhaspati became angry with him. During the Yajña, performed by Saṁvarta, he became extremely furious for the destruction of all the worlds. But he was pacified by the gods : Marutta the emperor obtained Nariṣyanta as his heir.

8. Nariṣyanta's successor was king Dama who held the sceptre (rod of chastisement). His son Rāṣṭravardhana was a well-known king.

9. Sudhṛti was his son and Nara was born of Sudhṛti. Kevala was his son. Bandhumān was the son of Kevala.

10-11. The son of Bandhumān was the righteous-souled king Vegavān. Budha was the son of Vegavān and Tṛṇabindu was the son of Budha. He became a king at the beginning of third Tretāyuga. Iḍaviḍā was his daughter who became the mother of Viśravas.

12. Viśāla, the son who was born to him became a king extremely virtuous, liberal in gifts and well renowned for heroism and great power. The city of Viśālā (Vaiśālī) was built by him.

13. The son of Viśāla was Hemacandra, a king of great strength. The successor of Hemacandra became famous by the name Sucandra.

14. Sucandra's son was a renowned king named Dhūmrāśva. The learned Sṛñjaya was born as the son of Dhūmrāśva.

15. The glorious Sahadeva of great exploits was the son of Sṛñjaya. Kṛśāśva, the son of Sahadeva, was extremely righteous.

16. The son of Kṛśāśva, viz. Somadatta was excessively brilliant and valorous. The son of the saintly king Somadatta was Janamejaya.

17-20. Janamejaya's son named Pramati was well-renowned. On account of potentiality of Tṛṇabindu all the Vaiśālaka kings with Viśālā as their capital were long-lived, noble-souled, heroic and very virtuous. Śaryāti begot twins. The son was well-renowned by the name of Ānarta. His daughter was Sukanyā who became the wife of Cyavana. Ānarta's heir named Reva was very powerful. His realm was called Ānarta and the capital city was Kuśasthalī (later Dvārakā).

Raivata was the son of Reva. Another name of his was Kakudmin. He was virtuous.

21-22. He was the eldest of a hundred brothers. After obtaining the kingdom and the capital Kuśasthalī, he went near Brahmā accompanied by his daughter. In the presence of Brahmā, he listened to Gāndharva Music for a short while (A Muhūrta i.e. 48 minutes) as reckoned by the lord of the Devas, but many Yugas according to human calculation. He returned to his city still a young man. The city then was inhabited by the Yādavas.

23. It had been renamed Dvārāvatī. It was protected by the Bhojas, Vṛṣṇis and Andhakas, the chief of whom was Vasudeva.

24. On hearing the story with all facts, Revata (Raivata) the suppressor of foes gave his daughter of good holy rites named Revatī to Baladeva in marriage. Thereafter, he went to the peak of Meru and became engaged in penance.

25. Rāma, the noble one, sported with Revatī.

On hearing that story the sages asked him subsequently.

The sages asked :

26-28. How was it that old age did not affect Revatī or Kakudmin, O highly intelligent one, even after the lapse of a long time viz. many Yugas?

We are desirous of listening to this. Tell us Gāndharva (the science of Music) too.

Sūta said :

To a person who goes to the world of Brahmā there is neither old age nor hunger nor thirst not even the fear from death. No ailments afflict him. Since I have been asked about Gāndharva (the science of Music). O great and excellent sages of good holy rites, I shall explain it accurately in details.

29. The *Svara-maṇḍala*[1] (the whole group in regard to notes) consists of seven notes (*Svaras*), three *Grāmas*[2] (Basic scales), twentyone *Mūrcchanās*[3] and forty-nine *Tānas*.[4]

---

1. The word *maṇḍala* suggests the ascent and descent of seven notes (known as *svara-saptaka*) (see V. 30)

2. *Grāma* : *Grāma* means the group of seven notes. In the Purāṇas three Grāmas are mentioned. They are, the *Ṣaḍjagrāma*, the *Madhyamagrāma* and the *Gāndhāragrāma*. These three were the basic scales. The *Sā*-scale, the *Ma*-scale and the *Ga*-scale had the notes *Sā*, *Ma* and *Ga* as the starting notes respectively. The *Sa*-scale would have notes, *Sā*, *Ri*, *Ga*, *Ma*, *Pa*, *Dha*, *Ni*; the *Ma*-scale would have the notes *Ma*, *Pa*, *Dha*, *Ni*, *Sa*, *Ri*, *Ga* and the *Ga*-scale would have the notes *Ga*, *Ma*, *Pa*, *Dha*, *Ni*, *Sā*, *Ri*. Out of these three basic scales, the *Ga*-scale fell into disuse afterwards. The ancient scholar Dattila states that it is not found in this world. The later scholars say that it went into heaven. The reason of its disappearance is given as it had extremely high and low notes. But from its description given by the later authors like Śārṅgadeva, it seems that it was not perfect in the aspect of consonance, which was vitally essential for the melodic music of India. Bharata in his *Nāṭya-śāstra* describes the *Sa*-scale and the *Ma*-scale on the basis of the consonance of the fourth (*Sa-Ma Saṁvāda*) and the consonance of the fifth (*Sa-Pa Saṁvāda*). In the *Sa*-scale the consonance of the fifth was more prominent (*Sa-Pa*, *Ri-Dha* and *Ga-Ni*) while that of the fourth in the *Ma*-Scale (*Sa-Ma*, and *Ri-Pa*). The number of *śrutis* (the microtones) in the *Saptaka* fixed by Bharata is 22. The *Śruti*-intervals were distributed in the notes as follows :

Sa scale $_4$*Sa* $_3$*Ri* $_2$*Ga* $_4$*Ma* $_4$*Pa* $_3$*Dha* $_2$*Ni*=22

Ma-scale $_4$*Ma* $_3$*Pa* $_4$*Dha* $_2$*Ni* $_4$*Sa* $_3$*Ri* $_2$*Ga*=22

The *Sa-Ma* consonance has the interval of 9 *śrutis* and the *Sa-Pa* consonance that of 13 *śrutis*.

3. *Mūcchanā*:

The *Mūrcchanā* was the gradual ascent and descent of the seven notes of the basic scale. The word is derived from the root—*Mūrcch*-meaning to increase or to pervade. As the *Mūrcchanās* started from each note of the scale, there were seven *Mūrcchanās* of each scale. Thus the *Mūrcchanās* of the three *Grāmas* numbered twentyone.

E.g. The *Sa*-scale *Mūrcchanās* would be :

(1) *Sā Ri Ga Ma Pa Dha Ni* ...

(2) *Ni Sā Ri Ga Ma Pa Dha*...

(3) *Dha Ni Sā Ri Ga Ma Pa* ... etc.

The *Sāman*-scale was descending having the notes *Ma Ga Ri Sā Dha Ni Pa* as per the *Nāradīya-śikṣā* (I.5. 1 and 2). Due to the influence of the

30. [The names of the notes :] *Ṣaḍja* (*Sā*), *Ṛṣabha* (*Ri*), *Gāndhāra* (*Ga*), *Madhyama* (*Ma*), *Pañcama* (*Pa*), *Dhaivata* (*Dha*) and also *Niṣāda* (*Ni*) should be (carefully) known (as the notes).

31-32. (and part of 33) : [The Text is corrupt and obscure. As emended from Vā P. and other Purāṇas, it gives the names of *Mūrchhanās* of the Ma-scale as follow :]

The *Mūrcchanās* of the *Ma-scale* are known as Sauvīrā, Madhyama-grāmā, Hariṇāsyā (*Hariṇāśca* in Bd. P. is wrong), Kālopabalopetā (also known as 'Kālopanatā'), Śuddha-madhyamā, Śārṅgī and Pāvanī (*nagniṁ ca pauṣā vai* in the text is not correct) and Hṛtyakā Dṛṣṭvā kām' in the text), in order.

Contd. from p. 806

Sāman-scale, there was the descending order followed in the case of starting notes of the *Mūrcchanās*. The *Mūrcchanās* served as the basis of different types of songs. They also brought in, the notes of the low (Mandra) and high (*Tāra*) registers (*Sthānas*).

If the first *Mūrcchanā* of the *Ma*-scale is rendered taking *Ma* as the *Ṣaḍja* and the remaining notes accordingly, then it would be indicated as—

$_4Sa\ _3Ri\ _4Ga\ _4Ma\ _2Pa\ _3Dha\ _2Ni = 22$ *śrutis*.

This gives the Gāndhāra of 4 Śrutis called *Antara Ga*. Its consonant note would be *Ni* of 4 *śrutis* called *Kākali Ni*. These two were called the *Sādhāraṇa* notes. Their use was restricted. Their employment was allowed when the songs had the two *śruti Ga* and the two śruti *Ni* notes in small measure. The *Mūrcchanās* with these two *Sādhāraṇa* notes were called as *Sādhāraṇīkṛta Mūrcchanās*.

4. *Tāna* is like *Mūrcchanā* in which one or two specific notes are dropped. When one specific *Svara* (note) is dropped, it is called *Ṣāḍava Tāna* (one consisting of six notes) and when two specific notes are dropped, it is called *Auḍuva Tāna* (one consisting of five notes). According to Purāṇas, there were twenty *Tānas* of Madhyamagrāma, fourteen of Ṣaḍjagrāma and fifteen of Gāndhāragrāma. Thus the number of *Tānas* of the three *grāmas* is given as forty-nine.

According to Bharata (*Nāṭyaśāstra* (Baroda edition Vol. P. 27), when the single note *Sa*, *Ri Pa* or *Ni* is dropped from the *Mūrcchanās* of the Ṣaḍjagrāma, there would take place twentyeight *Ṣāḍava Tānas* ($7\times4=28$). Similarly when the note *Sa Ri* or *Ga* is dropped from the *Mūrcchanās* of the Madhyamagrāma, twenty-one *Ṣāḍava Tānas* would be effected ($7\times3=21$). By dropping *Sa,Pa*, *Ga,Ni* or *Ri,Dha* from the *Mūrcchanās* of the *Sa*-scale twenty-one *Auḍuva Tānas* would be effected ($7\times3=21$). When *Ri,Dha* or *Ga, Ni* are dropped from the *Mūrcchanās* of the *Ma*-Scale, there would take place fourteen *Auḍuva Tānas* ($7\times2=14$). Thus the total number of the *Tānas* of two *grāmas* is eighty-four according to Bharata. These are given as *Śuddha Tānas* by later Ācāryas.

33-34a. Now understand the Mūrcchanās of *Sa*-Scale (*Ṣaḍja-grāma*) : (1) Uttara—mandrā, (2) Rajanī and also as (3) Uttarāyatā (for *Unnarāyátā* of Bd. P.), (4) Madhya-Ṣaḍja (but Vā. P. *Śuddha Ṣaḍja*) and also the other one is (5) Abhirudgatā (for *Abhi-mudgaṇā* in the Bd. P.*)

34b. Know the Mūrcchanās of the *Ga*-scale (*Gāndhāra-grāma*)** viz. Śyāmā as are described.

35-37. (The names of the *Tānas* are as follows :)

(1) Agniṣṭomika, (2) Vājapeyika, [Vā. P. adds (3) Pauṇḍraka, (4) Aśvamedhika], (5) Rājasūyaka (conjectural emendation for '*yava-rātasūyastu*' in the text). The sixth is 'Suvarṇaka,' the Seventh is 'Gosava', the eighth is Mahāvṛṣṭika, the ninth is 'Brahmadāna,' the next (10) is Prājāpatya, (11) Nāgayakṣāśraya, (12) Gottara, (13) Padakrānta (Vā. P. 'Haya-Krānta'), (14) Mṛgakrānta, (15) the charming Viṣṇukrānta, (16) the most desirable (*vareṇya*) Sūryakānta (Vā. P. reading for the obscure *Sūryakānta-dhareṇya* in Bd. P. is accepted), (17) the well-known Mattakokila (*Matta-kokila*) of Vā. P. is accepted for *Santakokila* in the text).

38a.***: Obscure and untraced in Vā P. and elsewhere.

38b. (The names of *Tānas* continued :)

(18) Sāvitra, (19) Ardha-sāvitra (20) Sarvatobhadra [After 38-b. here-of Vā. P. adds the following *Tānas* : Suvarṇa, Sutandra, Viṣṇu, Vaiṣṇuvara, Sāgara and Vijaya which is charming to all].

39. (21) The charming Adhātrya, (22) Gandharvānupata (23) Alambuṣeṣṭa, (24) Viṣṇu (25) Vaiṇavara.

---

*Note—The Purāṇa does not mention the remaining two viz. *Matsarīkṛtā* and *Aśvakrāntā*.

**Strangely enough, this Text and Vā. P. are silent about other Mūrcchanās of this scale. The NP. II. 50.35b.36a records them as follows :

Nādī, *viśālā* *Sumukhi*, *Citrā*, *Citravatī*, *Mukhā* and *Balā*. Leaving Ga-scale with mention of one Mūrcchanā, the text now enumerates *Tānas*. The omissions in the Bd.P. are made good by reference to Vā. P.

The Purāṇic concept of a *Tāna* is different from that of the present day one.

***The line is as follows :
tenavānityapavaśapiśācālīvanahyapi.

40a. (26) 'Sāgaravijaya' which is charming to all beings (Vā. P. gives 'Sāgara' and 'Vijaya').

40b. (27) Hatosṛṣṭa and (28) know the likable 'Skandha'*

41. (Repeats mostly the above verse 39 and adds) Alambuṣeṣṭa and also (29) Nārada-priya.

42a. As recounted by Bhīmasena (30) Nāgarapriya (dear to citizens), (*nāgarāṇāṁ yathā priyaḥ* in Vā. P. It is more clear than the obscure '*nāgaratānayapriyaḥ*' in the text).

42b. **(The *Tāna*) called (31) Vikalopanīta-vinatā Śrīḥ (32) Bhārgavapriya.

43a*** The fourteen; similarly they desire here fifteen (according to) Nārada.

43b. (Obscure but from Vā. P. it appears that the presiding deities of the *Mūrcchanās* are now enumerated. The Bd. P. text may tentatively be interpreted—on the basis of Vā. P. as follows)

(Mūrchanā Gāndhārī) along with Sauvīrā is hence sung by god Brahmā.

44a. And also of the Uttarādi-Svara, god Brahmā is the presiding deity here. [*devatāstrayaḥ*' of the Bd. P. is probably '*devatātra ca*', as in Vā. P.]

44b. *Hariṇāsyā* is originated in the region of Hari.

45a. The *Mūrcchanā Hariṇāsyā* has the Moon-god as the presiding deity (but Indra as per Vā. P.)

45b. The Mūrcchanā *Karopanītavitatā* is sung by Maruts in the *svara-maṇḍala* (group of notes).

46a. That is *Kalopanītā* and hence its presiding Deity is Māruta emended as : *Mārutaścātra daivatam*, as in Vā. P.).

46b. *Śuddha-madhyamā* (emended as per Vā. P. for *Śuddhamātmanā*) mūrcchanā is originated in Manu (Maru) *deśa* (After 46 b Vā. P. adds :)

---

*For 40b here of, Vā. P reads : Haṁsa, Jyeṣṭha and Tumburupriya.

**For this Vā. P. adds : Abhiramya, Śukra, Puṇya, Puṇyāraka. There are twenty (*Tānas*) in *Ma*-scale and fourteen in *Sa*-scale.

***For this Vā. P. states: They desire similarly fifteen belonging to *Ga*-grāma.

Śuddha Madhyamā is the note here and the deity is Gandharva. It moves along with the deer for the guidance of Siddhas.

47a. Hence, on account of *Mṛgas* (deer) it (the Mūrcchanā is called *Mārgi* and the Lion is its deity.

47b : Obscure :

(Tentative meaning : 'That is associated with hermitages and various human voices' (?)]

48a. As the *Mūrcchanā* is associated with *rajas* (atmosphere/mist), it is called *Rajani.*

48b. Obscure (If allied with Vā. P. :)

Uttaramandrā is known as having *Ṣaḍja* as its deity.

49. Obscure (If allied with Vā. P.) :

Hence *Uttara-tāla* is known first as well extended.

Hence, it is *Uttara-mandrā* whose deity indeed is Dhruva.

50. Obscure (emended from Vā. P.)

Because of its extension and being later (in the order) *Uttarāyatā* having *Dha* (*Dhaivata*) as the starting point, is the *Mūrcchanā,* the deity of which is the manes, the deities of Śrāddha.

51a. The great sages worship the Fire-god with the *Śuddha* Ṣaḍja (Pure *Sa-*) note. Hence, one should know it as *Śuddha-Saḍjikā* (Vā. P. : This *Mūrcchanā* starts from the *Pañcama* note).

51b. is obscure, hence the reading in Vā. P. is followed.

52a. In this manner employing these *Mūrcchanās* in which he has got such Bhāvanā (particular faith).

52b. The mūrcchanās belong to Yakṣīs (female Yakṣas) are called *Yakṣikā* mūrcchanās (*Ya* in the Ms seems to have been read as *Pa,* as in writing in Devanāgarī script *Pa* & *Ya* look similar).

53a (Obscure but if allied with Vā. P.)

The Mūrcchanās do not approach the songs affected by the poisonous sight of the serpents (Nāgas).

53b (Corrupt and obscure but with the help of Vā. P.)

And there are many *Sādhāraṇa mūrcchanās** (and also six

**Mūrcchanās* with *Sādhāraṇa Svaras* are called so. The *Sādhāraṇa Svaras* are :

(1) *Antara Gāndhāra* i.e. Modern *Śuddha Gāndhāra.*
(II) Kākalī Niṣāda=Mod. *Tīvra Niṣāda.*

only (?) are known thoroughly, (The reading Vaḍavātrividastathā in the text is obscure. Vā. P. gives *Ṣaḍevānuvidastathā*).

CHAPTER SIXTYTWO

The Science of Music

1. After knowing the views of earlier teachers, I shall expound the well-known embellishments in music in due order. Please listen to them, while I am explaining.

2. The embellishments are to be spoken of along with their *Varṇas* (movements of notes such as 'steady', 'ascending and others) as their specific basis and also alongwith their associated configuration (*saṁsthāna*), always in regard to dramatic[1] performance etc.

3a. The fulfilment of embellishment[2] is achieved by the implications of sentences and ·connotations of the word-combinations.

3b. The words of the song are said to be either preceding or following the embellishment.

4a: (Bd. P. text corrupt & obscure but Vā. P. reads) One should know that the following three are the places of Utterances viz. the chest, throat and head.[3]

4b. In these three places, the best procedure (of producing notes) functions.

5a. In the original stage (*Prakṛtau*), there are four *Varṇas* (tone-patterns) having fourfold movements.

---

1. *Vide Nāṭyaśāstra* (Baroda) Vol. IV. pp.79-92.
2. Vā.P. reading : *alaṅkārasya* accepted.
3. Bd. P. reads Sthatonitiraro nīddīmanaḥ. Vā. P. reads : *sthānāni trīṇi jānīyāt urāḥ* etc.

As the whole chapter is full of corrupt readings and obscurities the reading from the Vā.P. are accepted. But the readings are not quoted as is done above in ch.61 but simply translated indicating the source viz. Vā.P.

5b. The alternative movements are eightfold[1]; and gods know them as sixteenfold.

6. (The names of *Varṇas*:)

The first *Varṇa* is *Sthāyin*, the second is *Prasañcārin*, the third is *Avarohaṇa* (=*Avarohin*) and the fourth *Varṇa* is known by the experts in the knowledge of *Varṇas* to be *Ārohaṇa*[2] (=*Ārohin*).

7a. There is one (*Varṇa* i.e. *Sthāyin*) which has steady employment. The *Sañcāra* is the mixed movement.

7b. One should indicate the descent of *Varṇas* (i.e. *Svaras*) as *Avarohana.*

8a. (Vā. P.) And the experts in the knowledge of *Varṇas* know (that varṇa) as the *Āroha-Varṇa* by the ascent of notes.

8b. Now know then the embellishments of these specific *Varṇas.**

9. There are four embellishments viz. *Sthāpanī, Kramarejana, Pramāda* and *Apramāda.* I shall explain the characteristics of these.[3]

10. (Names of *Alaṅkāras* continue as follows:) *Visvara, Aṣṭakala* which has an interval of one place (from its original place?); *Āvarta* and *Kramotpatti*—These two should be effected according to their proportion.

11a. One should know the other one to be *Kumāra* and also *Vistara.*[4]

11b. And this indeed is the *Apāṅga* (*alaṅkāra*) and *Kutareka* (?) possesses one more *Kalā* (Time-measure)

12a. (Vā. P.) *Śyena* is originated as having one interval and situated in the midst of *Mātrās* of a *Kalā*.

---

1. These are referred to only in the Purāṇas. Later writers do not mention them.

2. The exigencies of metre have led to the change in the order. The order should have been (1) *Sthāyin* (i.e. *Sā Sā Sā*), (2) *Ārohin* (e.g. *Sā ri ga* etc.), *Avarohin* (e.g. *ni dha pa* etc.) and (4) *Sañcārin* (e.g. *Sa ri sa ri ga ri sa* etc.

*Although the Section on *Alaṅkāras* (I. Vi.) in the *Saṅgīta Ratnākara* is referred to, to interpret these *alaṅkāras* only a few like *Śyena* (p. 133 of S. R.) throw some light. Though S. R. is much later than Bd. P. or Vā. P. he has preserved some of the Purāṇa traditions.

3. But the anthor has not given them anywhere.

4. The texts of Bd. P. and Vā. P. are obscure here.

12b. (Vā. P.) In it there abides the increase in the order of the note different from it (e.g. *Sā—Pā,—Ri—Dha, Ga—ni*).

13a. (Vā. P.) The descent of the *Śyena Alaṅkāra* is called *Uttara*.

13b. (Vā. P.) The *Alaṅkāra* called *Bindu* is originated due to the measure of Kalās.

14a. One *Kalā* (a measure of time) should be employed of the *Varṇas*. Then it would be *Sthāpita* (established ?).

14b. *Durghaṭita* is that which has the note even in the reverse order.

15a. *Ekottara-Svara* has the highest note from *Ṣaḍja*.

15b. *Ākṣepāskandana* should be effected as having high amplitude like the (harsh) crowing of the crow.

16a. The two *Santāras* belong to *Sañcārin Varṇa* either as the cause or the effect.

16b. *Ākṣipta* belongs to the category of the descending (*Avarohin*) *Varṇa*.

17. The *Alaṅkāra* called Preṅkholita has the twelfth place of Kalā having one interval. Thus it is endowed with the notes (?)

18a. (Vā. P.) *Puṣkala* is said to be due to the transfer of notes.

18b. *Prakṣipta* is due to *Kalā*... (?)

19a. It is called *Bhāṣita* in which there is the use of two *Kalās* as before.

19b. *Visvarārūḍhā* (*Visarārūḍhā*) has got eight notes in ascendance.

20a. *Vāpa* (?) certainly is due to the descent from the high or low register (?).

20b. These are placed verily with one interval and have the same note at the end.

21. *Makṣi-praccheda* (?) is declared to have a group of four *Kalās*. Thus, these are the thirty Alaṅkāras explained.

22. Due to employment of *Varṇa* and *Sthāna* having the measure of *Kalā* and *Mātrā* are the configuration, proportion, modification and characteristics.

23-24a. This should be known as the purpose of embellishment which is fourfold[1]. Just as in the case of embellishment if it is used at the wrong place it is censured, similarly to beautify even the *Varṇas* unfavourably, the producer by oneself (?) would be blamed.

24b-25a. Just as due to the use of various ornaments, a woman gets herself beautified, the embellishment is the decoration of Varṇa born of itself (?).

25b. The ear-ring is not seen (worn) on the feet, nor the girdle round the neck.

26. Thus the embellishment if used in a wrong place is censured. When the embellishment is effected, it should indicate the *Rāga* (melody).

27a. Just as the characterisation of the path intended to be undertaken is enjoined by indicating it with a brush.

27b. (?)

28a. I shall describe realistically (as it is).... ?

28b. Obscure.

29a. Obscure (both in the Bd. P. and Vā. P.)

29b. The division of these two (viz. *Ṣaḍja* and *Madhyama*) as the dominant notes brings about the Charm of the songs.

30a. Obscure.

30b. (Vā. P.) The reverse would take place in the case of the order of seven notes.

31a. (Vā. P.) The four *Madraka Gitas* are sung with *Gāndhāra* as the keynote.

31b-32a. In *Madraka Gitas* we know the notes *Pañcama* (*Pa*), *Madhyama* (*Ma*), *Dhaivata* (*Dha*), *Niṣāda* (*Ni*), *Ṣaḍja* (*Sā*) and *Ṛṣabha* (*Ri*) as the remaining notes.

32b. One should know two *Aparāntika* Songs (?) (The Rest is obscure).

33a. In the *Aparāntika* songs *Gāndhāra* (*Ga*) is employed in the original (*Śuddha*) form and its modified form.

33b. (Vā. P.) The *Pada* has got three forms (?). The *Kaiśiki* song has seven forms.

---

1. *vide Saṅgīta-ratnākara* I.6.64 which enumerates *Rakti-lābha* etc.

34a. With the entire use of *Gāndhāra* as the keynote procedure of which is declared.

34b. This is also the order intended for its *Madhyama* as the keynote.

35. The songs which have been mentioned and particularly those of fourfold form (?) should be effected with seven notes and the *Kaiśikī* of sevenfold form.

36a. This is called as the pointing out of the components (of songs ?).

(*The Topic of Tāla* :) There are two even measures *Caturasra* (of four beats and eight Mātrās) and *Tryasra* (four beats and six Mātrās).

36b. Obscure (in Bd. P. & Vā. P.)

37. (Vā. P) In *Uttara* songs in the original form, the Mātrā is thus deleted (the rest is obscure).

38. With one foot in the Mātrā and deficiency in one foot... when there is the *Upahanana* (error ?) of numbers in it, it is called *Yāna*.

39. The second break in the foot is well-established with *Graha* (the starting point of the song) and in the *Aparāntika* the first, eighth, third and second are established with *Graha* ?

40. In the *Uttara* and in *Mandraka* songs in their original form, the *Pāda-bhāga*[1] and also along with one and a quarter (of a Pāda) (?) is in *Uttara* and *Mandraka*.

41a. In *Mandraka* songs the Kalā exists as explained of the *Dakṣiṇa mārga*[2] also.

---

1. *Pādabhāga* means the fourth part. Three forms of the *Tāla* were *Ekakala*, *Dvikala* and Catuṣkala.

e.g. *Ekakala Tāla* was indicated as :

S S S S; *Dvikala* as : SS SS SS SS, and *Catuṣkala* as : SSSS SSSS SSSS SSSS.

l=*Laghu*=one *mātrā*; S= *Guru*=2 *mātrās*; S=Pluta=3 mātrās. Mātrā was the time required for the utterance of five short syllables. In *Dvikala* form there were *Pāda-bhāgas* of two *Gurus* each, and in *Catuṣkala* form, of four *Gurus* each.

2. There were three *Mārgas* (ways of the *Tāla*-procedure) namely *Citra*, *Vārttika* and *Dakṣiṇa* having the *Kalā* of two *mātrās*, four *mātrās* and eight *mātrās* respectively. The forms *Ekakala*, *Dvikala* and *Catuṣkala* were associated with *Mārgas*.

41b. Obscure (in both the Purāṇas).

42a. Obscure (in both the Purāṇas).

42b-43a. When there is the use of one and the use of two, O best of Brāhmaṇas, and when there is the combination of many, Patākā[1] etc. are declared.

43b. There are three *Vṛttis—Citrā*, *Vṛtti* and *Dakṣiṇā*[2]

44a. (Vā. P.) The *samavāyas* (combinations of (?) are eight and similarly, the Mūrcchanā is Sauvīrī.

44b. Obscure : Last foot. Thus the *Svara-maṇḍala* (the whole group of notes in music) is explained.

CHAPTER SIXTYTHREE

*The Ikṣvāku Dynasty**

Sūta said :—

1. When Raivata, otherwise known as Kakudmin, went to that world (of Brahmā), his city, Kuśasthalī, was completely over-run and captured by Puṇyajanas (Yakṣas) and Rākṣasas.

2. The hundred brothers of that virtuous and noble-souled king were afflicted by arrows. Therefore, they fled in every direction due to fear.

---

1. *Paṭākā* was one of the eight *mātrās*, which was indicated by moving the hand upwadrs. These *mātrās* were to be employed in the *Mārgas* as specifically directed.

2. The *Vṛttis* (styles of rendering songs with accompaniment) were three namely *Citrā*, *Vṛtti* and *Dakṣiṇā*. They were associated with the three *Mārgas* : *Citra*, *Vārtika* and *Dakṣiṇa*, the three *Layas* (tempi), and *Grahas* etc.

In *Citrā* the music of stringed instrument was prominent and song subservient, in *Dakṣiṇā*, the song was prominent and instrumentation subservient; and in *Vṛtti* both were employed equally.

**vide* Vā.P.Ch.88.

3. O excellent Brāhmaṇas, the dynasty of these Kṣatriyas who fled due to excessive fright, is very great. They are present in different places.[1]

4. They are well-known in all the quarters as Śaryātas. They are righteous. The line of Dhṛṣṭa is called Dhārṣṭika. All the members were bold and aggressive in battle.

5-6. That clan of those noble-souled Kṣatriyas consisted of three thousand (families). Nabhāga's heir was the hero named Nābhāga. Ambarīṣa was the son of Nābhāga. His son was Virūpa. Pṛṣadaśva was the son of Virūpa and his son was Rathītara.

7. These were born of Kṣatriyas but are remembered as having become Aṅgiras. The excellent members of Rathītara family were Brāhmaṇas as well as Kṣatriyas.

8. Formerly, when Manu sneezed, Ikṣvāku was born. Ikṣvāku[2] had a hundred sons who distributed much wealth as religious gifts.

9. Vikukṣi, Nimi and Daṇḍa, these three were the most excellent among them. He had fifty sons, the chief of whom was Śakuni.

10-11. They were the kings protecting Uttarāpatha Northern territory. Forty-eight of them, the father of whom was Virāṭa were the defenders of Dakṣiṇāpatha (Southern territory), in the Southern quarter.

---

1. VV. 3-7. Though the present chapter deals mainly with the Ikṣvāku dynasty, these verses mention the dynastic list in the pre-Yayāti period i.e. before Circa 3000 B.C. as per *Vedic Age* p. 276 (BVB=Bharatiya Vidya Bhavan, Bombay).

Thus Śaryātas ruled in Ānarta (Gujarat and part of Malwa) with its capital at Kuśasthalī or Dwarka (De, 7), Dhārṣṭikas ruled over Vāhīka (between the Bias and Sutlej) in Panjab (De, 15). The descendants of Nābhāga were probably in the midlands of the Gangetic doab, but their special feature was the attainment of Brahminhood as Aṅgirasas, indicating the fluidity of caste system of that period.

2. From V. 8, the author describes the dynasty of Ikṣvāku. His three sons Vikukṣi, Nimi and Daṇḍa founded dynasties at Ayodhyā (U.P.), Videha (Bihar) and Daṇḍaka (North Deccan).

Once, at the performance of the *Aṣṭaka*[1] (a kind of *Śrāddha*), Ikṣvāku commanded Vikukṣi thus.

The King said :—

12. "Fetch flesh for the sake of *Śrāddha*, O highly powerful one, after killing animals. The *Śrāddha* of *Aṣṭaka* has to be performed by me surely."

13. At the instance of the intelligent one, he went for hunting. After killing thousands of animals, the powerful prince became tired.

14-15. Vikukṣi who had gone for hunting, ate a rabbit. When Vikukṣi returned with the meat and his army, the king urged Vasiṣṭha saying "Let the meat be sprinkled (with holy water)". Vasiṣṭha said "So be it". On being urged thus the meat was duly presented by the king. On seeing the meat polluted, Vasiṣṭha became angry and spoke to him :—

16-18. "This meat has been defiled by your son, O king. By eating the rabbit, O king of great splendour, the meat cannot remain unpolluted. O sinless one, rabbit has been eaten earlier by this wicked fellow. Therefore, O excellent king, this meat intended to be offered to the Pitṛs is defiled".

Thereupon, Ikṣvāku became furious and spoke this to Vikukṣi :

19-21. "Directed by me in connection with the holy rite of the Manes, you went for hunting. But you ate the flesh of the rabbit in the forest earlier to-day. You have been unkind (in this context), Hence, I am banishing you. Go anywhere else alongwith your own fate".

Thus he was abandoned by Ikṣvāku. He came to be known by the name Śaśāda (one who eats rabbit). Later, the son became extremely virtuous. When Ikṣvāku passed away he got the entire Earth at the instance of Vasiṣṭha. He became the ruler of Ayodhyā.

---

1. Aṣṭaka is a Śrāddha performed on the 8th day of the dark halves of the months of Mārgaśīrṣa, Pauṣa, Māgha, Phālguna (*Āśvalāyana* Gr.S. II.4.1), but most other *Gṛhya sūtras* regard the first three as the Aṣṭaka days. Flesh is to be offered to Pitṛs in this Śrāddha (Gobhila Gr.S.III.10.48). Hence, Ikṣvāku's order to Vikukṣi to bring flesh *vide* v.12. Now, no flesh is served in Śrāddha.

22-23. Urged and guided by Vasiṣṭha, he ruled over the kingdom for some time. Even when he was ruling over the kingdom, the king was fully afflicted by this sin. After some time, he fell into the hell, having waves of urine and faeces. After reading this anecdote, a learned man should understand (its implications). He should not eat anything against the Vedic injunction.

24. Learned men explain the etymological meaning of *Māṁsa*[1] (flesh) thus :—

(The being) whose flesh I am eating here shall eat me (*Māṁ*—me, *sa*—he *bhakṣayitā*—shall eat) in the next birth. This is the *Māṁsatva* (state of being flesh) of meat.

25-26. Śaśāda's heir was a heroic king named Kakutstha. Formerly, there was the *Āḍibaka** fight. In it Indra took the form of a bull. This king seated himself on the hump of the bull (Indra). (*Kakut*—hump, *tstha*—occupant) and won the war. Hence, he is remembered as Kakutstha.[2]

Kakutstha's son was Anenas and Pṛthu was the son of Anenas.

27-28. Dṛṣadaśva was the son of Pṛthu. The powerful (king) Andhra (came) after him. Yuvanāśva was the successor of Andhra. Śrāvasta was born as his son. Śrāvasta became a king by whom the city of Śrāvastī [Mod. Sahet-Mahet on the Rapti River in Oudh U.P] was founded. Śrāvasta's heir was Bṛhadaśva of great renown.

29. Bṛhadaśva's son was renowned as Kuvalāśva. This king later on came to be known as Dhundhumāra since he slew the demon Dhundhu.

---

1. A popular etymology—a special feature of this Purāṇa. But this is a quotation from Manu V.55.

**Āḍibaka*—The deadly combat fought by Vasiṣṭha and Viśvāmitra after assuming the form of *Āḍi* and *Baka* (two aquatic birds). Devas and Asuras fought with each other after taking sides of Vasiṣṭha and Viśvāmitra.

2. Kālidāsa, however, explains the epithet *Kakutstha* (as 'one who occupies a prominent place among kings', *vide Raghuvaṁśa* VI.71 *Ikṣvākuvaṁśyaḥ kakudaṁ nṛpāṇāṁ kakutstha ityāhitalakṣaṇobhūt.*

The sages requested :—

30. We wish to hear in detail, O sage of great intelligence, how Dhundhu was killed, on account of which Kuvalāśva came to be called Dhundhumāra.

Sūta replied :—

31-33. Kuvalāśva had twenty-one thousand sons. All of them were experts in different lores. They were strong and unassailable. All of them were righteous. They performed sacrifices and distributed plenty of monetary gifts. Bṛhadaśva the elderly ruler enthroned Kuvalāśva in that realm. Kuvalāśva was very powerful, excellent and virtuous. After transferring the royal position and splendour to his son, the king entered the forest.

34. Uttaṅka the Brahminical sage, prevented the great king Bṛhadaśva who was brave, excellent and virtuous, from going to the forest.

Uttaṅka said :—

35. "The duty of protecting people should be carried out by you. It behoves you to do it. O king, I am unable to perform penance unperturbed.

36. Near the precincts of my hermitage, on the other side of Meru, the ocean is filled with sand, O king.

37-38. A great Asura named Dhundhu is lying underground there hidden by the sands. He cannot be killed by the Devas. He has a huge body and is very powerful. He is the son of Rākṣasa Madhu. After performing terrible penance, he stays there for the destruction of the people.

39. When he exhales at the end of a year, the ground there quakes and shakes along with the forests.

40-41. A great column of dust is raised by the air exhaled by him. It envelops the path of the sun. The Earthquake continues for a week. It is extremely terrifying, as it is accompanied by sparks, flames and fumes. Hence, O king, I am unable to stay within my hermitage.[1]

42. Resist him, O king of great powerful arms, with a desire for the welfare of the worlds. Your brilliant splendour is already great. Viṣṇu will develop it further by contribution of his own splendour.

43. Indeed, you alone are capable of slaying him, O lord of the Earth. Let the worlds become happy and relieved with that Asura slain.

44-45. O sinless one, formerly, a boon had been granted to me (that you would help me by killing him). Indeed, Dhundhu of excessive virility and power, cannot be over-powered completely by any one of insignificant brilliance or even by rulers of the Earth, though they may fight with him for hundreds of years. His prowess and strength is very great, difficult to be approached even by the Devas".

46. On being told thus by the noble-souled Uttaṅka, that saintly king gave him Kuvalāśva for the task of warding off Dhundhu.

47. "O holy lord, I have laid down my arms. This is my son, O excellent Brāhmaṇa. He will undoubtedly become the slayer of Dhundhu".

48. He ordered his son to carry out the task of slaying Dhundhu with any step. The king of praiseworthy holy rites, went to the forest itself for the sake of penance.

49-51. Abiding by the order of his father, Kuvalāśva accompanied by his twenty-one thousand sons and Uttaṅka proceeded ahead for resisting Dhundhu. Lord Viṣṇu entered him with his own divine splendour. When, being urged by Uttaṅka and with a desire for the welfare of the world, the unassailable king marched out, there arose a great din and commotion in the sky.

---

1. B.C. Law regards this legend as a natural phenomenon. He conjectures that this volcanic pit near the western sea was sub-merged with sea water and the volcanic action ceased by the efforts of Kuvalāśva (*Tribes in Ancient India*, p. 126), while Pargiter regards this as a shallow sand-filled sea in Rajasthan which prevented Aryan expansion (AIHT. pp. 260-61).

52. "This king shall become Dhundhumāra (slayer of Dhundhu) with effect from today". The Devas showered him all round with divine flowers.

53-55. Then the divine Dundubhis (war-drums) were sounded loudly.

The heroic lion among men went along with his sons and dug up the vast inexhaustible ocean filled with sands. Dhundhu who had concealed himself beneath the sands, was found out by his sons who were digging the sands on the Western side.

That infuriated Asura appeared to upset the worlds by means of fire coming out of his mouth.

56. By means of his Yogic power that great and excellent Asura let flow water like the great ocean blending its currents and waves together at the time of moon-rise.

57-60a. All his sons were burnt down completely; only three survived that battle.

Then that king of enormous strength and great splendour approached that immensely mighty Rākṣasa Dhundhu who killed his kinsmen. The king, O dear one, who was a Yogin, suppressed his forceful flood of water let loose by him my means of his Yogic power and subdued fire by means of water. In the end the king killed that aquatic demon of huge body, by means of his prowess. After accomplishing his task the king pointed the Rākṣasa to Uttaṅka.

60b-63. Uttaṅka granted boon to that noble-souled king that the more he gave as gifts the more would be his wealth ever lasting. The other boons he granted were the invincibility (in battle) by the enemies, perpetual interest in Dharma and never-ending residence in the heaven. He granted the everlasting worlds in heaven to his sons who were killed by the demon.

Out of the three of his sons who survived, the eldest is called Dṛḍhāśva. Bhadrāśva and Kapilāśva are remembered as the younger ones. Dṛḍhāśva is known as Dhaundhumāri (i.e. son of Dhundhumāra) and Haryaśva was his son.

64. Haryaśva's son was Nikumbha who was always devoted to the duties of a Kṣatriya. Saṁhatāśva, who was an expert in battle, was the son of Nikumbha.

65-66. Kṛśāśva and Akṛtāśva were the two sons of Saṁhatāśva. His wife was the chaste Haimavatī and his mother Dṛṣadvatī was well-known in the three worlds. His (?) son was Prasenajit. Yuvanāśva, his son, was famous in the three worlds.

67. His wife Gaurī was an extremely virtuous and chaste lady. But she was cursed by her husband and was converted into the river Bāhudā*.

68. Her son Gaurika (i.e. son of Gaurī) became an emperor. Māndhātṛ, the son of Yuvanāśva, was a king who conquered the three worlds.

69-72. In this context the Brāhmaṇas well-versed in the Purāṇas cite the following stanza :—

The entire space where the sun rises and establishes itself is called the territory of Māndhātā, son of Yuvanāśva.

His wife was the daughter of Citraratha (?) and Śaśabindu. She was a chaste lady named Bindumatī. In beauty she was unrivalled on the Earth. This chaste lady was the eldest sister of ten thousand brothers. Lord Māndhātā begot of her three sons viz. Purukutsa, Ambarīṣa and Mucukunda who was well-known.

73. Another Yuvanāśva is remembered as the heir of Ambarīṣa. He was born of Narmadā. Sambhūta was his son.

74. The valorous Anaraṇya was the bosom-born son of Sambhūta. He was killed by Rāvaṇa by whom all the three worlds had been conquered before.

75. (Defective text) Tenadṛśya (?) (prob. Trasadasyu) was the son of Anaraṇya**. Haryaśva was Trasadasyu's son. King Sumati was born of Dṛṣadvatī and Haryaśva.)

76. His son was a virtuous king named Tridhanvā. The son of Tridhanvā was the scholarly lord Trayyāruṇi.

77-79. A son of great strength named Satyavrata was born to him. After killing the heaven-dwellers (?), Vidrabha's

*mod. Burha-Rāptī, a feeder of Rāptī river in Oudh.

** The Text *tenadṛśyonaraṇyaya* is wrong. Identical verse Vā.P. 88.75 reads *Trasadasyonaraṇyasya*'—Trasadasyu was the son of Anaraṇya'.

wife was abducted by him. This sin was committed by that intelligent one out of lust, strength and great delight, forcibly out of delusion and due to the power of the inevitable future. This was done by him when the Mantras of the wedding ceremony had not been concluded.* His father Trayyāruṇa banished him because he had been sinful.

80-81. Becoming infuriated with him, he exclaimed many times "This is disgrace and degradation".

He asked his father again and again, "I am alone. Where shall I go?".

The father told him, "Go and live along with Cāṇḍālas, O defiler of the family. With you as my son, I am not a seeker of a son now. Although I seek sons, they should not be like you".

82. On being told thus, he went out of the city at the instance of the lord, the king. Vasiṣṭha, the exalted sage, did not prevent him from going.

83. Satyavrata who was intelligent and bold, lived near the abodes of Cāṇḍālas on being abandoned by his father. His father went to the forest.

84. On account of this sin, Indra did not shower rain in that country for full twelve years.

85. Viśvāmitra, a sage of great penance, left his wife in the territory of that king and performed extensive penance in the marshy shores of the Sea.

86. His wife tied her own bosom-born middle son with a rope round his neck and offered him for sale in exchange for a hundred cows. She wanted to sell him in order to sustain and bring up the remaining sons.

87-88. The excellent king of holy rites and virtuous soul saw the son of the great sage tied round the neck and offered for sale. Thereupon, he released him.

For the sake of satisfying Viśvāmitra and arousing his sympathy, Satyavrata, of great intellect, sustained him and brought him up too.

89. That boy who had been tied round the neck became a sage of great penance named Gālava. That Kauśika

---

* Vide verse No. 96 below.

(one belonging to the family of Kuśika) was redeemed by that heroic king.

90. On account of his (?) holy vow, devotion, mercy and solemn declaration, the king who adhered to rules of discipline, sustained Viśvāmitra's wife also.

91. He used to kill deer, boars, buffaloes and aquatic beings and bring their meat near the hermitage of Viśvāmitra.

92-93. At the instance of sage Vasiṣṭha Satyavrata's father undertook *Upāṁśuvrata* (a secret vow) and for that purpose took initiation extending to twelve years. When the king went to the forest, Vasiṣṭha protected Ayodhyā, the harem and the whole realm from the evil contact and injustice arising from Satya-vrata.

94. On account of his childishness as well as due to the force of inevitable future, Satyavrata bore a grudge against Vasiṣṭha due to grief.

95. When Satyavrata was banished from the realm by the father, Sage Vasiṣṭha did not prevent this, due to a specific reason.

96. The conclusion of the wedding Mantras shall be only at the seventh step (*Saptapadī*). Ṭhinking thus Satya-vrata abducted her (?) at the seventh step.

97. "Despite being conversant with Dharmas, Vasiṣṭha wishes for fresh chanting of the Mantras",—saying thus Satyavrata became angry with Vasiṣṭha, in his mind.

98. The Saintly lord Vasiṣṭha performed penance for their welfare. But Satyavratra did not understand his secret vow.

99. The fury of his noble-souled father was excessively directed to his son. Therefore, Indra did not shower rain for twelve years.

100-101. "Atonement can be made in the family by me if I take up initiation which is very difficult to undertake on the earth now". So thought Vasiṣṭha. He did not prevent the banishment of the son by the father thinking thus—"when he passes away, I shall crown him". In the meantime that king of potentiality undertook initiation extending to twelve years.

102-105. When there was no meat readily available, the son of the king espied the divine cow of the noble-souled Vasiṣṭha that milked every one of desires of devotees.

The most excellent one among powerful ones, who was hungry due to fatigue, adopted the policy of thieves and killed the cow on account of his anger (towards Vasiṣṭha) and delusion too. He himself made the sons of Viśvāmitra eat the meat. On hearing about it, Vasiṣṭha cast him off. The holy lord Vasiṣṭha said thus to the prince.

106-108. "If you had not already had three sins, O base one among men, I would have made you fall down, O cruel one, after inflicting another sin.

You have committed sins in three ways viz. — "You made your father dissatisfied, you killed the cow of your preceptor, you made use of what had not been sacrificed by the sprinkling of holy water."

Thus the sage of great power of penance saw the three sins (*Śaṅkus*) and called him Triśaṅku. Therefore, the king is remembered as Triśaṅku.

109-112. Viśvāmitra who returned (from his penance) became delighted with Trisaṅku because he had sustained his wife (during the absence of the sage). He granted him a boon. When he was pressed to choose a boon the prince chose him as his preceptor and requested for this boon—"I shall go to heaven along with this physical body." When there was a danger of draught extending to twelve years, the sage crowned him in his hereditary kingdom. Even as the Devas as well as Vasiṣṭha were watching, the lordly saint Viśvāmitra made him ascend heaven.

113-114. It was all the more surprising because it happened even as Vasiṣṭha was watching. In this context persons well-versed in the Purāṇas cite this stanza :

"Due to Viśvāmitra's favour and on account of the blessing of that intelligent sage, Triśaṅku of great splendour shines in heaven alone with the Devas.

115. His wife named Satyavratā, born of the family of Kaikeyas, gave birth to Hariścandra, a sinless son.

116. King Hariścandra is well known as Traiśaṅkava.

(son of Triśaṅku). As a performer of Rājasūya sacrifice, he became famous as an Emperor.

117. Hariścandra had a heroic and powerful son named Rohita. Harita was the son of Rohita and Cañcu is mentioned as the son of Harita.

118. Vinaya and Sudeva were the two sons of Cañcu. Sudeva was the conqueror of all Kṣatriyas. Hence, he is remembered as Vijaya.

119. Ruruka was his son. He was a king proficient in details regarding Dharma and Wealth (*Artha*). Vṛka was the son of Ruruka and Bāhu was born of him.

120. Since that king indulged in vice, he was dethroned by the Haihayas, Tālajaṅghas, Śakas, Yavanas, Kāmbojas, Pāradas and Pahlavas.

121. Even when the Yuga was conducive to the development of virtue, that king was not much of a righteous person. Sagara was the son of Bāhu. He was born along with poison.[1]

122-123. It was at the hermitage of Bhṛgu that he was born. He was protected by Aurva. After acquiring the *Āgneya Astra* (a missile the deity of which is fire-god) from the grandson of Bhṛgu (viz. Aurva) king Sagara went over the whole of the Earth and killed Tālajaṅghas and Haihayas. The unerring king repudiated the Dharma (code of conduct etc.) of the Śakas and Pahlavas.

124-125. (Sagara) who was conversant with the real Dharma cast out the Dharma of the Kṣatriyas called (Pāradas) i.e. excommunicated them from Kṣatriya-hood.

The sages enquired :—

How was the king Sagara born along with poison ? What for did the infuriated king who never committed a fault banish them from the hereditary and traditional codes of conduct of Śakas and others who were Kṣatriyas of great prowess ?

Sūta explained :—

126. It has already been mentioned that the kingdom

1. *Sa-gara* (with poison) : The etymology of the King's name.

of Bāhu who indulged in vice, had been formerly seized by the Haihayas and Tālajaṅghas who came along with the Śakas.

127. The Yavanas, Pāradas, Kāmbojas. Pahlavas (and Śakas), these five clans (of kings) attacked for and on behalf of the Haihayas.

128. When he had been deprived of his kingdom, Bāhu renounced his abode and entered the forest. Accompanied by his wife, the noble-souled king performed a penance.

129. Once that king, though disabled, went to fetch water. On account of old age and weakness, he passed away in the middle.

130. His wife, a member of the family of Yadu, was pregnant and she had gone after him. Poison had been administered to her by her co-wife with a desire to kill the child in the womb.

131. She lit the funeral pyre of her husband and got on to it. On seeing her, Aurva, the grand-son of Bhṛgu, made her desist from it out of mercy.

132. She gave birth to the child developed in her womb along with the poison. She gave birth to a righteous son named Sagara who became very powerful.

133. Aurva performed *Jātakarman* and other post-natal holy rites of the noble-souled prince. He taught him Vedas and Sacred scriptures. Thereafter, he taught him how to discharge missiles and miraculous weapons.

134. After that the king determined to exterminate the Śakas, Yavanas, Kāmbojas, Pāradas, and Pahlavas.

135. On being hit, hurt and killed by the noble-souled, heroic Sagara, all of them sought refuge in Vasiṣṭha, desirous of shelter.

136. On seeing them filled with humility, the great sage granted them freedom from fear and restrained Sagara.

137. Remembering his own vow and on hearing the prescriptive words of his preceptor, Sagara struck off their customary observances of caste and other characteristics, and made them change their guise and garments.

138-139.[1] He shaved half of the heads of Śakas and discharged them. He shaved off the heads of Yavanas and Kāmbojas completely. The Pāradas were compelled to keep their hairs dishevelled and the Pahlavas were made to grow their moustache and beard. All of them were deprived of the study of the Vedas and the utterance of the Vaṣaṭkāra Mantras, by that noble-souled king.

140-141. The Śakas, Yavanas, Kāmbojas, Pahlavas, Pāradas, Kalisparśas, Māhiṣikas, Dārvas, Colas and Khaśas —the customary observations of their castes and conventions of all these groups of Kṣatriyas were prohibited formerly by the noble-souled Sagara at the instance of Vasiṣṭha.

142. After conquering the whole of the Earth by means of righteous victory, the king took initiation for the horse sacrifice and made the sacrificial horse go round the world.

143. As he made it go round, the horse was stolen away near the shore of the South-Eastern Ocean and made to enter beneath the earth.

144-145. The king got that place completely dug up by his sons. Digging up the bed of the great ocean, they met with the primordial being, Lord Viṣṇu in the form of Kapila, the lord Hari, Kṛṣṇa, the lord of subjects, lord Haṁsa, lord Nārāyaṇa.

146. After coming within the path of his vision and being afflicted by its fiery splendour, all those princes were burned; only four sons survived.

147. They were Barhiketu, Suketu, Dharmaratha and the heroic Pañcajana. They perpetuated the line of the lord.

148-150. Hari, Nārāyaṇa granted him boons viz— ever-lasting status to his race, ability to perform hundred horse sacrifices, the all pervading ocean as a son, and the eternal residence in heaven.

Fetching the horse with him, the ocean, the lord of rivers, saluted him. By that activity of his, he got the name Sāgara.

---

1. VV.138-139 describe the ways of hair-dressing etc. of these tribes.

After getting back the sacrificial horse from the ocean, the king performed horse-sacrifices again and again making up the total of one hundred.

151-152. His sixty thousand sons were burned by the anger of the lord Kapila. We have heard that the noble-souled sixty thousand sons entered the brilliant lustre of Nārāyaṇa.

The Sages asked :—

153. Tell us by what procedure were the numerous, highly mighty and valorous sons of Sagara, sixty thousand in number were born.

Sūta replied :—

154. Sagara had two wives who had dispelled their sins by means of their penance. The elder of the two was the daughter of Vidarbha named Keśinī.

155. His younger wife was the daughter of Ariṣṭanemī. She was extremely virtuous and unparalleled in beauty throughout the world.

156-159a. On being propitiated by means of austerities, the lordly sage Aurva granted them these boons viz.—One of them would give birth to a desired son who would perpetuate the line and the second would give birth to sixty thousand sons.

On hearing the words of the sage, Keśinī chose the single excellent son who would perpetuate the line, O king, in the assembly. Sumati, the sister of Suparṇa, of exalted good fortune, delightedly chose the sixty thousand sons.

159b-160. As time passed on, the elder queen gave birth to the eldest son of Sagara well known by the name of Asamañja, the scion of the family of Kakutstha. Sumati of great renown gave birth to a pot-gourd like the lump of foetus.

161. The sixty thousand sons emerged from the gourd-like lump of foetus. He then placed them (the pieces of the foetus) in the pot filled with ghee.

162-163. The king engaged as many nurses (as there were pieces) in order to nurture them individually. Thereafter, in nine months, all those sons of exalted fortune fully developed comfortably increasing the pleasure of Sagara. After a long time, they entered the prime of youth.

164-165. The other son of Sagara born of Keśinī was Barhiketu of great strength well known as Asamañja. Since he was engaged against the interests of citizens, he was banished from the city by his father. The heroic son of Asamañja was named Aṁśumān.

166. His noble-souled son was well known as Dilīpa. Bhagīratha, a hero of great splendour, was born of Dilīpa.

167. It was by him that Gaṅgā, the most excellent of all rivers, rendered splendid by aerial chariots, was brought here (in this world) and assigned the status of his daughter by the lord of Suras (Brahmā).

168-169. In this context, persons well-versed in the Purāṇas cite this verse. "By means of his active endeavour Bhagīratha brought Gaṅgā to the Earth. Hence Gaṅgā is called Bhāgīrathī by those excellent persons who are conversant with genealogy." Bhagīratha's son was named Śruta.

170. Nābhāga was his heir. He was always engaged in virtuous activities. Ambarīṣa was his son and Sindhudvīpa was the next king.

171-172. It is well known that persons of yore conversant with the Purāṇas and genealogy sing thus :— 'The Earth protected by the arms of Ambarīṣa, son of Nābhāga became perfectly free from the three distresses". Ayutāyu was the heroic son of Sindhudvīpa.

173. Ṛtuparṇa of great renown was the heir of Ayutāyu. This strong king who was conversant with the divine Mantra *Akṣahṛdaya* (the heart of dice) was a friend of Nala.

174. Two Nalas of steadfast holy vows are well known in the Purāṇas : the one, the son of Vīrasena and the other the prominent member of the family of Ikṣvāku.

175. Sarvakāma, the lord of the people, was the son of Ṛtuparṇa. King Sudāsa, his son, became a friend of Indra.

176. Sudāsa's son, the king named Saudāsa became well-known as Kalmāṣapāda. He is known by the name Mitrasaha also.

177. For the perpetuation of the line of Ikṣvāku, Vasiṣṭha of great brilliance, begot Aśmaka of the wife of Kalmāṣapāda.

178-179. Mūlaka was the bosom-born son of Aśmaka. In this context too they cite this, concerning king Mūlaka :—

"Indeed, because he was afraid of Paraśurāma, that king remained surrounded by women. Desirous of protection, the lord who was devoid of robes had women for his coat of mail.

180. The righteous-souled king Śataratha is remembered as the son of Mūlaka. Iḍaviḍa, the powerful king, was born of Śataratha.

181. The valorous Kṛtavarmā was the glorious son of Iḍaviḍa. His son Viśvasaha was born of Putrīkasī (?).

182-183. Dilīpa[1] was his son. He became well known as Khaṭvāṅga. Having attained a span of life extending to a Muhūrta, he returned from Heaven and combined the three worlds on account of his intelligence and truthfulness. Dīrghabāhu was his son. Raghu was born of him.

184. Aja was the son of Raghu. The heroic king named Daśaratha was born of him. He was the delighter of the members of the family of Ikṣvāku.

185. Rāma, Bharata, Śatrughna and Lakṣmaṇa of great strength were the sons of Daśaratha. Rāma was heroic, conversant with Dharma and well-known in the worlds.

186. Śatrughna went to Madhuvana and killed Lavaṇa, son of Madhu. There the city of Mathurā was founded by Śatrughna.

187. Subāhu and Śūrasena were the sons of Śatrughna. They were born of the princess of Videha. They ruled over the city of Mathurā.

188. Aṅgada and Candraketu were the two sons of Lakṣmaṇa. Their territories at the border of the Himalaya mountain were very prosperous and flourishing.

189. In the territory of Kārāpatha (?) the city of Aṅgada was called Aṅgada. Candracakra, the splendid city of Candraketu is well known.

---

1. This is Dilīpa II. Dilīpa I was the father of Bhagīratha (see v.166).

190. The heroic Takṣa and Puṣkara were the sons of Bharata. The cities of those two noble souls were situated in the realm of the Gandharvas.

191. The city of Takṣa was well known in all the quarters by the name of Takṣaśilā. The city of the heroic Puṣkara was well known as Puṣkarāvatī.

192. Those people who are conversant with the Purāṇas sing this Gāthā (lyrical verse). It concerns Rāma. It consists of facts due to the greatness of that intelligent one.

193-195. "Rāma was dark-complexioned and youthful. He had red eyes and bright face. He was a person of few words. His arms extended as far as his knees. He had splendid face, leonine shoulders and long brawny arms. He ruled over the kingdom for ten thousand years.

In his kingdom the sound of the chanting of Mantras of Ṛk, Sāman and Yajus as well as that of— "Let it be given, let it be enjoyed" was incessant and unbroken.

While living in Janasthāna (Nasik in Maharashtra) Rāma accomplished a task of the Devas.

196. Earlier, proceeding in search of Sītā's whereabouts, Rāma the bull among men (the powerful leader), the king of great fame slew (Rāvaṇa) the descendant of Pulastya, the demon who had committed sins.

197. He had Sattva (purest) qualities (or he had great inherent strength). He was richly endowed with good qualities. He shone with his own brilliance. Thus Rāma, the son of Daśaratha, shone surpassing the sun and fire.

198. The two sons of that powerful king were like him. They are well known as Kuśa and Lava. Understand their territories.

199. Kośala was the kingdom of Kuśa and his city was Kuśasthalī.[1] This beautiful city was built by him on the sides and ridges of the Vindhya mountain.

200. Uttarakośala was the kingdom of the noble-souled Lava. His city Śrāvastī is well known in all the worlds.

Understand the line of Kuśa.

---

1. De identifies it with Ujjain but our text locates it on the ridges of the Vindhya mountain.

201. Atithi, the virtuous-souled son of Kuśa was fond of entertaining guests. The famous king named Niṣadha was the son of Atithi.

202. Nala was the son of Niṣadha. Nabhas was the son of Nala. Puṇḍarīka was the son of Nabhas and Kṣemadhanvan is remembered as the king after him.

203. The valorous king Devānīka was the son of Kṣemadhanvan. Lord Ahīnagu was the son of Devānīka.

204. Ahīnagu's heir was Pāriyātra of great fame. Dala was his son. King Bala was born of him.

205. The noble-souled son of Bala was Ulūka.[1] Vajranābha was his son and his son was Śaṅkhaṇa.

206. Śaṅkhaṇa's son was a scholar well known as Vyuṣitāśva. It is said that king Viśvasaha was the son of Vyuṣitāśva.

207. Hiraṇya-nābha alias Kauśalya (belonging to Kośala) was his most excellent son. In the Prācya Sāman Mantras, he is remembered as the disciple of Pauṣyañji.[2]

208. He learned five hundred Saṁhitās from Pauṣyañji. Yoga was learnt from him by the intelligent Yājñavalkya.

209. Puṣpa (Puṣya), his son, was a scholar. His son was Dhruvasandhi. Sudarśana was his son. Agnivarṇa was born of Sudarśana.

210-211. Śīghra was the son of Agnivarṇa, Maru is remembered as the son of Śīghra. Maru practised Yogic exercises and stayed in Kalāpagrāma.

This lord was the person who made the Kṣatriyas function in the twentyfirst Prayuga (? subsidiary Yuga).

Prabhusuta (Prasuśruta-Vā.P.) was the son of Maru and Susandhi was his son.

1. Vā.P.88.205 calls him Auṅkha while in the AIHT list of Ayodhyā kings (p. 149) he is recorded as Uktha.

2. Pauṣyañji—a teacher of Sāma-veda. He was a disciple of Sukarman Jaimini. He taught 500 branches of Sāmaveda (PCK—*Prācīna carita kośa* I.9.624).

It is seen that most of the kings in this chapter are listed in Pargiter's AIHT, pp.145-149.

212. Susandhi's son was Marṣa (Amarṣa ?) otherwise known by the name of Sahasvān. The son of Sahasvān was a king named Viśrutavān.

213-216. King Bṛhadbala was the son of Viśrutavān.

These are the sons and heirs of Ikṣvāku. They are remembered to be hundreds in number. Those who were very important have been recounted on account of their importance.

If a person reads this creation of Āditya Vivasvān (the sun) he becomes endowed with children. He attains Sāyujya merging with Manu, the son of Vivasvān, who is known as Lord Śrāddhadeva and who grants nourishment to the subjects.

He shall be rid of his sins and *Rajas* qualities. He shall become long-lived. He shall never swerve from the righteous path.

CHAPTER SIXTYFOUR

*The Description of Nimi Dynasty.**

Sūta said :—

1-2. Understand (the details of) the line of Nimi who was the younger brother of Vikukṣi. He built a city well-known by the name Jayanta, comparable to the city of the Devas. (It was) near the hermitage of Gautama. It was in his family that there was born the excellent king Janaka.

3. Ikṣvāku of profound brilliance had a son named Nimi, a highly pious soul who was saluted by all living beings and who became a great king.

4-5. On account of the curse of Vasiṣṭha, he became *Videha* (devoid of physical body). His son named Mithi was produced in the course of three Parvans. This king of great fame was born of *Araṇi* (the wood from which fire is kindled for sacrificial purpose) while it was being churned. He is well-

*This chapter corresponds to chapter 89 of Vā.P.

known by the name Mithi. He became Janaka due to the act of *Janana* (procreation in such a way).

6. Mithi was indeed a king of great prowess. It is from his name that this capital city became known as Mithilā[1] Another name of this king was Janaka and Janaka's successor was Udāvasu.

7. The virtuous-souled son Nandivardhana was born of Udāvasu. The valorous and virtuous son named Suketu was born of Nandivardhana.

8. The noble-souled son of great strength, Devarāta was born of Suketu. The pious-souled son well known as Bṛhaduktha was born of Devarāta.

9. Mahāvīra was the valorous son of Bṛhaduktha. Dhṛtimān was the son of Mahāvīrya and Sudhṛti was his son.

10. Dhṛṣṭaketu, the suppressor of his enemies, was the noble-souled son of Sudhṛti. The son of Dhṛṣṭaketu was well-known by the name Haryaśva.

11. Maru was the son of Haryaśva. Pratimbaka[2] was the son of Maru. It is remembered that the righteous-souled king Kīrtiratha was the son of Pratimbaka.

12. The son of Kīrti-ratha is also known by the name Devamīḍha. Vibudha was the son of Devamīdha. Mahādhṛti was the son of Vibudha.

13. The son of Mahādhṛti was the valorous king Kīrtirāta. The learned son of Kīrtirāta was well-known by the name Mahāroman.

14. The famous king Svarṇaromā was born of Mahāromā. The son of Svarṇaromā named Hrasvaromā became a king.

15. The learned son of Hrasvaromā was wellknown as Sīradhvaja. Sītā of great reputation, rose out of the ground when that king ploughed it.

16-18. She was the chaste queen of Rāma. She was a lady of good holy rites and vow of self-restraint.

---

1. Modern Tirhut, also called Janakpur, in Darbhaṅgā Dist. Bihar.

2. Pargiter records Pratīndhaka for this (AIHT. p. 147)

Vaiśampāyana enquired :—

How was Sītā of great reputation raised up from the ground on being ploughed. What for did the king plough? Where was the field ?

Sūta replied :

The site of the sacrificial fire in the horse-sacrifice of the noble-souled king was being ploughed energetically in accordance with the injunction. She rose up from it. The Prince of Mithilā named Bhānumān was the younger son of Sīradhvaja.

19. His brother was Kuśadhvaja. He was the king and overlord of Kāśī. (Saṁkāśya Pradyumna was the valorous son of Bhānumān.

20. Muni was his son. It is remembered that Ūrjavaha was born of him. Sanadvāja was born of Ūrjavaha and Śakuni was his son.

21. Svāgata was the son of Śakuni.[1] It is proclaimed that Suvarcas was his son. His heir was Sutoya[2] and his son was Suśruta.

22. Jaya was the son of Suśruta. Vijaya was the son of Jaya. Kratu[3] was the son of Vijaya. Sunaya is remembered as the son of Kratu.

23. Vītahavya was born of Sunayā. Dhṛti was the son of Vītahavya. Bahulāśva was born of Dhṛti. Kṛti[4] was the son of Bahulāśva.

24. The line of the noble-souled scions of the family of Janaka came to a close with him. Thus the Maithilas have been recounted. Understand the line of Soma now.

---

1. It appears our text jumped twelve generations downwards and declared Svāgata as the son of Śakuni. AIHT, p. 144.

2. Pargiter records the name Śruta for Sutoya of our text.

3. Ṛta according to Pargiter—*ibid.*

4. Kṛtakṣaṇa in AIHT, p. 149.

CHAPTER SIXTYFIVE

The Nativity of Soma and Saumya

Sūta said :—

1-3. The lordly sage Atri became the father of the moon, O Brāhmaṇas. He stayed steady surrounded by his own brilliance. He performed only auspicious things, mentally, verbally and physically. He stood steady like wood, a wall or a piece of rock with his arms raised. He possessed excessive refulgence. We have heard that formerly for a period of three thousand years according to the reckoning of gods, he performed a penance that was very difficult to be performed by the worlds.

4. That Brāhmaṇa was highly intelligent. He had sublimated his sexual urge. He stood without even winking his eyes. His body attained the status of Soma.

5. The sage of sanctified soul in the state of Soma rose up to the sky.

6. Ten delighted divine ladies (i.e. ten quarters) gathered there together and duly bore that foetus in their wombs. But they were unable to hold it.

7. The foetus held up by those ten ladies, the ten quarters, fell down illuminating the worlds. It was the cool-rayed moon, the sanctifier of all.

8. When the ten ladies were unable to hold that foetus, the moon fell down to the Earth along with them.

9. Seeing him falling down, Brahmā, the grand-father of the worlds, placed him in a chariot, with a desire for the welfare of the worlds.

10. O Brāhmaṇas, we have heard that he was a righteous-souled one, truthful to his promise and identical with the Vedas. He seated himself in a chariot yoked with a thousand horses.

11-13. When that son of Atri of great soul had fallen, the Devas, the seven famous mental sons of Brahmā, the Aṅgirasas and the sons of Bhṛgu, eulogised him by means of many Ṛks, Yajus, Atharvan and Aṅgirasa Mantras.

The satisfying, nourishing and developing refulgence of the lustrous moon who was being eulogised, extended to all the worlds around.

14. By means of that prominent chariot, he circumambulated the ocean-encircled Earth twentyone times (and became) excessively famous.

15. The increased and developed refulgence (of the moon) that reached the Earth, created the medicinal herbs. The firmament is ablaze with that brilliance.

16. This moon nourishes the worlds and the four types of living beings. O excellent Brāhmaṇas, lord Soma is indeed the nourisher of the Universe.

17. The highly fortunate one performed penance for nine hundred years. By means of penance, by means of his own Karmans and on account of those eulogies he acquired more brilliance.

18. By means of his own Karman as well as through the joy of those gold-complexioned goddesses who sustain the Universe, lord Soma became famous.

19. Then, O excellent Brāhmaṇas, god Brahmā, the most excellent one among those who know Brahman, granted him the kingdom of seeds, medicinal herbs, Brāhmaṇas and waters.

20. On being crowned the exceedingly brilliant king of kings who was endowed with great refulgence and who was the most excellent one among those who blazed, sanctified the worlds through his great kingdom.

21. Dakṣa, the son of Pracetas, gave in marriage to the Moon the twentyseven Dākṣāyaṇīs (daughters of Dakṣa) of great holy rites, whom they know as the stars.

22. After getting that big kingdom, Soma the lord of those who possess Soma (juice), began a Rājasūya sacrifice where a hundred thousand gold coins were distributed as monetary gifts.

23-24. Hiraṇyagarbha acted as Udgātṛ (the chanter of Mantras), god Brahmā took up the post of Brahmā (in sacrifice the presiding dignitary). The member of the sacrificial council consisted of lord Hari Nārāyaṇa, surrounded by the ancient Brahminical sages with Sanat-kumāra as their leader.

25. We have heard, O Brāhmaṇas, that Soma gave three worlds as monetary gifts to *Sadasyas* (members of the sacrificial assembly) consisting of important Brahmanical sages.

26. Nine goddesses served him viz. Sinī, Kuhū,[1] Vapsu, Puṣṭi, Prabhā, Vasu, Kīrti, Dhṛti and Lakshmī.

27. After undergoing the holy valedictory bath called *Avabhṛtha*, the leading Rājan (i.e. the moon) who was devoid of agitation and who was worshipped by the Devas and sages, excelled in his lustre illuminating the ten quarters.

28. When he acquired that luxurious glory which was difficult to get and which was praised by the sages, O Brāhmaṇas, his mind became involved in unrighteousness and hence went astray from the path of moral discipline.

29. He disregarded the sons of Aṅgiras and suddenly abducted the renowned wife of Bṛhaspati named Tārā.

30. Even after being requested by the Devas and divine sages, he never let-off Tārā to Bṛhaspati, the son of Aṅgiras.

31-33. Uśanas took up his (Soma's) side and Bhava (Śiva) that of Aṅgiras (i.e. Bṛhaspati), for that person of great brilliance was the disciple of the father of Bṛhaspati formerly. It was out of this affection that lord Rudra became the ally of Bṛhaspati and took the bow Ajagava.

A great miraculous missile named Brahmaśiras was discharged by that noble-souled one after aiming at the Devas, whereby their reputation was destroyed.

34. There a well-known battle between the Devas and Dānavas took place. It was known as Tārakāmaya[2] (concerning Tārā). It was destructive of the worlds.

35. The Devas who survived this battle are remembered

1. The first two viz.: Sinī and Kuhū are deities presiding over the day preceding the new moon day on which the moon rises with scarcely visible crescent (Sinīvālī) and the new moon day when the moon is invisible (Kuhū).

2. Out of the twelve wars between Devas and Asuras, this was the 5th war. For other wars see Introduction : Vaiṣṇavism, last footnote.

as Tusitas. They sought refuge in god Brahmā, the primordial lord, the grandfather of the world.

36. Then the grandfather (i.e. Brahmā) himself came there and prevented Uśanas and Rudra, from fighting. He restored Tārā to Aṅgiras (Bṛhaspati).

37. On seeing Tārā, the lady of moon-like face, pregnant, the Brāhmaṇa Bṛhaspati said—"You cast off the foetus immediately.

38. Your womb belongs to me and therefore no other child should ever be born there". So Tārā discharged the child in the womb that was blazing like fire.

39. The moment he was born that lord assumed the body of the Devas. Therefore the Suras became suspicious and told Tārā.

40-41. 'Tell the truth whose is the son ? Of the moon or of Bṛhaspati ?'

Out of shyness she did not say anything to the Devas good or bad. Then the boy *Dasyuhantama* (the greatest destroyer of demons) was about (lit. began) to curse her. Preventing him, Brahmā asked Tārā regarding his suspicion.

42-44. "O Tārā speak out what is the truth here ? Whose son is this ?" With palms joined in reverence she said to lord Brahmā, the bestower of boons.

"Of the Moon". She said this regarding the noble-souled son named Dasyuhantama.

Thereafter, sniffing at the head of his son, the lord Soma, the Prajāpati, named his intelligent son 'Budha'.

Every day Budha (Mercury) rises in the sky.

45. The daughter of the king (i.e. Ilā) gave birth to his son. Therefore Pururavas, the son of Ilā, became his son of great splendour.

46-47. Six sons of very great powers were born to him by Urvaśī.

At that time, violently attacked by pulmonary consumption, he (Soma) became helpless. Then over-whelmed by consumption, the moon's disc became pale and weak. He therefore, sought refuge in his own father Atri.

48-50. Atri of great fame subdued his disease. He was freed from pulmonary consumption. He shone with splendour all round.

This is the nativity of Soma recounted unto you O excellent Brāhmaṇas. Understand his race which is being recounted by me, O excellent Brāhmaṇas.

The nativity of Saumya (Mercury) is conducive to wealth, health and longevity. It is holy and it dispels sins. On hearing this, one gets rid of all sins.

CHAPTER SIXTYSIX

Description of Amāvasu Dynasty

Sūta said :—

1-3. Budha was the son of the Moon and Budha's son was Pururavas. He was brilliant and liberal in charitable gifts. He used to perform sacrifices distributing much wealth as monetary gifts. He was an expounder of Brahman. Possessing valorous exploits, he was invincible to the enemies in battle. This king regularly performed *Agnihotra* and many (other) *Yajñas*. He was truthful in speed and righteous in mind. He was very lustrous. His sexual indulgence was only in secret. In handsomeness he was perfectly unrivalled in all the three worlds.

4. Setting aside her personal prestige, Urvaśī, the reputed (celestial damsel), chose as her husband that expounder of Brahman who had complete control of his sense organs, was conversant with *dharma*, and truthful in speech.

5-7. That vigorous king stayed with her for a period of ten years, eight years, seven years, six years, seven years, eight years, ten years and eight years at the Caitraratha forest, the beautiful bank of the Mandākinī, Alakā (Capital city of Kubera), Viśālā, Nandana, the excellent park, the feet (foothills) of mount Gandhamādana, the peak of the excellentmost mount Meru, Northern Kurus and the village Kalāpi (respectively).

8. The king of great vigour accompanied by Urvaśī sported with excessive joy in these important parks and forests frequented by the Suras.

The sages enquired :—

9. Tell us the misdemeanour of the king for which the Gandharva divine lady Urvaśī left off the king of human birth and came back to heaven.

Sūta said :—

10. Overwhelmed with the curse of a Brāhmaṇa (or of Brahmā), she came to the world of human beings. For the sake of getting herself released from the curse, she stipulated certain conditions.

11-13. (Defective text). "Not seeing him naked, sexual intercourse without passion (?) and she would keep two goats near her bed.[1] (She then said)—"My sole diet shall be ghee and that too once a day, O king. If these conditions are agreed to, O king, and as long as you closely adhere to this stipulation, I shall continue to stay with you. This is our mutual agreement." The king strictly adhered to her stipulation.

14-15. Thus she stayed with the son of Ilā and had intercourse with him. Deluded by the curse and on account of her devotion to him, she stayed for sixtyfour years.

Urvaśī came to the mortal world. Hence the Gandharvas became worried.

---

1. Urvaśī as her name implies was a resident of Ur, an ancient town in the middle east. It appears that fashionable ladies of B.C. 3300 of Ur used to keep a pair of rams as pets : A.J. Karandikar in his (marathi) *Background of the Mahābhārata* (*Mahābhāratācī Pārśvabhūmī*, Poona 1980. quotes from sir Leonard Wooley's excavations at Ur. Among the finds in a queen's tomb of 3300 B.C. deposited therein for the entertainment of the queen, 'The strangest perhaps was a pair of rams. They were beautifully and intricately made. Their bodies were covered with fleece of shell. . . . their heads and legs were of gold" (Intro. to Karandikar's book p. 8). This may be the cause of importance attached to this term of contract-marriage between Pururavas and Urvaśī.

The Gandharvas said :—

O fortunate ones, think about the ways and means whereby that excellent lady Urvaśī, the ornament of Heaven, may come back once again to the Devas.

16-19. Then a Gandharva of very great intellect named Viśvāvasu removed the two young kids belonging to her. After that, she left for heaven. The king began to wander (here and there) on account of separation from her and saw her at Kurukṣetra. He had a talk with her. She told him..."Rush up to the Gandharvas". He did so. Then they gave him a pot of fire. The king of great martial competency (literally—of great chariot) went to Heaven with it. Originally there was only one fire. But the son of Ilā made it three.

20-21. The son of Ilā, O excellent Brāhmaṇas, was a king of such ability and potentiality. The king of great fame established his kingdom at Prayāga on the northen bank of Yamunā in the city of Pratiṣṭhāna (modern Jhusi, near Allahabad) in a holy realm adorned by great sages.

22-23. Six sons were born to him. They had their splendour comparable to that of Indra. They are well-known in the world of Gandharvas viz.—Āyus, Dhīmān, Āmāvasu, Viśvāvasu, Śrutāyus and Ghṛtāyus. These were the sons of Urvaśī.

The formidable king Bhīma, the conqueror of the Universe, was born of Amāvasu.[1]

24. The glorious king Kāñcanaprabha was the heir of Bhīma. The learned Suhotra of great strength was the son of Kāñcana (i.e. Kāñcanaprabha).

25-27a. Jahnu, born of the womb of Keśinī was the son of Suhotra.

While his elaborate sacrificial rite was going on, the river Gaṅgā turned her course and flooded that territory on account of the vision of inevitable future.

On seeing the sacrificial chamber entirely flooded with (the waters of) the Gaṅgā, the infuriated son of Suhotra, the king, drank up the Gaṅgā.

---

1. As noted by Pargiter, Amāvasu was the founder of Kānyakubja kingdom (AIHT. p. 144).

27b-28. On seeing the Gaṅgā drunk up by the saintly king, the celestial sages brought out the highly fortunate river (Gaṅgā) as his daughter (and known as) Jāhnavī. Jahnu married Kāverī the grand-daughter of Yauvanāśva.

29. Through the curse of Yuvanāśva, Gaṅgā gave birth from half of her part to Kāverī the praise-worthy wife of Jahnu, the most excellent of all rivers.

30. Jahnu begot of Kāverī a beloved son of great virtue named Sunaha. His son was Ajaka.

31. Ajaka's heir Balākāśva of great fame, became a habitual hunter. Kuśa is remembered as his son.

32. Kuśa had four sons of divine lustre and refulgence viz. Kuśāmba, Kuśa-nābha, Amūrtarayasa and Vasu.

33. Kuśika (? Kuśanābha) the excellent king performed a penance seeking a son. When a hundred years were completed, Indra noticed him.

34-35. On seeing him performing severe penance, the thousand-eyed lord Indra, the eternal one who was himself capable of causing a son to be born unto him became his son himself. The chastiser of Pāka (i.e. Indra) became the son of Kuśika under the name Gādhi.

36. Paurukutsī (daughter of Purukutsa) became the wife of Gādhi. At first a splendid girl of exalted fortune was born of her known by the name of Satyavatī.[1]

37-38. King Gādhi gave her (in marriage) to Ṛcīka who was desirous of a son. Being pleased with her, her husband, the delighter of the members of the family of Bhṛgu, himself a descendant of Bhṛgu, prepared Caru (consecrated cooked rice) for the sake of a son to himself as well as to Gādhi.
Then Ṛcīka, the descendant of Bhṛgu, spoke to his wife.

39-42a. This Caru should be eaten by you, O splendid lady and that Caru by your mother. To her will be born a lustrous son. a bull among Kṣatriyas, who can never be conquered by Kṣatriyas in battle and who will be able to slay even prominent Kṣatriya warriors. So you also, O lady of

1. Pargiter gives Kuśāśva as the name of Kuśa's son and Kuśika was Kuśāśva's son (AIHT, p.144).

good weal, this Caru will cause the birth of a son of great courage, a great ascetic of quiescent nature, an excellent Brāhmaṇa.

After saying this to his wife, Ṛcīka, the delighter of the members of the family of Bhṛgu who was always engaged in penance, entered the forest for penance.

42b-45a. At that time, in the course of his pilgrimage, Gādhi, the king, accompanied by his wife came to the hermitage of Ṛcīka in order to see his daughter. Taking up the two vessels of consecrated Caru of the sage, the delighted Satyavatī intimated to her mother the words of her husband quietly, without any excitement.

As fate would have it, the mother gave her own Caru to her daughter. Due to ignorance she swallowed her daughter's Caru herself.[1]

45b-50. Then with her bright and lustrous body Satyavatī conceived in her womb a splendid son, the future annihilator of Kṣatriyas. She became terrible to behold. On seeing her and reflecting by means of his Yogic power, Ṛcīka the excellent Brāhmaṇa spoke to his wife, the lady of excellent complexion :—

"O gentle lady, you have been deceived by your mother by the inter-change of the Carus. An extremely terrible son of cruel activities will be born to you. Your mother will give birth to an ascetic of such a nature as I have mentioned before. The entire Brahminical splendour had been instilled into the the Caru by me through my power of penance".

On being told thus by her husband, Satyavatī of exalted fortune and dignity sought the favour of her husband saying—"A base Brāhmaṇa like this should not be born as my son through you".

51. On being told thus, the sage said "O excellent lady, this has never been thought of by me or by you. This has never

---

1. This exchange of *caru* seems an explanatory device to justify the militant nature of the Brahmin Paraśurāma and the Brahmanical transformation in the Kṣatriya Viśvāmitra.

been wished for by me or by you. A son shall become ruthless in his activities usually on account of his mother or father".

52-55. On being told thus, Satyavatī spoke again like this—"If you wish, O sage, you can create even worlds, why not a son ? It behoves you, O husband to give me a son of quiescent nature. If it cannot be altered, O excellent Brāhmaṇa, of good holy rites, let our grandson be like this (i.e. terrible and ruthless)".

Thereupon, by means of the power of his penance, he made her pleased and contented saying—"Whether it is my son or my grandson, O lady of excellent complexion, I do not see any difference. It shall be as you have said, O gentle lady".

56. Therefore, Satyavatī gave birth to Jamadagni, a son of the Bhṛgu family, of quiescent nature, having perfect control over his sense-organs and devoted to the performance of penance.

57. Formerly, there had been an interchange of the Carus belonging to Rudra and Viṣṇu. Since he ate (i.e. since he was born as a result of his mother eating) the fire (Caru) belonging to Viṣṇu, he became Jamadagni

58. After getting Viśvāmitra as his heir, Gādhi the son of Kuśika (or descendant of Kuśika) attained the status equal to that of a Brahminical sage. He was chosen by Brahmā (as such).

59-60a. Satyavatī of great sanctity and devoted to truthful vows and observances flowed as the great river named Kauśikī. Kauśikī the most excellent and distinguished river began to flow.

60b-64. There was a king named Reṇuka born in the family of Ikṣvāku. His daughter of great fortune Reṇukā was otherwise known by the name of Kamalī. By means of his power of penance, fortitude and concentration of mind, Jamadagni, the son of Ṛcīka, begot of Reṇukā alias Kamalī a son of great terrific nature (named) Rāma who was very excellent, who (later) mastered all lores and the science of archery, who was to kill the Kṣatriyas who resembled well-kindled blazing fire.

Thus Jamadagni of lofty (noble) mind, the most excellent one among the knowers of Brahman, was born of Satyavatī, due to the vigour of the penance of Ṛcīka, son of Aurva. Śunaḥśepha was the middle and Śunaḥpuccha was the youngest son*

65. Viśvāmitra of noble soul was otherwise known by the name Viśvaratha. It was through the grace of (the scion of the family of) Bhṛgu that he was born as the perpetuator of the line of Kauśikas.

66-67. Viśvāmitra's son Śunaḥśepha was a sage.[1] He was intended (appointed) as the sacrificial animal in the *Yajña* of Hariścandra. He was given back to Viśvāmitra by the Devas. Since Śunaḥśepha was given back by the Devas he became Devarāta.

68-69. Among the sons of Viśvāmitra,[2] Sunaḥśepha is regarded as the eldest. Madhucchanda and others, Kṛtadeva, Dhruva, Aṣṭaka, and Pūraṇa also were the sons of Viśvāmitra. The spiritual lines (Gotras) of those noble-souled Kauśikas are numerous.

70-73. They are as follows :—

Pārthivas, Devarātas, Yājñavalkyas, Samarpaṇas, Udumbaras, Vātadyas, Talakāyanas, Cāndravas, Lohinīs, Reṇus, Kārīṣus, Babhrus, Paṇins, Dhyāna-Japyas, Śyāmāyanas, Hiraṇyākṣas, Sānkṛtas, Gālavas, Devalas, Yāmadūtas, Śālaṅkāyanas, Bāṣkalas, Lālāṭyas, Bādaras and others belonged to the Gotras of the intelligent Viśvāmitra.

Many descendants of Kauśikas (i.e. those of the spiritual lines of Viśvāmitra) who have to enter into marriage alliance with other sages are also proclaimed.

---

*In Vā. P. 91.92 also Śunaḥśepa and Śunaḥpuccha are the names of Jamadagni's brothers.

1. As *Aitareya Brāhmaṇa* notes Śunaḥśepa was adopted as a son by Viśvāmitra.

2. A comparison of this list with that given in Mt.P., Baudhāyana, Āśvalāyana, Āpastamba and Kātyāyana shows that our author is not exhaustive in giving the Gotras of the Kuśika clan. (*vide 'Mt.P.—a Study' pp.* 406-409)

74-75. They are Kauśikas, Sauśrutas, Saindhavāyanas and others. They belong to the *Gotra* of the holy Brahminical sage Kauśika, the lord of Yogic practice.

Among the sons of Viśvāmitra, Śunaḥśepha is remembered as the eldest. Aṣṭaka was the son of Dṛṣadvatī and Viśvāmitra. Lauhi was the son of Aṣṭaka. Thus the group of Jahnu has been recounted by me.

The sages enquired :—

76-78. The status of Brāhmaṇas has been acquired by Viśvāmitra and other kings. What is the nature of *Dharma* (virtue, piety), penance or learning through which they acquired this ? Under what names did the Kṣatriyas attain the status of a Brāhmaṇa ? We wish to know the difference through penance or charitable gifts.

On being asked thus, he spoke these meaningful words.

79. A rich man desirous of religious merit and virtue may invite excellent Brāhmaṇas and perform Yajñas with wealth acquired by unjust means. But he does not attain the benefit of the righteous act.

80-82. A person overwhelmed by passion and delusion, who had been always without any check or restraint due to covetousness for wealth, may in the end desire to sanctify himself and for this purpose he may perform *Japa* (chanting of Mantras etc.) intensely and distribute gifts also. But the charitable gifts made by him may become fruitless. That wicked man prone to violence may be inclined to perform meritorious deeds. After acquiring wealth thus (by unjust means), he may distribute charitable gifts and perform *Yajñas* out of delusion. The tarnished gift of that wicked soul does not stand in good stead.

83-85a. If a man gives to the deserving persons wealth accumulated through just means, if a person worships and distributes gifts without cherishing desires in his mind, he acquires the fruit of those charitable gifts. That gift results in pleasure and happiness. One attains worldly pleasures through charitable gifts. One goes to heaven through truthfulness. One pervades the worlds and stands eternally by means of penance performed duly.

85b. Truthfulness is more conducive to welfare than penance. Knowledge is remembered weightier, more efficacious than that.

86a-90. It is reported that the twice-born castes who were born as Kṣattriyas achieved (Brahminhood) through penance. (For example) king Viśvāmitra, Māndhātṛ, Saṅkṛti, Kapi, Kāśya, Purukutsa, Śala, lord Gṛtsamada, Ārṣṭiṣeṇa, Ajamīḍha, Bhargavyoma, Kakṣīvān, Auśija king Śiśira, Rathāntara, Śaunaka, Viṣṇuvṛddha and other kings had been Kṣatriyas, but these are remembered to have attained the status of sages by means of penance.[1] All these saintly kings had attained great Siddhis (spiritual accomplishments).

Henceforth, I shall recount the line of the noble-souled Āyus.

CHAPTER SIXTYSEVEN

*The Origin of Dhanvantari**

1. Āyus had five noble-souled sons of great strength. Those kings were born of Prabhā, the daughter of Svarbhānu.

2. Nahuṣa was the eldest among them. Kṣatravṛddha is remembered as the son next to him. Rambha, Raji and Anenas are well-known in the three worlds.

3. Kṣatravṛddha's son was Śunahotra of great reputation. Śunahotra had three sons who were very much righteous.

1. This is an evidence of social mobility in ancient India.

*This chapter describes the line of Āyu that ruled at Kāśī. In this dynasty was born Dhanvantari, the famous physician-king, the founder of Āyurveda. He learnt the science from Bharadvāja but due to his systematic presentation of that science, due credit is given to him. Hence, the title of this chapter specially refers to Dhanvantari. His period viz.: "second Dvāpara Yuga" is merely a Purāṇic way of stating time.

4. They were Kāśa, Śala and lord Gṛtsamada. The son of Gṛtsamada was Śunaka from whom Śaunaka was born.

5. Brāhmaṇas, Kṣatriyas, Vaiśyas and Śūdras were born in his family, O Brāhmaṇas, on account of their diverse Karmans.

6. Ārṣṭiṣeṇa was Śala's son. His son was Śiśira. The Śaunakas and the Ārṣṭiṣeṇas were Brāhmaṇas mixed with Kṣatriyas.

7-8. King Dīrghatapas was the ruler of Kāśī and son of Kāśya. Dhanva was the son of Dīrghatapas and the scholar. Dhanvantari was born of him. This brilliant son was born to the intelligent king in his old age, at the close of his penance.

Thereupon, the sages spoke these words to Sūta.

The sages said :—

9. Who is Dhanvantari, the lord who was born among human beings? We wish to know this. Recount that unto us, O scorcher of enemies(?)

Sūta replied :—

10-13a. Let the origin of Dhanvantari be heard, O Brāhmaṇas. He was born formerly when the ocean was being churned, for the sake of nectar. At the outset, he was born before the Kalaśa (pot). He was encircled by a halo of glory all round. On seeing him having accomplished his task suddenly, Viṣṇu who was standing by said—"You are born of water". Hence, he is remembered as *Abja* (water-born). *Abja* said to Viṣṇu—"O lord, I am your son. Allot me my share and place in the world, O excellent god."

13b-19. On being told thus, the lord said after review in the factual position, "The division of the Yajña has already been made by the sons of Diti as well as the Suras. The due performance of *Homas* etc. has been laid down in the Vedas by the great sages. It is not possible to get *Homa* performed unto you at any time. As you are born subsequent to Vedas O god, you have no Mantra (assignable to you). O lord, in your second incarnation you will earn reputation in the world. Then you will attain the super-natural powers like *Aṇimā* (minuteness) and others. O lord, you will attain Devahood with this selfsame body. Brāhmaṇas (and other twice-born ones) shall worship you with *Caturmantras* (i.e. Mantras from the four Vedas), ghee offerings and *Gavyas* (materials of worship obtained from milk, milk products). You will once again reproduce the Āyurveda (the Science of Medicine). These incidents and events are inevitable and have already been visualised by the lotus-born lord (Brahmā) earlier. Undoubtedly you will be born in the second Dvāpara Yuga". Therefore, after granting the boon, Viṣṇu disappeared.

20. When the second Dvāpara arrived, king Dīrghatapas, the ruler of Kāśī, a descendant of Śunahotra being desirous of a son, performed a penance.

21. The king desired to propitiate lord Dhanvantari for the sake of a son. Thereupon, Dhanvantari urged the king to choose a boon as he pleased.

The king said :—

22. "O lord, if you are pleased with me, be my son, bestower of my goal". After saying "So be it", the lord vanished there itself.

23-24. Lord Dhanvantari was then born in his abode. He was a great king, the ruler of Kāśī, the dispeller of all ailments. He learned the science of Medicine—Āyurveda along with its therapeutics from Bharadvāja. He classified it into eight sections and taught them to different disciples.

25. The son of Dhanvantari became well known as Ketumān. The son born to Ketumān became king Bhīmaratha.

26. The son of Bhīmaratha became an intelligent lord of the subjects. Well-renowned as Divodāsa,[1] he became the lord of Vārāṇasī.

27. At this time, a Rākṣasa named Kṣemaka, colonised the city of Vārāṇasī which had been a desolate and tenantless place.

1. He is regarded as a contemporary of Daśaratha of Ayodhyā. During his reign, Vārāṇasī was made desolate by a demon-like Gaṇa of god Śiva—the whole episode (described later in this chapter) is not creditable to the great God Mahādeva.

28. Earlier, the city had been cursed by the noble-souled Nikumbha, again and again—"This city will be void of people and a deserted place for a thousand years".

29. When this city was cursed, Divodāsa, the lord of the subjects, colonized another beautiful city at the border of his realm, on the banks of Gomatī.

The sages said :—

30. What for did Nikumbha curse Vārāṇasī formerly? Why did Nikumbha the noble-souled one curse the holy place of the Siddhas?

Sūta said :—

31. The saintly king Divodāsa lived in that flourishing city after obtaining it. The ruler of men of great brilliance lived there in that prosperous city.

32. It was at this very same time that Maheśvara took a wife unto him. Desirous of doing some thing pleasing to the Goddess Umā, the lord lived near his father-in-law.

33. At the behest of the lord, the Pāriṣadas (attendants) of various kinds of forms, the ascetics began to delight goddess Umā (Maheśvarī) by adopting the forms and guise as mentioned before.

34. Mahādeva was delighted on account of them. But Menā was not delighted. She treated the lord and the goddess with contempt.

35. She said—"Your husband Maheśvara has no manners or good conduct even in my presence. He is always indigent in every respect. Alas, he is not ashamed".

36. On being told thus by her mother in so many words, Pārvatī did not brook it, that being the natural characteristic of women. Smilingly, the goddess who bestowed boons, went near Hara.

37. With a sorrowful face, the goddess spoke to Mahādeva—"O lord, I will not stay here, Take me to your abode".

38. On being told thus, Mahādeva examined all the worlds, O excellent Brāhmaṇas and desired to take up residence on the Earth.

39-41a. The great lord Bhava of great lustre, came to know that the city of Vārāṇasī, the spot of spiritual masters, was occupied by Divodāsa. He called the lord of Gaṇas standing at his side and said thus—"O lord of Gaṇas, go to the city of Vārāṇasī and make it evacuated by using gentle means. That king possesses excessive heroism and strength".

41b-44a. Then Nikumbha went to the city of Vārāṇasī at outset. He appeared before a Brāhmaṇa named Maṅkaṇa in dream and said—"I shall do something for your welfare, O sinless one, find out a suitable place for me. Make an idol of mine and instal it at the outskirts of the city".

After getting permission of the king, the Brāhmaṇa did everything duly as he was instructed in dream. He installed the idol, at the gate of the city.

44b-47a. Worship was carried on every day on a grand scale, with fragrant garlands, sweet scents, incense, offerings of cooked food and many other beautiful things worthy of being seen. That was really a wonderful thing. Thus the lord of Gaṇas was worshipped there every day. Therefore, he granted thousands of boons to the citizens such as sons, gold, land, etc, —nay all that they wished for.

47b-50. The excellent queen of the king, named Suyaśā, who was chaste and renowned, and who was urged by the king, came there for the sake of a son. After performing the worship elaborately, the gentle lady begged for sons, visiting (the temple) again and again for many times for the sake of sons. Nikumbha did not grant her sons with a reason behind it. His idea was to do something destructive, if the king were to get furious.

Then after a long time, the king was overwhelmed with anger.

51-55. He thought thus:—"This great *Bhūta* (Goblin, Spirit) at the gateway grants hundreds of boons with great pleasure, to the citizens. But he does not give us anything. He is always being worshipped by my own people in my own city. He has been requested by the queen many times for sons, but he has not granted a son. Really he is ungrateful despite eating a lot. Hence, he does not deserve at all any worship from me. Therefore, I shall destroy the abode of that wicked being".

After resolving thus, the evil-minded sinful king destroyed the abode of that lord of the Gaṇas. On seeing his shrine shattered, the lord cursed the king.

56. "Since, without any fault on my side, my abode has been destroyed by you, O king, your city shall become a deserted wasteland suddenly".

57. Thereupon, on account of that curse, Vārāṇasī became a void then. After cursing the city, Nikumbha brought Mahādeva there.

58. Mahādeva of great and noble mind made that deserted vacant city equal to the city of the Devas by means of its wealth and luxury, and made it his abode as well as that of the goddess.

59. The goddess sported and diverted her mind there itself. She was wonder-struck at the affluence. For the sake of sports and pastime of the goddess, lord Īśāna spoke these words :—

60. "I will not leave off my abode. Indeed my abode is *Avimukta*". Laughingly he said to her—"My abode is *Avimukta*. I will not go elsewhere, O gentle lady, after leaving thus.

61. Sport along with me in this holy spot, O resplendent lady who has no one superior to you". Hence that (holy place) was called *Avimukta* by the lord himself.

62-63. Thus Vārāṇasī was cursed and glorified as *Avimukta*. It was here that the noble-souled Maheśvara lived in the three Yugas along with the goddess. That city of that great Soul vanishes in the Kali age.

64. When that city vanished, it was built once again and colonized. Thus Vārāṇasī was cursed and colonized once again.

65. King Divodāsa colonized it after killing a hundred sons of Bhadrasena, who were excellent wielders of bows.

66-67. The kingdom of Bhadrasena was destroyed by that powerful king. There was a son of Bhadrasena named Durmada who was let off with contempt and mercifulness that he was only a boy. The heroic son Pratardana was born of Dṛṣadvatī and Divodāsa (Divodāsa II).

68. He was attacked by that boy, the son (of Bhadrasena) O great king, who was desirous of wreaking vengeance.

69. Pratardana had two sons, Vatsa and Garga who became very famous. Alarka was the son of Vatsa and Sannati was his son.

70-71. This verse has been sung by persons of yore about the saintly king Alarka :—

'The young and excellent king of Kāśī, Alarka, was richly endowed with beauty for sixty thousand and six hundred years. By the grace of Lopāmudrā he attained the greatest span of life.'

72. At the end of the period of curse, the king of powerful and great arms killed the demon Kṣemaka and got rehabilitated the city of Vārāṇasī.

73. The heir of Sannati was a pious person named Sunītha. The heir of Sunītha was a righteous person named Kṣaima (Kṣema ?).

74. Ketumān was the son of Kṣema. Suketu was his son. The son of Suketu was known as Dharmaketu.

75. The heroic warrior Satyaketu was the heir of Dharmaketu. The lord of subjects named Vibhu was the son of Satyaketu.

76. Suvibhu was the son of Vibhu. It is remembered that Sukumāra came thereafter. Dhṛṣṭaketu was the extremely virtuous son of Sukumāra.

77. The heir of Dhṛṣṭaketu was the lord of subjects Veṇuhotra. Veṇuhotra's son named Gārgya[1] was very famous.

78-79. Gargabhūmi was the son of Gārgya. This is the line of Vatsa, the intelligent one. Their sons were Brāhmaṇas and Kṣatriyas. They were exceedingly righteous. They were valorous and powerful and had leonine exploits. Thus the Kāśyapas have been recounted. Understand the descendants of Raji too.

1. Recorded as Bharga in AIHT, p.149. The line is shown to have closed there, but our text records Gargabhūmi as the son of Gārgya (VV. 78-79).

80. The heroic Raji had five hundred sons. This group of Kṣatriyas is well known as Rājeya on the Earth. Indra was afraid of them.

81. At that time a very terrible battle between the Devas and the Asuras took place, when the Devas and the Asuras asked Brahmā.

82. "Who will be victorious, O holy lord in the battle between us ? Tell us, O lord of all worlds. We wish to hear."

Brahmā said :—

83. "There is no doubt that those, on whose behalf Lord Raji will take up his arms and fight, will conquer the three worlds.[1]

84. Where there is Raji, there will be Lakṣmī (fortune, wealth), where there is Lakṣmī there is fortitude. Where there is fortitude there is *Dharma* (virtue) and where there is *Dharma* there is victory."

85-86. On hearing about Raji's success in battles, all the Devas and the Dānavas, desirous of their own victories, approached the excellent king and eulogised him.

Delighted in their minds, all those Devas and Dānavas said—"You, please take up your excellent bow for the sake of our victory".

Raji said :—

87. "I shall defeat, O Daityas, the Devas with Indra at their head I shall become Indra with a virtuous soul. Therefore, I shall fight in the battle-field.

88. Our Indra is Prahlāda. We shall win the battle for his sake. Abide by this agreement urged by our lord."

89. Even as he was about to say "So be it", he was urged by the Devas too—"After winning the war, you will become Indra". He was thus invited by the Devas too.

---

1. This is the twelfth war between Devas and Asuras (*vide*-Intro.—Vaiṣṇavism—last footnote).

90-91. He killed all the Dānavas who had been armed with thunderbolts and who could not be killed. That king of great splendour and perfect control over his sense-organs redeemed the lost glory of the Devas after killing all Dānavas. Lord Raji redeemed it. Accompanied by the Devas, Indra spoke to Raji. "I am the son of Raji". After saying like this, he spoke these words once again.

92-93. "You are Indra of all Devas. There is no doubt in this. I shall, O king, O slayer of foes, attain reputation since I am your son". On hearing these words of Indra he was deceived by his illusion.

94-95. "So it shall be", said the delighted king to Indra.

When the king who was on a par with the Devas went to heaven, the sons of the preceptor of Raji, seized their share in the legacy from Indra (?). The hundreds of sons attacked the heavenly world Triviṣṭapa, the abode of Indra, several times.

96-98. Then, after the lapse of a great deal of time, Indra of great strength whose kingdom had been taken away and whose fortune had been spoilt spoke to Bṛhaspati—"Make my *Puroḍāśa*(sacrificial offering) at last as big as the jujube fruit, O Brāhmaṇa sage, whereby I can remain alive after being revived by means of splendour. O Brāhmaṇa, I am emaciated and dejected in mind because my kingdom has been taken away and my seat removed. I have been rendered weak and devoid of prowess in the battle by the sons of Raji. Be pleased with me."

Bṛhaspati said :—

99-101. "If only you had urged me earlier in this matter, O Indra, O sinless one, there would have been no work on my part that should not have been done, for the sake of your pleasure.

I shall endeavour, O lord of Devas of great splendour, for the sake of what is conducive to your welfare.

Ere long, you will attain your kingdom and share in the Yajña offerings.

So Indra I shall go. Let not your mind be dejected."

102-104. Thereafter, he performed great holy rites that caused the development of his splendour. The preceptor of excellent intellect caused delusion to sons of Raji.

When they became extremely deluded, intoxicated due to passion, haters of Brāhmaṇas, followers of heretic views and deprived of heroism and exploits, he regained the excellent abode of Indra and the affluence of Asuras after killing the sons of Raji who were engrossed in activities of lust and fury.

105. If anyone were to listen and narrate the details of dethronement and re-establishment of Indra, he shall never attain the state of wretchedness.

CHAPTER SIXTYEIGHT

The Story of Yayāti

The sages asked :—

1. How was his daughter given to a king by the noble-souled Maruta (rather Marutta)[1]?. Of what heroic ability were the noble-souled persons born of the daughter of Maruta ?

Sūta replied :—

2. That lord of subjects desirous of cooked food, performed the sacrifice *Marutsoma*. That king of great splendour performed it every month for sixty years.

3. The gods, Maruts, were pleased by the sacrifice *Marutsoma* of that king. Delighted in their heart, they give never-failing cooked food with all the other articles he should desire.

---

1. VV. 1-6 speak of Maruta and Mitra-Jyoti. But these have no connection with any dynasty in this chapter.

4. His food taken in once did not get wasted for a day and a night* (i.e. people eating it will not be hungry for twenty-four hours). Starting at sunrise, he used to give food to crores of people (?)

5. To the daughter of Mitra-jyoti and the intelligent Maruta were born many sons who were conversant with *dharma*, could realize salvation and who were endowed with great intrinsic strength.

6. They renounced the rites and vows pertaining to the householder and adopted *Vairāgya* (non-attachment to worldly desires or objects). After taking up the duties of recluses they attained salvation.

7. Kṣatra-Dharma was the valorous son of Anenas.[1] Pratipakṣa of great penance was born as the son of Kṣatra-dharma.

8. Sṛñjaya, the son of Pratipakṣa, became well-known. Jaya was the son of Sṛñjaya. Vijaya was born to him.

9. Jaya the second, was the son of Vijaya. Haryaśvaka is remembered as his son. The valorous king Sahadeva was the son of Haryaśva.

10. The righteous-souled son of Sahadeva was famous by the name of Ahīna. Jayatsena was the son of Ahīna. His son was Saṅkṛti.

11. The righteous-souled Kṛtadharman of great fame was the son of Saṅkṛti. These are the descendants of Āyus of Kṣatriya qualities. Now understand the line of Nahuṣa.

12. Nahuṣa had six sons whose splendour was comparable to that of Indra. They were Yati, Yayāti, Saṁyāti, Āyāti Viyāti and Kṛti.

13. Yati was the eldest among them. Yayāti was his younger brother. Yati got as his wife the daughter of Kākutstha, named Gau.

---

*Vā. P. 93 reads *pakvam* for *bhuktam* hereof. It means 'food once cooked for twentyfour hours does not get exhausted even if served to millions of people from sunrise.'

1. This dynasty of Anenas (also given in Vā.P.93. 7-11 and Brahma P.11.27-31) was limited and could not be properly located. Bh.P.IX.17 gives a different line of Anenas.

14. Yati adopted the path of salvation. He became a sage and became one with Brahman. Among the other five, it was Yayāti who became king.

15. He got Devayānī, the daughter of Uśanas, and Śarmiṣṭhā the Asura lady and daughter of Vṛṣaparvan, as his wives.

16-18. Devayānī gave birth to Yadu and Ṭurvasu. Śarmiṣṭhā, the daughter of Vṛṣaparvan, gave birth to Druhyu, Anu and Pūru, sons of great prowess and comparable to the sons of the Devas.

Indra who was delighted gave him an extremely refulgent chariot. It would not get stuck up anywhere. It was divine and golden. It was fitted with horses having the speed of the mind. It was in this chariot that he brought the virgin for marriage (?). Indra gave him two great quivers too wherein the arrows would be inexhaustible.

19. With that pre-eminent chariot, he constantly conquered the different kingdoms on the earth. Yayāti was invincible in battle to the Devas, Dānavas and human beings.

20-21. That chariot continued to be with all the kings of Pūru's line upto Janamejaya, the son of Kaurava dynasty. That chariot disappeared when it reached Pārīkṣita, the king who was the grandson of Kuru. It disappeared due to the curse of the intelligent Gārgya.

22. That king Janamejaya who was evil-minded and who was known as Lohagandhī (Having the odour of iron) also, killed a boy, the son of Gārgya.

23. Abandoned (Banished) by the citizens and people of the outlying districts, that king Lohagandhī ran about here and there. He did not get happiness or mental peace anywhere.

24. Distressed with sorrow and misery as he was, he did not get sympathetic understanding from anyone anywhere. Utterly dejected he sought refuge in the sage Śaunaka.

25-26. This sage of liberal and exalted intellect was famous under the name Indrota. For the sake of sanctity, Indrota Śaunaka made king Janamejaya perform a horse-sacrifice, O excellent Brāhmaṇas. After reaching the stage of *Avabhṛtha* (valedictory bath after horse-sacrifice) the king Lohagandhī died.

27-28. That divine chariot was taken away from him and given to (Uparicara) Vasu, the king of Cedi, by Indra who was pleased with him. Bṛhadratha got it from him.

Bhīma, the scion of the family of Kuru, killed Jarāsandha and gladly gifted that excellent chariot to Vāsudeva.

29. That saintly king Yayāti, the son of Nahuṣa, attained old age. He then spoke these words to Yadu, his eldest and the most excellent son.

30. "Dear son, wrinkles, grey hair and other infirmities of old age have overpowered (lit. encircled) me on account of the curse of Uśanas. But I am not content with the pleasures of youth.

31. O Yadu, accept my sin along with my old age. Accept my old age."

Yadu replied to him.

32-36. "A request for alms (of an unspecified nature) by a Brāhmaṇa has been promised but not fulfilled by me. It can be accomplished only through physical exertions. I will not take up your old age. There are many deficiencies and ailments in old age caused by food and beverage. Hence, O king, I dare not take up your old age. I do not wish to be afflicted by old age, while in youth, along with the people with sacred threads (i.e. aged Brāhmaṇas)(I do not want to be) a wretched fellow having a white beard and moustaches, rendered infirm by old age aud having wrinkles covering up the whole body. (And old man) is desperate, weak in physique and incapable of doing his daily work (I do not wish to be so in my youth). I do not like old age at all. You have many sons, O king, dearer to you than I. Let them accept (the old age), O king conversant with Dharma (piety and virtue), choose some other son".

37. On being told thus by Yadu, he became extremely furious. (The king) who was the most excellent among the eloquent ones spoke to the eldest son after censuring him.

38. "O evil-minded one, what other devout rite do you have for which you disregard me, your preceptor (and father)? What other Āśrama (stage of life) can you have ?"

39-40. After saying this to Yadu, the angry father cursed him—"In spite of your being born of my bosom, you are not passing on your youthful age unto me. Hence, O foolishly deluded one, your progeny will not be entitled to the kingdom.

O Turvasu, accept my sin along with my old age".

Turvasu said:—

41-44. "I do not desire to accept old age, O father. It is destructive of all worldly pleasures of love. There are many defects in old age caused by food and beverage. Hence, O king, I am not eager to take up your old age."

Yayāti cursed :—

"In spite of your being born of my bosom, you are not cxchanging your youthful age with me. Hence, O Turvasu your progeny will be cut off from (all rights to the kingdom). O deluded one, you will be the ruler among men of mixed religious rites aud practice opposed to ours, among people of mixed castes, meat-eaters and others. Undoubtedly, your residence, O sinner, will be among barbarians and outcastes—men engaged in outraging the modesty of their preceptors' wives, men (destined to be born) among animals of lower strata."

Sūta said :—

45-47. After cursing Turvasu, his own son, thus, Yayāti spoke these words to Druhyu, the son of Śarmiṣṭhā :—

"O Druhyu, you take up my old age that destroys handsome features and complexion. Give me in exchange your prime of youth for the period of a thousand years. When the period of a thousand years is complete I shall give you back your youth. I shall also take back my sin once again along with the old age."

Druhyu said :

48. "An old man cannot drive a chariot or ride a horse. He cannot enjoy women. He has no pleasure. Therefore, I do not desire old age".

Yayāti said :

49-51. "Since you, born of my own bosom, do not give me your own youthful age, O Druhyu, none of your desires will be realised anywhere. You will always be compelled to move about in boats, rafts, canoes etc. Though born in the family of kings, you will stay there as a non-king.

O Anu, you accept my sin along with the old age. I shall move about with your youthful age for the period of a thousand years."

Anu said :

52. "An old man is as weak and feeble as a child. He is always unclean. He does not perform *Homa* in the sacred fire at the proper time. I do not like that type of old age."

Yayāti said :

53-57. "Since you, born of my own bosom, do not give me your youthful age and since the defects of old age have been recounted by you, you will have to meet with the (infirmities of) age. You will be prematurely old O Anu, your progeny will die after attaining youth. You will have to devote to the scattering of fire like this (i.e. you will have to cremate your own children).

O Pūru, accept my sin along with my old age. Defects of old age, wrinkles and grey hairs have encircled me, O dear one, due to the curse of Kāvya Uśanas. I am not satisfied with the enjoyment of pleasures of youth. With your youthful age, I shall enjoy worldly pleasures for some time. When the period of a thousand years is complete, I shall give back to you your youth. I shall also take back my own sin along with my old age."

Sūta said :—

58-61a. On being told thus the son replied to his father immediately :

"I shall do as you wish, O dear father. I shall accept, O king, your sin along with your old age. Take from me my youthful age and enjoy worldly pleasures as much as you wish.

I shall be disguised by your old age, wearing your form and age. After giving you my youthful age, I shall move about (as naturally as) I have become old in reality."

Yayāti said :—

61b-62a. "O Pūru, welfare unto you. I am pleased with you. Being delighted I am granting you this. Your progeny shall be rich. They will realize their desires. They will rule over the kingdom."

Sūta said :—

62b-64. With the assent of Pūru, king Yayāti then transferred his old age to him. With the blessings of Bhārgava, with the grandeur and with youthful age, Yayāti son of Nahuṣa, the excellent one among men, became delighted and enjoyed all worldly pleasures, according to his desire, in conformity with his eagerness, at the proper time and occasion and attained happiness.

65. The king was his own real self as before (in the performance of religious rites). He enjoyed pleasures without any prejudice to Dharma and according to his capacity. He propitiated the Devas by means of sacrifices and the Pitṛs by means of Śrāddha rites.

66. He delighted his wives by means of all favours desired by them. He made excellent Brāhmaṇas pleased by granting them everything they desired. He pleased guests by means of foodstuffs and beverages and the Vaiśyas (the merchant class) by according them benign administration.

67. He delighted Śūdras by avoiding cruelty and preventing their harassment by others. He controlled decoits by giving punishments and restraining them otherwise. He delighted all subjects duly according to the injunctions of *dharma*.

68-70a. Yayāti protected the kingdom like another Indra.

That king of leonine exploits and youthful in age enjoyed worldly pleasures without coming into conflict with *Dharma* (Righteousness, piety). He attained excellent happiness. Seeking excellent happiness in the passionate indulgence because he failed to notice the defects thereof, he sported about in the company of Viśvācī in the Nandana park as well as Vaibhrāja park.

70b-73a. When the king saw that his desires for pleasures were increasing (despite his indulgence),[1] he approached Pūru and took back his old age. After attaining his desired pleasures, the king was satiated as well as dejected. The king remembered the stipulated period of a thousand years. He counted even the Kalās and Kāṣṭhās (small units of time) and thinking that the stipulated period of time was complete, said to his son Pūru.

73b-74. "With your youthful age, O son, O suppressor of foes, worldly pleasures have been enjoyed by me at the proper time, in accordance with my eagerness and in a way conducive to happiness. I am pleased with you, O Pūru. Welfare unto you. Take back your youthful age.

75-76a. You may take up the administration of the realm. Indeed, you alone among all the sons carried out my wish in order to please me." King Yayāti, the son of Nahuṣa took back his old age. Pūru regained his youthful age.

76b-77a. When the king was desirous of crowning his youngest son Pūru, the people of all castes with the Brāhmaṇas being the chief of them, spoke to him these words.

77b-79.[2] "Why do you set aside the claim of the eldest son Yadu, the son of Devayānī, the grandson of Śukra, and hand over the kingdom to Pūru. Yadu is your eldest son. Turvasu was born after him. Druhyu is the son of Śarmiṣṭhā. Anu was born after him and only then Pūru. How does the youngest son deserve kingdom superseding the claims of the elder brothers? We are reminding you. Abide by *Dharma*."

1. The story of Yayāti requesting his sons to exchange their youth for a period of 1000 years for his old age is given in details in *Mbh.Ādi*. Chs 84 and 85. The immortal verse :

na jātu kāmaḥ kāmānām upabhogena śāmyati'

is quoted by other Purāṇas as well.

2. VV.77-90 show that kings in ancient India had to seek some sort of public sanction, before appointing a heir apparent to the throne.

Yayāti said :—

80-86. "O people of all castes with the Brāhmaṇas as chief ones, all of you listen to my words. Understand why the kingdom should not be given at all to the elder ones by me. The bold son who carries out the words of his parents is praiseworthy. My behest was not obeyed by my eldest son Yadu. The son who is antagonistic to his father is not honoured or approved of by good men. He is the real son who behaves like a son unto his father and mother. I have been slighted and insulted by Yadu, Turvasu. I have been treated with great contempt by Druhyu and Anu. My words have been carried out by Pūru and I have been particularly honoured. This youngest son shall be my heir, because my old age was taken over by him. All my desires have been fulfilled by Pūru of meritorious activities.

A boon has been granted by Śukra Kāvya Uśanas. "O king of great intellect the son who obeys you shall be the king".

The Subjects said :—

87-90. "Let Pūru approved of by your majesty be crowned as a ruler of the kingdom.

Even if he be the youngest, the son who is richly endowed with good qualities, and who does everything for the welfare of his parents, deserves all good things. He deserves to be the lord.

Puru who is your favourite son, and who has done every thing to please you, deserves this kingdom. Due to the boon granted by Śukra, nothing more can be said contradicting it".

When this was declared by the satisfied citizens and people of the outlying districts, the son of Nahuṣa (Yayāti) crowned his son Pūru in his own kingdom (i.e. the hereditary kingdom). He established Turvasu in the South-eastern quarter.[1]

1. VV.90-94 show that despite the disobedience of his sons Yayāti gave parts of his kingdom to his sons, though the hereditary throne was given to the youngest son Pūru.

91. The king established the eldest son Yadu in the South-Western quarter. He assigned the Western quarter to Druhyu and the northern quarter to Anu.

92. After conquering the Earth consisting of seven oceans and continents, King Yayāti, the son of Nahuṣa, divided it into five divisions and distributed them among his sons.

93. The entire Earth consisting of towns and seven continents is being protected by them righteously without encroaching on other territories as they were conversant with *Dharma*.

94. After dividing the Earth among his sons and after transferring the royal glory to his sons, the king, the son of Nahuṣa, became delighted.

95. After laying aside the bow and the arrows, after entrusting the kingdom to his sons and after allotting the duties and responsibilities to his kinsmen, the king became pleased.

96. In this context the following verses have been formerly sung by Yayāti, the great king. By following the advice therein one should restrain and withdraw lustful desires like a tortoise that withdraws his limbs.[1]

97. "Never can lust subside by enjoying the pleasures. Just as the fire is ablaze all the more by ghee offerings so also the desires get increased by indulgence.

98. All the food-grains and barleys, all the gold, all the animals and all the women in the world—all these are not sufficient even for one. One who realizes this does not become deluded.

99. If one has no inauspicious feelings towards all living beings, if one is not ill-disposed towards anyone mentally, verbally or physically, one realizes the Brahman then.

100. If one does not terrify others, if one is not afraid of others, if one neither desires nor hates, one realizes the Brahman then.

---

1. VV.97-103 are often quoted and have become in a way, immortal verses.

101. Happiness befalls one who eschews *Tṛṣṇā* (thirst, covetousness) which cannot be got rid of by evil-minded persons, which does not subside even when one becomes old and infirm and which can be considered an ailment that lasts till our vital airs last (or that causes death).

102. When one becomes old, one's hair become rotten and decayed; when one becomes old, one's teeth decay, but the desire to live and the greediness to earn wealth do not subside even when one becomes old.

103. The pleasure of love in the world, the great pleasure of heaven, do not deserve to be on a par with a sixteenth part of the pleasure of destruction of covetousness."

104-107. After saying thus that saintly king went to the forest along with his wives. After performing a penance on the peak Bhṛgutuṅga,[1] and after observing the holy vow of sages, that king of great fame attained heaven. These five lines of kings belonging to his family are meritorious. They are honoured by the Devas and sages. The entire Earth is pervaded by them as with the rays of the sun. The man who reads or listens to Yayāti's life story in full shall become blessed and is blest with progeny, long life and fame, O excellent Brāhmaṇas.

CHAPTER SIXTYNINE

*The Birth of Kārttavīrya**

Sūta continued :—

1. I shall recount the line of Yadu, the eldest (son of Yayāti) of excellent splendour in detail and in the proper order. Even as I recount it, listen and understand.

---

1. A mountain in Nepal on the eastern bank of the Gandak. Here was the hermitage of sage Bhṛgu (De. 34).

*This chapter describes the Haihaya line of Yadu. in which the great king Kārttavīrya Arjuna was born. The chapter is named after that great emperor.

2. Yadu had five sons comparable to the sons of the Devas viz.—Sahasrajit the excellent one (or the eldest), Kroṣṭu, Nīla, Añjika and Laghu.

3. The son of Sahasrajit was the glorious king named Śatajit. The three sons of Śatajit became well-known as extremely virtuous.

4. They were Haihaya, and the king Veṇuhaya. Haihaya's heir was well-known as Dharmanetra.

5-6. Kunti was the son of Dharmanetra, Saṁjñeya was his son. Saṁjñeya's heir was the king named Mahiṣmān. Bhadrasena was the valorous son of Mahiṣmân. He was the king and ruler of Vārāṇasī and he has already been mentioned.

7. Bhadrasena's heir was the king named Durmada. Durmada's intelligent son named Kanaka was well known.

8-9. Kanaka's heirs were four and they were very famous in all the worlds. They were Kṛtavīrya, Kṛtāgni, Kṛtavarman and Kṛtaujas who was the fourth. Arjuna was the son of Kṛtavīrya. This king became the overlord of seven continents with a thousand hands.

10. Kārttavīrya performed penance for ten thousand years. His penance was extremely difficult to be performed. By means of this penance, he propitiated Datta, born of Atri.

11. Datta granted him four excellently glorious boons. He chose at the out-set the first boon viz. a thousand arms.

12-13. (His second boon was) the ability to prevent one from evil the moment he plans (lit. meditates upon) it. His third boon was protection of the Earth virtuously after conquering it righteously. His last boon was "I must be able to conquer in many battles. I must kill thousands of enemies. My death should be in a battle while fighting."

14. This entire Earth consisting of seven continents and many towns, and encircled by seven oceans was conquered by him in a manner befitting the Kṣatriyas.

15. He possessed a thousand arms by means of his Yogic power and that too while fighting. Just as the Yoga manifests in the case of the lord of Yogas, so also the thousand arms appear by means of Māyā.

16. O excellent sages, it is heard that seven hundred sacrifices were duly performed by that king in the seven continents.

17-18. All the *Yajñas* of that powerful king had plenty of splendour and grandeur. Gold altars were used in all of them. All of them were performed with sacrificial posts made of gold. All the *Yajñas* were graced by their presence by the Devas of exalted fortune seated in aerial chariots. They were always rendered splendid and attractive by the Gandharvas and Apsaras.

19. After observing the greatness and conduct of life of that saintly king, Nārada, a Gandharva, sang the following verse about that king :

20-22. "Definitely human beings will not be able to attain the goal achieved by Kārttavīrya by means of sacrifices charitable gifts, austerities, exploits and learning."

That king is seen everywhere in the seven continents moving about by means of his Yogic power. He is armed with bow, sword or with bows and arrows. He moves about in his chariot along with his followers.

On account of the prowess of that great king the subjects were protected virtuously. They did not have any misery or perturbation. They suffered no less in their assets and properties.

23. He was the overlord of the people for eighty-five thousand years. He was an Emperor, the suzerain over many kings. He was the enjoyer of all gems.

24. He was the protector of animals. He was the defender of the fields. On account of his Yogic power, he was the *Parjanya* (lord of clouds and rain) through rain.

25. On account of his thousand arms rendered tough and rough by the frequent contact with the bow-string, he shone like the autumnal Sun with his thousand rays.

26. With a thousand elephants, that king attacked and conquered the Royal assembly of Karkoṭaka in Māhismatī and built his city there.

27. (Defective verse) That lotus-eyed king used to check the speedy waves of the ocean during the rainy season.

Sportingly he used to spew out its waters and make an artificial rainy season.

28. Shaken and tossed about by him while playing, the Narmadā, having garlands with golden fillets approached him in an apprehensive manner and produced a loud cry of distress released through the waves.

29. Once he waded through the great sea and tossed up the waves and tides by means of his thousand arms, creating an untimely high tide as though blown up by the wind.

30. When the great ocean was being agitated by his thousand arms, the great Asuras in the Pātāla (nether-worlds) remained hidden and motionless.

31-32. With his thousand arms, the king stirred up the ocean in the same manner as the Devas and the Asuras churned up the ocean of milk. A great number of fishes concealed under the great waves were crushed down to pieces. The foams were tossed up and down. The sea became rough and unbearable when so many whirlpools and eddies were caused, when it was stirred up by Kārttavīrya.

33-34. The agitation of the sea by the king was like that of the ocean of milk churned with the Mandara mountain, for the sake of producing nectar.

On seeing the excellent king of terrifying appearance, the great serpents became frightened. They hung down their heads and fled immediately. When they hung down their heads they appeared like the stumps of plantain trees in the evening that remain motionless in a place devoid of wind.

35-36. In strong and steady bows, he tied the string firmly and fitted five hundred arrows. With his prowess he rendered Rāvaṇa, the king of Laṅkā, senseless along with his army. He defeated him in the battle and subjugated him. After gaining control over him, he brought him to Māhiṣmatī and tied him there. Pulastya, thereupon, approached Arjuna, propitiated him and pacified him.

37-38. On being requested by Pulastya, the king set Paulastya (i.e. Rāvaṇa, the grandson of Pulastya) free.

The twanging sound of the bowstring produced by his thousand arms, resembled the thundering sound of the groups of bursting clouds at the end of Yuga.

Indeed, Bhārgava was a warrior of great prowess and heroism, because in the battlefield, he cut off his thousand arms as though they were a forest of golden palmyras.

39-41. Once, he was earnestly requested by the fire-god who was thirsty and hungry. The lord of subjects granted seven continents as alms unto the firegod. Fire blazed at the tips of his arrows with a desire to consume the cities, villages, towns and cowherd colonies.

With the help of valorous exploits of Kārttavīrya the leading man firegod of great fame burned mountains and forests.

42-44. The firegod accompanied by Haihaya (i.e. Kārttavīrya) arrogantly burned down the vacant hermitage of Varuṇa's son entirely. Vasiṣṭha was the name of that son whom Varuṇa obtained. He was excellent and brilliant. He became a famous sage by the name Āpava. The saintly lord Āpava then cursed Arjuna out of anger.[1]

45-47. "Since this forest of mine has not been spared by you, O Haihaya, another king named Arjuna, son of Kuntī who will become a king will supersede the difficult task achieved by you.* Rāma the most excellent one among those who strike (with weapons) will cut off thousand arms (of Sahasrārjuna). Rāma a sage, a Brāhmaṇa of great strength and prowess will crush Arjuna and kill him."

48. On account of the curse of that intelligent sage, Rāma became the cause of his death. In fact this boon had been chosen by that king himself formerly.

49-50. He had a hundred sons. Five of them were very great warriors. They were very strong, heroic, well-versed in wielding weapons, famous and virtuous-souled viz. Śūra, Śūrasena Vṛṣāsya, Vṛṣa and Jayadhvaja. It was Jayadhvaja who perpetuated his line. He was the ruler of Avanti.

---

1. The curse motif was very popular with Purāṇa-writers to explain any miraculous or unlikely event, here the killing of a great hero like Kārttavīrya. The explanation of Kārttavīrya's anti-sage action is given in the next chapter VV.1-14.

*Probably the idea is that Arjuna will gain a better reputation in this task in the context of Khāṇḍavadāha.

51-53a. Tālajaṅgha was the valorous son of Jayadhvaja. He had a hundred sons. It is reported that they were well-known by the name of Tālajaṅghas. Thus five groups of the noble-souled Haihayas have become famous viz. Vītihotras, Bhojas, Āvantis, the valorous Tuṇḍikeras and the Tālajaṅghas.

53b-57. The son of Vītihotra was the king named Ananta. Durjaya, his son, became a destroyer of his enemies. That king had received the boon of never losing his wealth. With his great power, the great king protected his subjects. He never lost his wealth. He regained whatever was lost.

If a person were to recount the birth story of Kārttavīrya, the intelligent one, his riches will increase. His piety will develop further. He will be honoured in heaven like a person who performs sacrifices and like a donor.

CHAPTER SEVENTY

Dynasties of Jyāmagha and Vṛṣṇi

The sages enquired :—

1. Why was the forest of Āpava, the noble-souled one, burnt by Kārttavīrya forcibly ? Tell us this in details even as we ask.

2. We have heard that saintly king was the protector of the subjects. Protector of subjects as he was, how could he destroy the penance-grove ?

Sūta replied :—

3. Āditya (the Sun-god) approached Kārttavīrya in the guise of a Brāhmaṇa and said, "Give me food till I am satisfied. Because I am undoubtedly the Sun-god."

The king said :—

4. O lord, tell me, with what will you be satisfied, O Sun-god ? What type of food should I serve you ? I shall do so after hearing from you.

The Sun said :—

5. "Give unto me as food all immovable beings, O most excellent one among donors. I shall be satisfied with it, O king, and not with anything else."

The king submitted :—

6. "All the immovable beings cannot be burnt by the fiery splendour of a human being, O most excellent one among those who blaze, I make my obeisance unto you."

The Sun said :—

7-8. "Pleased with you I shall give you inexhaustible quiver of arrows that can face in all directions (i.e. that can be discharged in every direction). On being discharged, they will blaze, charged with my refulgence. Assailed by my brilliance, all immovable beings shall become parched up. O king, I shall reduce everything to ashes in a moment."

9-11. Then the sun-god gave many arrows to Arjuna. After receiving those arrows from him, the volleys of arrows thus discharged from his bow, O king, burned all the immovables such as hermitages, villages, colonies of cowherds, cities, penance-groves, beautiful forests, parks and gardens etc. The Earth was burned and rendered devoid of trees and grass by the fiery splendour of the Sun.

12-13. In the meantime, Āpava, the great sage of highest splendour, who had already performed holy rites in fire and had undertaken a *Vrata* (holy vow) of staying under water for ten thousand years, had come out from water after completing his *Vrata*. The great sage then saw his hermitage burned down by Arjuna.

14. Out of anger, he cursed the saintly king in the manner already recounted to you by me.

Now listen to the line of the saintly king Kroṣṭu, consisting of many excellent persons.

15. He was the king in whose family was born Vṛṣṇi the leading member of the Vṛṣṇi dynasty.

Kroṣṭu had only one son, Vṛjinīvān of great fame.

16. Svāhī, the most excellent one among Svāhāvāns (i.e. those who perform *Yajñas* where the Mantra 'Svāhā' is repeated) was the son of Vṛjinīvān. Svāhi's son Ruśeku* became a king and the most excellent one among donors.

17. Desirous of the birth of sons, Ruśeku of sanctified soul, performed great sacrifices of different types with plenty of requisite monetary gifts.

18-19. Citraratha was born as his son who performed many holy rites. Śaśabindu was the son of Citraratha. He was a great warrior. He performed sacrifices, distributing large sums of money. He practised the highest (most excellent) activities of saintly kings. He had the most exalted character and great prowess. He was an emperor and had many children.

The following verse has been sung by men of yore regarding his line :—

20-22. "Śaśabindu had ten thousand sons. They were glorious with plenty of wealth and brilliance. They were in all respects worthy as his successors".

Among them six were the most important. All these were very strong and powerful. They performed many sacrifices.

They were Pṛthuśravas, Pṛthuyaśas Pṛthukarman, Pṛthuñjaya, Pṛthukīrti and Pṛthudānta. They were kings born of Śaśabindu.

23. Persons conversant with Purāṇas praise Akṣara** as the son of Pṛthuśravas. Suyajña was the son of Akṣara and Uśanas was his son.

24. Uśanas was virtuous and pious. After getting the Earth (i.e. after coming to the throne), he performed a hundred horse-sacrifices conferring the most excellent monetary gifts (as Dakṣiṇā).

25. Marutta[1] was his son. He followed the footsteps of saintly kings. Vīrakambala-Barhiṣ is remembered as the son of Marutta.

---

*Ruśadgu in AIHT, p. 144.

**Antara in AIHT, p. 144.

1. Our text dropped Śineyu as the son of Uśanas and named his grandson Marutta as the son of Uśanas *vide* AIHT, p. 144.

26-27. Rukmakavaca was the learned son of Kambalabarhiṣ. With his sharp arrows, Rukmakavaca, at the very outset, killed many warriors with coats of mail and bows, in battle and attained the most excellent glory. That king of great fame distributed much wealth to Brāhmaṇas in his horse-sacrifice.

28. Five sons of great strength and prowess were born to Rukmakavaca. They could pierce the enemies and kill inimical warriors.

29. They were Rukmeṣu, Pṛthurukma, Jyāmagha, Parigha and Hari. The father established Parigha and Hari in the land of Videha.

30. Rukmeṣu became king (as successor to his father,[1]) and Prthurukma became his dependant. Thus cheated (and defeated) by them, Jyāmagha[2] lived in a hermitage though (he was entitled to be) a king.

31-32. He was calm (by temperament). In a great forest, he incurred the antagonism of a Brāhmaṇa. He took up his bow. Seated in a chariot and flying his own banner, he went to another country. Alone, the king went to the Narmadā, then to the land of Mekala (?), the Mirikā forest, the mountain Ṛkṣavān and ultimately reached Muktimān.

33. The wife of Jyāmagha named Śaibyā was a very powerful woman. Though he had no son, he did not marry another woman.

34. In a battle he was victorious and brought a girl as his prize. Afraid of his wife that he was, the king told his wife "This is your daughter-in-law."

35. On being told thus, she replied "To which son does she belong to be called my daughter-in-law ?

(The king replied)—"She will be the wife of the son who will be born to you".

36. By means of her severe and terrible penance, the exalted noble lady Śaibyā, in her old age, gave birth to her son Vidarbha.

---

1. AIHT.p.146 names Parāvṛt instead of Rukmeṣu as the successor to Rukmakavaca.

2. Jyāmagha is noted as a hen-pecked husband in Purāṇas. *vide* vv.33-36 below.

37-38. The prince Vidarbha begot of that girl two learned sons Kratha and Kaiśika. They were heroic experts in battle. Afterwards he begot Lomapāda, the third son. Babhru was the son of Lomapāda and Ākṛti was his son.

39. Cidi was the son of Kaiśika. The sons and descendants born of him were kings and are remembered as Caidyas. Kunti was the son of Kratha who (as had been already mentioned) was Vidarbha's son.

40. Dhṛṣṭa was born as the son of Kunti. He was courageous and valorous in battle. Nirvṛti was the virtuous son of Dhṛṣṭa. He was a slayer of inimical warriors.

41. His son was Daśārha who had great strength and exploits. Vyoma was the son of Daśārha. Jīmūta is mentioned as coming after him.

42. Vikṛti was the son of Jīmūta. His son was Bhīmaratha. Rathavara, it is said, was the son of Bhīmaratha.

43. He was always engaged in making charitable gifts, acquiring learning and practising good conduct.

His son was Navaratha and it is remembered that Daśaratha came thereafter.

44. His son was Ekādaśaratha and Śakuni was his son. The archer Karambhaka came thereafter, and Devarāta succeeded him.

45. King Devakṣatra of great fame was son of Devarāta. Devana, the delighter of all Kṣatriyas, was born as the son of Devakṣatra.

46. Madhu was born of Devana. Puruvasu was the extremely brilliant son of Madhu whose intellect was the source of his wealth.

47-49. Purūdvān, the excellent man, was the son of Puruvasu. Purūdvaha was the son of Bhadravatī and Purudvān. His wife was Aikṣvākī and Sattva was his son born of her. Sātvata, the increaser of fame and endowed with Sattva quality, was born of him. After perfectly understanding this creation of Jyāmagha of noble-soul, one shall attain progeny and identity with the intelligent 'King' Soma.

CHAPTER SEVENTYONE

The Vṛṣṇi Dynasty

Sūta said :—

1-2. Sons of great strength were born to Sātvata and Kauśalyā. They were Bhajamāna, Bhaji, Divya, Vṛṣṇi, Devavṛdha, Andhaka and Mahābhoja who was well-known, truthful of speech and a patron of Brāhmaṇas. Their creations (descendants) are fourfold. Listen to them in detail.

3-6. (Defective text) Sṛñjaya was the son of Bhajamāna* (?) Sṛñjaya had two daughters. He gave them in marriage to Bāhyaka. Those two sisters his wives, gave birth to many sons namely Nimloci, Kiṁkaṇa, Dhṛṣṭi and Parapurañjaya** They were born (as the great grandsons) of Bhajamāna and the sons of the daughter of Sṛñjaya. The sister of Bāhyaka's first wife gave birth to Ayutājit, Sahasrājit and Śatājit. Among the sons of Sātvata, Devavṛdha performed a severe penance with the intention "A son endowed with all good qualities should be born to me".

7-8. After engaging himself thus in the Yogic practice, he touched the waters of the river Parṇāśā.[1] Since the king was endowed with auspicious qualities, the excellent river became delighted at his touch when the king ceremoniously sipped the waters.

9-10. She (the river) became engrossed in thought and finally resolved thus—

"I shall not come in the way of that lady of whom a son endowed with all good qualities can be born to king Devavṛdha. Hence, I shall myself become his wife".

11-12. As her emotional attachment to him, as mentioned before welled up in her heart, she (assumed the form of)

---

*Acc. to Vā. P. 71.3 King Bhajamāna had from Sṛñjayā two sons Bāhya and Bāhyaka.

**The list in Vā. P. is Nimi, Paṇava, Vṛṣṇi, Para-Purañjaya.

1. The river Banas in Rajasthan, is tributary to the Chambal—De 146.

a girl and wooed the king who was in a thoughtful mood. The king too liked her. The liberal-minded king begot a brilliant child of her.

13. In the ninth month, the most excellent river gave birth to Babhru, the son of Devavrdha. That son was endowed with all good qualities.

14. In regard to that race of kings, Brāhmaṇas conversant with the Purāṇas sing the following verses. They glorify the good qualities of the noble-souled Devavṛdha.

15-16. 'Inasmuch as we hear from a distance and see at close quarters, Babhru is the most excellent one among human beings and Devavṛdha is on a par with the Devas.

The number of men who gained immortality (? absolution) from Babhru and also from Devavṛdha is seventy thousand and sixtyfive.

17-18. Mahābhoja, a scion of the family of Sātvatas, was a great warrior. He was a performer of sacrifices, the chief of the most prominent ones among the donors of liberal gifts, firm of resolve, truthful in speech, a patron of Brāhmaṇas and the most famous among kings.

His line is very great. The kings of his line are well renowned on the Earth as "Bhojas".

Dhṛṣṭi (Prob. Vṛṣṇi*) had two wives viz. Gāndhārī and Mādrī.

19-21. Gāndhārī give birth to Sumitra who delighted his friends. Mādrī gave birth to Yudhājit, Mīḍhvān, and Anamitra and Śina—both excellent among men.

Nighna was the son of Anamitra. Nighna had two sons viz. Prasena and Satrājit of great fortune. The Sun-god was a friend of Satrājit as dear to him as his own life.

22. Once, at the close of night, that excellent person among riders in the chariot (a great warrior) viz. Satrājit went in his chariot to the banks (of the river) in order to take water for offering libations to the sun.

23. Even as he was going on with his worship of the sun, Vivasvān (The Sun god) stood in front of him. The form

*AIHT p. 107—The genealogy.

of the lord was very vivid and clear. The disc of the Sun-god with a circular effulgence was very brilliant.

24-25. Then the king addressed to Vivasvān (the Sun-god) who stood in front of him. "O lord of luminaries, I see you alike both in the sky as well as in front of me. You have the same circular effulgence. O Vivasvān, what is the difference in you when you have approached me as a friend?"

26. On hearing this, the Sun-god removed the excellent jewel Syamantaka[1] from his own neck and tied it round the neck of the king.

27. Thereupon, the king saw him in his physical form. On seeing him, he was delighted and he carried on a pleasant talk with him for a short while.

28-29. When Vivasvān started once again, Satrājit said to him—"It behoves you, O lord, to give me this excellent jewel whereby the people may see you in it having the splendour of fire.

The Sun-god gave him the jewel named *Syamantaka*.

30. The king wore that jewel when he entered the city. He made the entire city wonder-struck and entered his harem.

31. With great love, that king Satrājit gave that divine excellent jewel Syamantaka to his brother Prasena.

32. Parjanya (god of clouds and rain) would shower plenty of rain in that country where this jewel named Syamantaka happened to exist. There would be no danger from ailments or epidemics in that country.

33. Govinda (Kṛṣṇa) expressed his desire to have that excellent jewel Syamantaka from Prasena, but did not get it. Although he was powerful enough, he did not take it by force.

34. Once Prasena bedecked himself with that jewel and went for hunting. For the sake of Syamantaka (i.e. on account of it) he met with a terrible death from a lion.

35. Jāmbavān, the king of bears, killed that lion. He took the divine jewel and entered his cave.

1. Compare the story of Syamantaka in Bh.P.X.Chs 56 and 57.

36. Elderly persons among the Vṛṣṇis and Andhakas considered that murder of Prasena an act of Kṛṣṇa who was covetous of the jewel. They suspected him alone.

37. The lord, the destroyer of enemies, who was more powerful than they did not brook that false accusation. So he roamed about in the forest to trace Prasena.

38-41. Accompanied by a few citizens who were trustworthy and obedient to him, the lord roamed about in the forest where Prasena had been hunting and where Prasena's footprints could be traced. He searched the excellent mountains Ṛkṣavān and Vindhya and became tired. In the end the noble-minded lord saw Prasena who had been killed along with his horse. But he did not get the jewel there (on his person). Thereafter, the lion was seen killed by a bear not far from the body of Prasena. This had been indicated by the footprints of the bear. The Scion of the family of Yadu (i.e. lord Kṛṣṇa) traced the foot-prints to the cave of a bear.

42-44. In that large cave, he heard the words uttered by a young woman. The nurse had been playing with the infant son of Jāmbavān, O Brāhmaṇas, along with the jewel. The words *Mā rodiḥ* (Do not cry) were uttered by her.

The nurse said :—

"The lion killed Prasena. It was killed by Jāmbavān. O my excellent child, do not cry. This jewel is for you".

The words were very clear. He went into the cave immediately.

45-47. Near the cave (also) he saw (a few) torn (pieces of) Prasena.

Entering the cave of the bear suddenly, the liberal-minded lord saw Jāmbavān, the king of bears. For twentyone days, Govinda, the son of Vasudeva, had a hand-to-hand fight with Jāmbavān inside that cave. After Kṛṣṇa had entered the cave (those who had followed Kṛṣṇa) with Vasudeva at their head, returned to Dvārāvatī and announced that Kṛṣṇa had been killed.

48-50. After defeating Jāmbavān of great strength, Vāsudeva won Jāmbavatī, the honoured daughter of the king of bears.

Overwhelmed by the splendour of the lord, Jāmbavān gave the jewel and Jāmbavatī immediately to Viṣvaksena (i.e. Kṛṣṇa). He accepted the jewel Syamantaka in order to clear himself of scandalous accusation.

51-54a. After pacifying the king of bears, the lord came out of the cave. After redeeming the jewel thus and clearing himself of all scandals by his own efforts, the lord gave the jewel to Satrājit in the presence of Sātvatas. The slayer of Madhu married Jāmbavatī.

Thus Madhusūdana cleared himself of false accusation. If anyone understands this false accusation and its removal by Kṛṣṇa, he will never be a victim of false accusation and slanderous gossip.

54b-56. Satrājit had ten wives and ten thousand sons. Among them three were very famous. Bhaṅgakāra was the eldest. Vātapati was a great warrior and Tapasvī was a favourite of many people. Bhaṅgakāra's mother was Vīramatī by name. She gave birth to three daughters endowed with beauty and good qualities.

57. Satyabhāmā was the most excellent among women. She used to be steadfast in her holy rites and observances. She was a saintly woman. Her father gave her in marriage to Kṛṣṇa.

58-60. (Defective Text). On hearing that Kṛṣṇa did not take away the jewel from Satrājit, Akrūra, desirous of wealth coveted the jewel Syamantaka. Through Śatadhanvan of the Bhoja family, he requested for Satyabhāmā of unblamed beauty. Śatadhanvan of great strength then killed Satrājit at night, took away the jewel and gave it to Akrūra.

61-62. Akrūra, the most excellent among men, took the jewel and entered into an agreement (with Śatadhanvan). "This should not be known to anyone else. We shall make use of the wealth received from it. In case you are assailed by Kṛṣṇa, the entire city of Dvārakā will undoubtedly remain under my control.

63. When her father was killed, Satyabhāmā of great reputation became distressed with grief. She got into a chariot and went to the city of Vāraṇāvata.

64. After reporting to her husband (i.e. Kṛṣṇa) the activities of Śatadhanvan of the Bhoja family, the excessively distressed Satyabhāmā stood at the side of her husband and shed tears.

65. Hari (Kṛṣṇa) performed the obsequies of Pāṇḍavas who were supposed to have been burnt in the lac palace at Vāraṇāvata. He engaged Sātyaki in activities of welfare* (?) for the brothers.

66a. Madhusūdana (Kṛṣṇa) came to Dvārakā in a hurry. The glorious lord then spoke these words to his elder brother Halī (Balarāma).

66b-68. "Prasena was killed by a lion. Satrājit was killed by Śatadhanvan. Syamantaka should be searched for. O lord, I am the legal master of that gem. So get into your chariot quickly. After killing the very powerful scion of the family of Bhoja, O mighty one, bring the Syamantaka jewel. It should be common to you all.**

69. Then a fierce battle ensued between Bhoja and Kṛṣṇa. Śatadhanvā looked for Akrūra in every direction.

70. Akrūra left Bhoja and Śrīkṛṣṇa without bringing about any truce between them. Though he was able to fight, he did not own loyalty, due to perfidy.

71. Then Śatadhanvan became frightened. He decided to go away from that place. Hṛdayā (the mare of Śatadhanvan) ran more than a hundred Yojanas.

72. The mare named Hṛdayā belonged to Bhoja. It was reputed as one capable of going a hundred Yojanas. It was a divine mare with which he fought with Kṛṣṇa.

73. On seeing Hṛdayā exhausted due to the fast running at the close of the hundredth Yojana of the journey and on observing the misfortune (?) of the chariot, Śatadhanvan began to run on foot.

74. Then, due to fatigue and affliction, O Brāhmaṇas, that vital breath of that mare went up in the sky. Then Kṛṣṇa said to Rāma.

**Kalyārtha* is obscure. Vā. P. 96.63 reads *tulyārtha* 'for equivalence' in performance of rites.

** '*us all*' as per Vā. P. 96.66:

75. "O mighty one, wait here. I have found out that there is a defect in the mare. I shall go on foot and take away the excellent jewel Syamantaka".

76. Then Acyuta who was conversant with the use of the greatest missile went on foot and killed Śatadhanvan in a park in the city of Mithilā.

77. He did not see Syamantaka (with him). When Kṛṣṇa returned after killing Bhoja of great strength, the wielder of plough (i.e. Bala-Rāma) said to him "Give me the jewel".

78. Kṛṣṇa said—"It is not with me". Then Rāma became angry and replied to Kṛṣṇa using the word "Fie on you" many times.

79. "I tolerate this since you are my brother. Welfare unto you. I am going away. I have nothing to do with Dvārakā, you and the Vṛṣṇis."

80. Thereafter, Rāma, the suppressor of foes entered Mithilā. With the offering of all desirable objects he was honoured by the king of Mithilā himself.

81. It was at this time itself that Babhru (=Akrūra) the most excellent one among the intellectuals performed without any obstacle different kinds of Yajñas.

82. This intelligent noble-minded son of Gāndinī (Akrūra) adopted initiation along with Kavaca (coat of mail) as protection, for keeping Syamantaka.

83. Those sacrifices of that noble-souled one are famous as *Akrūrayajñas*. In all of them, food and monetary gifts were in plenty. All of them yielded everything one desired.

84. Then king Duryodhana went to Mithilā. The lord had a training in mace-fighting under Balabhadra. The training was usually of a divine nature.

85. Thereafter, Rāma was pacified and brought to Dvārakā by the noble-souled Kṛṣṇa and the leading warriors belonging to the families of Vṛṣṇis and Andhakas.

86. Akrūra, a powerful leader of men, came back along with the Andhakas after killing Śatrughna along with Bandhumān.

87-88. Two well-renowned and very mighty sons named Śatrughna and Bandhumāṇ were born to Bhaṅgakāra and

Narā, the daughter of Suyajña. They were the most excellent among men. Kṛṣṇa was not happy over this murder, because Bhaṅgakāra was a prominent member of Andhaka family.

89. Since he was afraid of a split amongst his kinsmen, he (Kṛṣṇa) ignored him (Akrūra). When Akrūra went away, Indra did not shower rain (as Akrūra took with him the Syamantaka gem).

90. Since the whole realm was ruined by the draught in various ways, the Kukuras and Andhakas pacified and consoled Akrūra.

91. When Dānapati (i.e. Akrūra) returned to Dvārakā once again, the thousand-eyed lord (Indra) rained everywhere (even) within the ocean.

92. In order to gain the love (of Kṛṣṇa), O leading sages, Akrūra, the glorious one gave his sister (in marriage) to Vāsudeva, a girl honoured by everyone for her good conduct.

93. By means of his Yogic power, Kṛṣṇa understood that the jewel Syamantaka was with Babhru (i.e. Akrūra). Hence, he spoke thus to Akrūra in the open Assembly hall.

94-95. "O lord, you are worthy of honour. Do not do anything mean or ignoble towards me. Hand over to me that jewel which is in your possession. Sixty years have passed. The anger that I had at that time has become firmly rooted (on account of) repeated (offences). A long time has elapsed now".

96. Then, at the instance of Kṛṣṇa, the highly intelligent Babhru handed over, without hesitation and mental strain, the jewel (to Kṛṣṇa) in the Assembly of all Sātvatas.

97. Then Kṛṣṇa, the suppressor of enemies, became delighted in his mind. He returned to Babhru the jewel he had obtained from Babhru, by a straightforward deal.

98. After obtaining from Kṛṣṇa the excellent jewel Syamantaka, the son of Gāndinī wore it and shone like the Sun.

99. He who understands this false accusation of the lord and the excellent way in which the lord cleared himself, will not at all be a victim of false accusation.

100. Śini was born of Anamitra who was the youngest son of Vṛṣṇi. His son was Satyaka who was truthful in speech and richly endowed with truthful habits.

101. Yuyudhāna was the son of Satyaka and Bhūti* was his son. Yugandhara was the son of Bhūti. Hence, he was famous as Bhautya.

102. Vṛṣṇi was born as the son of Yudhājit who was the son of Mādrī. Śvaphalka and Citraka were the two sons of Pṛśni.

103. There was no fear from ailments or drought in the place where the noble-souled great king Śvaphalka was present.

104. Once upon a time, O excellent Brāhmaṇas, Indra did not shower rain for three years in the realm of the king of Kāśī a powerful lord.

105. That king of Kāśī greatly honoured Śvaphalka and made him stay there. The chastiser of Pāka (i.e. Indra) showered rain on account of the stay of Śvaphalka.

106. Śvaphalka obtained as his wife the daughter of the king of Kāśi, named Gāndinī. Every day she gave a cow as a gift to a Brāhmaṇa.[1]

107. It is said that she was in the womb of her mother for many hundreds of years. She did not come out. The father then spoke to her even as she was in the womb.

108-109. "Welfare unto you. Be born quickly. Why do you stay behind ?". The girl in the womb said to him—"If you give as a religious gift a cow every day, I shall come out of the womb in three years". The father said "So be it" and fulfilled her desire.

110. Akrūra her son from Śvaphalka, was remembered as a liberal donor, a performer of sacrifices, heroic, learned, fond of guests and a person who distributed much wealth as monetary gifts.

111-112. (She had other children also viz.) Upamaṅgu, Maṅgu, Mṛduras, Arimejaya, Girirakṣa, Yakṣa, Śatrughna,

---

*Asaṅga according to AIHT, p. 107.

1. A popular etymology of Gāṁdinī.

Arimardana, Dharmavṛddha, Sukarman, Gandhamāda, Āvāha and Prativāha were the sons. The excellent lady Vasudevā was her daughter.

113. Two sons who were the delighters of the family and who resembled Devas were born to the daughter of Ugrasena and Akrūra. They were Devavān and Upadeva.

114-115. Citraka begot three sons. Pṛthu, Vipṛthu, Aśvagrīva, Aśvavāha, Supārśvaka, Gaveṣaṇa, Ariṣṭanemi, Aśvāsya, Suvarmā, Varmabhṛt, Abhūmi and Bahubhūmi. Śraviṣṭhā and Śravaṇā were his daughters.

116. The daughter of the king of Kāśī bore four sons to Satyaka viz.—Kukura, Bhajamāna, Śuci and Kambalabarhiṣ.

117. Vṛṣṇi was the son of Kukura; Kapotaroman was the son of Vṛṣṇi and Viloman was his son.

118. Andhaka was his son. It is well-known that he was a scholar and friend of Tumburu. Another name of his viz. Candanodakadundubhī* is also famous.

119-120. Abhijit was his son and from him was born Punarvasu. The excellent king performed a horse-sacrifice for obtaining a son. In the course of the holy rite of Atirātra, Punarvasu was born from the midst of assembly, Therefore, he became later on a great scholar, a liberal donor, a performer of sacrifices and one conversant with piety and virtue.

121. Thereafter, it is said, two more children were born to Abhijit viz. Āhuka and Āhukī.** They were the most excellent ones among intelligent persons and they were well-renowned.

122-124. They cite these verses in regard to Āhuka :— "He had ten thousand chariots having the rumbling sound of the cloud. They were fully equipped with *Upāsaṅgas* (quivers) *Anukarṣas* (axle-trees), banners and *Varūthas*(protecting ledges).

---

*AIHT, p. 150 records *Nandanodakadundubhi* as the name. His another name Andhaka given in our text is not given by Pargiter.

**According to the genealogy on p. 105 of AIHT Āhuka was the son of Punarvasu.

(In his land) there was no one uttering a lie, refraining from the performance of sacrifices or not giving thousands of coins. No one was unclean. No one was unrighteous, lean or devoid of scholarship."

We have heard that Dhṛti was the son of Ārdraka (?) (rather Āhuka—Vā. P. 96. 123).

125-128. (Defective partially). With this retinue Āhuka, the unrivalled, marched towards the eastern quarter displaying eighty lakhs of horses very young in age. Thereby he surpassed king Bhoja (although he had as many) elephants. (In this compaign he gained) twentyone thousand ropes made of silver and gold for binding elephants.

An equal number of thousand (of bells of elephants) of king Bhoja in the northern quarter made tinkling sound on his conquest.

Āhuka gave his sister Āhukī in marriage in the land of Avanti (i.e. to a Prince of Avanti).

Two sons were born to the daughter of the king of Kāśī and Āhuka.

129. They were Devaka and Ugrasena. Both of them were on a par with those born of divine womb. Heroic sons comparable to the Devas were born to Devaka.

130. They were Devavān, Upadeva, Sudeva, and Devarakṣita. They had seven sisters. He gave them to Vasudeva in marriage.

131-132. They were Dhṛtadevā, Upadevā, Devarakṣitā, Śrīdevā, Śāntidevā, Sahadevā and the youngest of all of them viz. Devakī. She had a charming appearance.

Ugrasena had nine sons. Kaṁsa was the eldest among them.

133-136. They were Nyagrodha, Sunāman, Kaṅka, Śaṅku, Subhūmi, Sutanu, Rāṣṭrapāla, Yuddhatuṣṭa and Tuṣṭimān.

They had five sisters viz. Kaṁsā, Kaṁsavatī, Sutanu, Rāṣṭrapālī and Kaṅkā.

Ugrasena had a large number of children. Thus the scions of the race of Kukura have been recounted.

A man who remembers this race of Kukura having many members of unlimited strength and prowess, makes his own family extensive with many children.

Vidūratha was the son of Bhajamāna. He was the most important among chariot-warriors.

137-138. Śūra was the son of Vidūratha. He became the king of kings. Very powerful sons were born to Śūra viz. Vāta. Nivāta, Śoṇita, Śvetavāhana, Śamī, Gadavarman and Nidānta. Indeed, he was a conqueror of his foes.

139. Pratikṣatra was the son of Śamī. Svayambhoja was the son of Pratikṣatra. Hṛdika was the son of Svayambhoja.

140-141. Hṛdika had ten sons of terrible exploits, Kṛtavarman was the eldest among them. Śatadhanvan was a son in the middle. (The others were) Devabāhu, Subāhu, Bhiṣak, Śvetaratha, Sudānta, Adhidānta, Kanaka and Kanakodbhava.

142. A scholarly son named Kambalabarhis was born to Devabāhu. Asamaujas was his son. (Another son) Susamaujas was very famous.

143. Kṛṣṇa gave Sucandra and Vasurūpa (as sons in adoption) to Asamaujas of whom no son was born.

Thus the Andhakas are remembered (have been recounted).

144. He who repeats the names of and glorifies this race of Andhakas every day, attains an extensive family of himself. There is no doubt in this matter.

145. Śūra begot Devamīḍhvan (Devamīḍhuṣa) of Aśmakī. Ten persons were born of Māriṣī from Śūra. Māriṣī belonged to the Bhoja family.

146-148. Vasudeva of mighty arms was born at the outset. He is known as Ānakadundubhi because when he was born a loud report of *Dundubhi* (War drum) was heard in the sky.

There was the loud sound of *Ānakas* (a type of war-drum) too in the sky. There was no one on a par with Vasudeva in the entire world of men in regard to the handsomeness of features.[1] He was the foremost among all

1. Vasudeva's unparalleled handsomeness is recorded not only in Brahmanical Purāṇas but in Jaina works also. According to Jaina records,

men of the Earth. His splendour was like that of the Moon.

149-152. The following were born after him viz. Devabhāga, Devaśravas, Anādhṛṣṭi, Vṛka, Nandana, Sṛñjaya, Śyāma, Śamīka and Gaṇḍūṣa. They had five excellent ladies as their sisters. They were Pṛthā, Śrutadevā, Śrutakīrti, Śrutaśravās and Rājādhidevī. These five were mothers of heroic sons. Śūra gave his daughter Pṛthā to Kuntibhoja by way of adoption. Hence, Pṛthā became the daughter of Kuntibhoja. She is remembered by the name Kuntī. Pāṇḍu, an important heroic scion of the family of Kurus, took her as his wife from him.

153-154. Thereafter, Pṛthā gave birth to three sons whose splendour was on a par with that of the three fires. They were heroes without compeers in the world. They had the prowess and exploit comparable to that of Indra.

Pṛthā gave birth to the son Yudhiṣṭhira from Dharma, Vṛkodara (i.e. Bhīma) from the wind god Māruta and Dhanañjaya from Indra.

155. This is well known that the Aśvins were born of Mādravatī. Nakula and Sahadeva were endowed with beauty of form, inherent strength and other good qualities.

156. The heroic son Dantavakra of great strength was born to Śrutadevā from Vṛddhaśarman the king of Karūṣa.

157. Santardana, the powerful one, was born to Śrutakīrti from the prince of Kekaya. Similarly, another pair of very powerful princes named Cekitāna and Bṛhatkṣatra were also born.

158-160. The brothers Vinda and Anuvinda who were very powerful were born of the prince of Avantī (? as sons of Rājādhidevī). Śiśupāla, the prince of Cedi, was born of Śrutaśravā as the son of saintly king Damaghoṣa. His manliness is well-known. Formerly, he had been the tenheaded

---

Vasudeva was banished by his father, as complaints were lodged by the citizens about the seductive effect of his beauty on their women. A work called *Vasudeva Hiṇḍi* (600 A.D) an authentic version of the (Paiśācī) Bṛbatkathā of Guṇāḍhya—makes Vasudeva (instead of Naravāhanadatta) a hero whose wonderings were a marriage-campaign.

(Rāvaṇa), the suppressor of foes. He was the younger brother of Vaiśravaṇa and Kumbhakarṇa had been his younger brother.

Thirteen excellent ladies were the wives of Vasudeva.

161-163. They were Pauravī, Rohiṇī, Madirā, Bhadravaiśākhī and the fifth one Sunāmnī. (These were perhaps the earlier wives). Then Sahadevā, Śāntidevā Śrīdevā, Devarakṣitā, Dhṛtadevā, Upadevā and Devakī the seventh one—these too were his wives. The thirteenth one was Sugandhā. (Besides these) Vanarājī and two other attandant ladies became his wives.

Rohiṇī and Pauravī were the younger sisters of Bāhlīka.

164-165. Rohiṇī of excessive magnificence and fortune was the eldest and the most beloved wife of Ānakadundubhi. She gave birth to eight sons out of whom Rāma (Balarāma) was the eldest. (The other sons were) Sāraṇa, Śaṭha, Durdama, Damana, Śubhra, Piṇḍāraka, Kuśītaka. A daughter called Citrā was also born to her.

166-168. Niśaṭha and Ulmuka were very famous. They were born as the sons* of Rāma. Similarly, Pārśvī, Pārśvamardī, Śiśu, Satyadhṛti and Mandabāhyā were also the sons of Rāma.

Girika, Giri, Śulkagulma, Atigulma and Daridrāntaka were the sons of Sāraṇa. He had five daughters too. Understand them by their names. They were Arciṣmatī, Sunandā Surasā, Suvacā and Śatabalā. These were the daughters of Sāraṇa.

169-170. Bhadrāśva, Bhadragupti, Bhadraviṣṭa Bhadrabāhu, Bhadraratha, Bhadrakalpa, Supārśvaka, Kīrtimān and Rohitāśva were the sons of Śaṭha.

171-172. Abhibhūta was the son of Durmada (? Durdama). The above are remembered as the persons born of the family of Rohiṇī.

Nanda, Upananda, Mitra, Kukṣimitra, Bala, Citra, Upacitra, Kṛtaka, Tuṣṭi and Puṣṭi—these were the sons of Madirā. They were born to Vasudeva of Madirā.

---

*grandsons according to Vā. P. 96. 164.
There appears to be some confusion in the text.

173. Bimba, Upabimba, Sattvadanta and Mahaujas—these four persons of great strength are well known as the sons of Bhadrā (?)

174-175. Śauri (i.e. Vasudeva) begot of Vaiśālī (?) (Vaiśākhī) the excellent son Kauśika. The following six sons were born of Devakī to Śauri viz. Suṣeṇa, Kīrtimān, Udarṣi, Bhadrasena, the fifth one Ṛjudāya or Bhadradeva, the sixth one Kaṁsa.

176. In these circumstances, Viṣṇu, the lord of worlds, became Prajāpati once again (being born) as the long-lived Kṛṣṇa.

177. Subhadrā, who used to speak pleasantly well (Bhadrabhāṣiṇī) was born subsequent to Kṛṣṇa. This lady who delighted the family of Vṛṣṇi became well renowned later as Kṛṣṇā and Subhadrā.

178-179. The great warrior Abhimanyu was born of Subhadrā to Pārtha (i.e. Arjuna). Understand by their (individual names, those sons of great heroism, who were born of those seven highly fortunate wives of Vasudeva.

Pūrva and others were born of Vasudeva as the sons of Sahadevā.

180. Śāntidevā gave birth to Janastambha the illustrious scion of the family of Śauri.

Āgāvaha the noble-souled one was born of Vṛkadevī (?)

181-182a. A son named Mandaka was born to Śrīdevā.

Devarakṣitā gave birth to two sons viz. Upāsaṅga and Vasu.

Thus there were ten sons of his. Kaṁsa got them also killed.

182b-183. Śiśirāvatī (?) gave birth to these noble-souled sons viz.—Vijaya, Rocana, Vardhamāna and Devala.

The seventh wife, the daughter of Devaka gave birth to the highly prosperous son Gaveṣaṇa of good name, who fought in a wonderful manner during the battle.

184-186. O Brāhmaṇa, formerly while moving about in the urban parks and forests, Vasudeva begot of the Vaiśya lady Śraddhādevī the son Kauśika who was economical.

Sugandhī and Vanarāji were (see V. 163) also the wives of Śauri.

Puṇḍra and Kapila were the sons of Sugandhī. Of these two Puṇḍra became a king and Kapila went to the forest.

187. To the other lady, a powerful heroic son of Vasudeva was born. He was the Niṣāda (forester) named Jara (?). He was the foremost archer.

188. Mahābhāga was the famous son of Devabhāgya (in V. 149 Devabhāga).

They call the son born of Devaśravas as one honoured by scholars.

189. Anādhṛṣṭi begot of Aśmakī, a powerful son Śrāddhadeva. He was a destroyer of enemies. All his enemies had receded from him.

190. Ekalavya, the highly lucky son, was born to Śrāddhadeva. He was brought up by Niṣādas (foresters) and so he was well-known as Naiṣādi.

191. With pleasure Kṛṣṇa gave his sons Cārudeṣṇa and Sāmba for adoption to Gaṇḍūṣa who had no children. These two sons were well up in the use of arms. They were endowed with highly laudable characteristics.

192-194. Ranti and Rantipāla were the two sons of Nandana.

Vasudeva, the son of Śūra, who was valorous gave his heroic sons Saumi and Kauśika to Vṛka who had no sons.

Dhanus and Virajas were the two sons of Sṛñjaya.

Śyāma had no children. Śamīka went to the forest treating his status of being born of the family of Bhoja with contempt. He secured the status of a Rājarṣi (a royal sage).

195. He who duly observes holy rites and reads this story of the birth of Kṛṣṇa or narrates it to a Brāhmaṇa, shall obtain great happiness.

106. Kṛṣṇa, the lord of the Devas, the Prajāpati (lord or procreator of subjects) who was originally Lord Nārāyaṇa, was born among human beings for the sake of sport.

197. The lotus-eyed lord was born to Devakī and Vasudeva on account of their previous austerities. The lord had four arms and was endowed with divine beauty, charm and splendour.

198. The lord who was originally *Avyakta* (Unmanifest) exhibited his characteristics clearly. The holy lord of Yogic powers came to light as Kṛṣṇa in a human form.

199. It was Nārāyana who turned what is *Avyaya* (the imperishable) into *Vyaya* (the perishable one i.e. the body of Kṛṣṇa). After becoming Hari (i.e. Kṛṣṇa), Nārāyaṇa resumed his original *Sanātana* (eternal) status.

200-203a. (Partially defective text). The lord had created Prajāpati (god Brahmā) the primordial Being from a lotus. The lord well-known as Viṣṇu became the younger brother of Indra after being born as the son of Aditi. Devas propitiated the omnipresent Lord for being born as the son of Aditi.

The family of intelligent Vasudeva born in the race of Yayāti became sacred and holy, because lord Nārāyaṇa took his birth therein for the sake of killing Daityas, Dānavas and Rākṣasas.

203b-206. While Janārdana incarnated, the oceans trembled and agitated, the mountains shook, and the sacrificial fires of *Agnihotra* blazed. Auspicious and lucky winds blew. Dust particles became settled down. The luminaries shone all the more brightly.

The asterism on the day when Janārdana was born was Abhijit by name. The night is called Jayantī (the 8th of the dark half of Śrāvaṇa, the asterism Rohiṇī rising at mid-night). The Muhūrta (auspicious period of 48 minutes) was Vijaya by name.

Hari the eternal, unmanifest lord Nārāyaṇa became Kṛṣṇa.

207. Causing delusion to the subjects through his Māyā (illusive Power), the lord incarnated and the lord of the Devas (i.e. Indra) caused shower of flowers from the sky.

208. With words full of auspicious purport and significance, thousands of great sages, along with the Gandharvas eulogised and prayed to Madhusūdana.

209-211. On seeing his son born at the night and on observing the characterisic curl of hair on the chest called Śrīvatsa, Vasudeva thought in his mind that it was Adhokṣaja

(Viṣṇu) himself on account of the divine characteristic marks.

Vasudeva said to him—"O lord withdraw this divine form. O beloved one, I am afraid of Kaṁsa. Hence, I say like this.

My sons of wonderful appearance, your elder brothers have been killed by him".

On hearing the words of Vasudeva, the lord withdrew his divine form.

212. Being permitted by the lord, the father took him to the abode of Nanda the cowherd (who was staying) in the house of Ugrasena and handed him to Yaśodā.

213. Yaśodā and Devakī had become pregnant at the same time. Yaśodā was the wife of Nandagopa, the head of cowherds.*

214. A girl was born to Yaśodā in the very night when the lord was born as Kṛṣṇa in the family of Vṛṣṇis.

215. Guarding the son born to him, Vasudeva of great fame, handed over his son to Yaśodā and took the girl with him.

216-218. After giving the child to Nandagopa, he requested "Protect this (child). This is your son. Everything will be auspicious unto the Yādavas. This is the child of Devakī. He will remove all my distresses."

Ānakadundubhi (Vasudeva) then intimated to the son of Ugrasena (i.e. Kaṁsa)—"This is a daughter of very auspicious and splendid characteristics."

Kaṁsa was not at all aware, that a son had been born to his sister.

219. The evil-minded (Kaṁsa) handed the girl back (to Vasudeva) and said with pleasure—"She is my daughter in the same way as yours. There is no doubt in this. O heroic one, I will not kill her. Let her go wherever she pleases".

---

*Syntactically *sā Nandagopateḥ* is tautologous. *Sā* should stand for Devakī but then *Nandagopateḥ* needs emendation like *Ānakadundubheḥ*. The emended text will be *sā'nakadundubheḥ*. 'she (Devakī) was the wife of Vasudeva.'

1. Contrast Bh.P.X.5.5-8 where Kaṁsa is said to have snatched away the girl from Devakī and tried to dash her on a slab of stone.

220-222. Honoured in the ancestral abode of the Vṛṣṇis that girl grew up very well. The gentle lady (Devakī) joyously brought up the goddess like her own son. Thus the people say that Prajāpati himself was born as Kṛṣṇa in this manner. It is for the protection of Keśava that she was born.

The Yādavas will respect and honour her with concentration of mind. The lord of the Devas with divine body, Kṛṣṇa himself had been protected by her.

The sages enquired :—

223. Wherefor did the Bhoja king Kaṁsa kill the infant sons of Vasudeva? It behoves you to clarify this.

Sūta said :

224-225. Listen why the foolish-minded Kaṁsa killed the sons of Vasudeva when they were born due to fear of the powerful Lord—why Kṛṣṇa was taken away elsewhere as soon as he was born and how Govinda, the supreme person, was brought up along with the cows.

226. At the marriage of Devakī and Vasudeva the intelligent Kaṁsa acted as the charioteer. At that time he was the crown-Prince.

227. Then in the sky rose the speech of some incomprehensible person. It was a divine speech. It was very loud and witnessed by the people of the world merely because the name of Kaṁsa was uttered by it.

228. "O Kaṁsa, out of affection, you are taking your sister by means of a chariot. The eighth child of that lady shall be your killer".

229. On hearing that aerial voice, Kaṁsa, the foolish one, became distressed. He drew his sword and became intent on killing her.

230. The Valorous Vasudeva of great power said to Kaṁsa the son of Ugrasena, out of friendship or love.

231. —"O scion of the family of Yādavas, you are a Kṣatriya and it does not behove you to kill a woman. In this matter (under reference) a certain remedy has been found out by me.

232. O lord of the Earth, I shall hand over to you the eighth son that will be born of her. With him, you can do what you deem proper.

233. O munificent one, do not behave now in the way you wish.

Or, as another alternative, I shall bring unto you all the children (born of her) severally (i.e. as and when they are born).

234. In this manner, O excellent one among men, this aerial voice too will not be erroneous".

On being told thus and consoled, he accepted the suggestion then.

235. On regaining his wife, Vasudeva became delighted. The foolish-minded Kaṁsa of evil deeds killed his sons.

The sages enquired :—

236-337. Who is this Vasudeva who begot Viṣṇu whom he addressed as "O dear one"? Who is this renowned Devakī who bore Viṣṇu in her womb ? Who is Yaśodā of great reputation who brought him up ? Who is this Nandagopa ?

Sūta said :—

238. Puruṣa became Kaśyapa and Aditi was his beloved Prakṛti. Kaśyapa was a part of Brahmā and Aditi that of Pṛthivī (the Earth).

239-240. Nanda is reputed as Droṇa and Yaśodā was Dharā*.

The mighty lord made the desires of Devakī flourish and entered a human body. The lord thus walked over the earth. The lord of Yogic soul caused delusion unto all living beings by means of his Yogic Māyā.

241. When Dharma (Virtue) became lost, Viṣṇu himself was born in the family of Vṛṣṇi in order to re-establish Dharma and annihilate Asuras.

---

*According to Bh.p.X.8.48-51 Nanda was a Senior Vasu called Droṇa in his previous birth and Dharā was his wife. God Brahmā gave them a boon whereby they became the foster-parents of Lord Kṛṣṇa and were devoted to him.

242-244. (Defective text) Rukmiṇī was the daughter of the king of Vidarbhas. Satyā was the daughter of Nagnajit. Satyabhāmā was the daughter of Satrājit. (These were the wives of Kṛṣṇa). Jāmbavatī, Rohiṇī (? prob. Lakṣmaṇā) Śaibyā and sixteen thousand other gentle ladies were also the blessed wives of Kṛṣṇa.

Fourteen groups of Apsaras (celestial women) have already been mentioned before. Indra held council with the Devas and the important ones were sent here for the sake of becoming the wives of Vāsudeva. They were born in palaces (rich families).

245-246. These prosperous and lucky ones are well known as the wives of Viṣvaksena.

The sons of Rukmiṇī were :—

Pradyumna, Cārudeṣṇa, Sudeva. Śarabha, Cāru, Cārubhadra, Bhadracāru and Cāruvidya. There was a daughter named Cārumatī.

247-248. The sons of Satyabhāmā were Sānu, Bhānu, Akṣa, Rohita, Mantravid, Jara, Andhaka, Tāmracakra, Saubhari and Jarandhara. Four sisters were born of the Garuḍa-emblemed lord (i.e. Kṛṣṇa) viz. Bhānu, Saubharikā, Tāmraparṇī and Jarandharā. Listen to the childern of Jāmbavatī.

249-250. Bhadra, Bhadragupta, Bhadracitra and Bhadrabāhu were the sons of Jāmbavatī*. The daughters were famous by the names of Bhadravatī and Sambodhanī. These should be known as the children of Jāmbavatī.

251. Saṅgrāmajit, Śatajit and Sahasrajit—these were glorified as the sons of Viṣvaksena born of Sudevī.

252. The children of the daughter of Nagnajit were these—viz. Vṛka, Vṛkāśva, Vṛkajit, Mitrabāhu and Sunītha were sons. Vṛjinī, the excellent lady, was her daughter.

253. These and others constitute thousands of sons. Understand that it is mentioned that Vāsudeva's sons were about a million.

254. Eighty thousand among them were great heroes and experts in war.

Thus the race of Janārdana has been duly recounted to you all.

255. Brhatī was the wife of Pūru. So also Sumadhyā and Sugati. She (? Bṛhatī) was the daughter of the noble-souled Bṛhaduktha, son of Śini.

256. Thereof her sons viz. Ānanda, Kanaka and Śveta were well-known. They shone splendidly in battles. She had a daughter also named Śvetā.

257. Citra, Śūra and Citraratha were the sons of Agāvaha. Citrasena was his son. He had a daughter Çitravatī

258. Tumba had two sons viz. Tumba (?) and Tumbavarcas.

Vajrāra and Kṣipra were the sons of Upāsaṅga.

259. Bhūrīndrasena and Bhūri were the sons of Gaveṣaṇa.

Sudhanus was his (?) son born of the daughter of Yudhiṣṭhira.

260. Kāśyā (Princess of Kāśī) bore five courageous and strong sons to Sāmba. They are glorified as five shining heroes beginning with Satya.

261-262. The grandsons of the noble-souled Yādavas were three crores in number. The entire family and those who stay in the family are under the protection and the lordly authority of Viṣṇu. Suras and human beings are bound by those who abide by his behests.

263. Those powerful Asuras who were killed in the battles between the Devas and Asuras are born here among human beings. They harass human beings.

264. It is for annihilating them that they are born in the family of Yādavas. A hundred branches of the family of the noble-souled Yādavas were born.

265. Thus the progeny of Vṛṣṇis has been glorified succinçtly and in detail. That must be glorified by one who is desirous of achievement of fame.

CHAPTER SEVENTYTWO

Praise of the Lord : Conclusion

Sūta said :—

1-3. Understand the Devas with human appearance and descent who are being glorified.

Saṅkarṣaṇa, Vāsudeva, Pradyumna, Sāmba and Aniruddha—these five are glorified as the five heroes of the race (of Vṛṣṇis).

The seven sages, Kubera, Yajña, Maṇivara, Śālūki, Nārada, the learned Dhanvantari, Nandins, Mahādeva, Sālaṅkāyana and Viṣṇu, the primordial God, along with these gods (Saṅkarṣaṇa etc.) (? are the Devas with human descent).

The sages said :—

4. What for was Viṣṇu born ? How many *Sambhūtis* (births or incarnations of Viṣṇu) are remembered ? How many of them are to occur in future ? How many are the manifestations of the noble-souled one ?

5. What for is he born again and again in excellent families of Brāhmaṇas and Kṣatriyas among beings. Recount it to us who (being inquisitive) enquire about it.

6-7. We wish to hear in detail about the activities of intelligent Kṛṣṇa, the destroyer of enemies. Kindly narrate duly the activities in the proper order. So also mention what are the manifestations of the lord.

8-11a. It behoves you to recount to us, O beloved one, his descent and source of origin. Why did Lord Viṣṇu, the annihilator of enemies, who was among gods (and had the status of God) was born in the family of Vasudeva ? How did the intelligent one attain the status of the son of Vasudeva ? Why did he leave the holy Devaloka (world of the gods) inhabited by the meritorious immortal ones and come down here to the mortal worlds ?

Hari who is the leader of the Devas as well as human beings, is the source of origin of god Brahmā (the creator of the world). Why did he make his divine self permeate a human form?

11b-13a. It is he alone who makes the mental cycle (*manomayaṁ cakram*) of human beings revolve and function. How is it that he, the most excellent among the wielders of discus, decided to be born among human beings.

It is he who accords protection all times to the Universe. How did that lord Viṣṇu come to the Earth and functioned as a protector of Cows?

13b-14a. He is Bhūtātmā (the immanent Soul of all living beings). It is he who created and sustained the *Mahābhūtas* (the great elements). He is *Śrigarbha* (having glory and splendour within). How was he accommodated in the womb by a woman walking over the Earth (i.e. ordinary human being)?

14b-16. It is he by whom the Devas had been made glorious and prosperous after conquering the worlds) one after another) in due order. The paths (i.e. diverse forms of activity worldly as well as spiritual) of the world have been established by him. A body that took three steps (traversing the three worlds within them) was assumed by him (in the Vāmana incarnation). This most excellent god handed over the earth conquered by him (from Bali) to gods again.

Hiraṇyakaśipu the demon of yore, possessing great prowess had been killed by him after adopting a leonine body and dividing it into two (as half-man-half-lion).

17. It is that all-pervading lord became the submarine fire called Aurva and Saṁvartaka. Stationed in the netherworlds and within the ocean, he drank the *Havis* offerings in the form of water.

18. In the different Yugas, they (the learned sages) call him the lord with a thousand feet, a thousand rays, a thousand forms) and a thousand heads.

19. It is from his navel as holy as the sacred *Araṇi* (the piece of wood used for kindling sacred fire by attrition that the abode of *Pitāmaha* (the creator Brahmā) took its origin when the whole world was a vast ocean. It was a *Paṅkaja* (lotus) but not born of any *Paṅka* (mud).

20-21a. It is he by whom all those Daityas were killed in the battle called Tārakāmaya (the war caused by the abduction of Tārā by Candra) after adopting a body consisting of (the essential spirit of) all Devas and holding all sorts of weapons. Kālanemi who was arrogant on account of his great prowess, was killed by him.

21b-c. It is he who after resorting to his eternal Yoga, and enveloping everything in the dense darkness (after deluge) lies down (in his Yogic slumber) in the northern areas of the milky ocean, the veritable ocean of nectar (or from which nectar was churned out).

22. Formerly, on account of the intensity of her austerities, Aditi, who is an Araṇī (i.e. source of origin) of the Suras (gods) accommodated in her womb the lord as well as Indra. It was the lord who kept the group of Daityas very much under check and restraint by the miscarriage of pregnancy (i.e. Daitya women became afraid of the lord so much so that they had abortions).

23. It was the lord who made Daityas lie down in water after making the regions (and worlds) the abodes of people, and after making Devas the shining residents of Heaven, he made Indra the lord of Suras.

24-29a. It was the lord who created all types of sacrifices and the necessary adjuncts thereof. He duly created the sacred fires of Gārhapatya and Āhavanīya and the monthly *Śrāddha* rite of Anvāhārya. He created the various adjuncts of sacrifice such as the *Vedi* (Altar), the Kuśa grass, the *Sruvā* (holy ladle), water for consecrating (Prokṣaṇīya etc.), the Śruta (holy texts and Mantras) and the *Āvabhṛthya* (holy water for purificatory bath at the conclusion of a sacrifice.

Then he created sages who offered shares in the oblations in the fire for gods in the sacrifice (shares in the oblations). He made the Suras the partakers of *Havya*, and the Pitṛs the partakers of *Kavya*. He made persons deserving enjoyment through the holy rite of *Yajña*. It is the lord himself who is termed *Yajña* in the course of the holy performance of *Yajña*.

He created the requisite materials of *Yajña* such as the *Yūpas* (sacrificial posts), *Samits* (holy twigs) *Sruvā* (sacred ladle), the Soma (the creeper as well as juice), the *Pavitra* (the sacred ring of Kuśa grass with a projecting tail) and *Paridhis* (the holy twigs of *Palāśa* etc. laid around the sacrificial fire). He created the sacrificial fires, the *Sadasyas* (the members of the holy assembly), the *Yajamānas* (performers of sacrifices), the *Udgātṛs* (those who sing *Sāman* Mantras and hymns) and others. He created excellent sacrifices such as Aśvamedha (horse sacrifices) and Rājasūya (imperial consecration) etc. of diverse kinds. By means of the *Pārameṣṭhya* (concerning Brahmā) holy rite he sustained the worlds and Yajñas.

29b-33. Many things have been created by the lord who is the immanent soul of all the groups of living beings—*Kṣaṇas*, *Nimeṣas*, *Kāṣṭhās* and *Kalās* (all units of time), the three periods of time (past, present and future), *Muhūrtas* (periods of 48 minutes), *Tithis* (lunar days), months, days, years, seasons, the auspicious Yogas of time, the three kinds of Pramāṇa (means of valid knowledge), the span of life, fields, strength, the beauty of form, the intellect, heroism, the ability to comprehend holy texts and three Vidyās (lyres), the three holy fires, the three units of time (past, present and future), the three holy rites, the three Mātrās (measures of times) the three Guṇas (i.e. Sattva, Rajas and Tamas) and the lords of the world have been created by some means or other. All the groups of Bhūtas (living Beings, Elements) have been created.

34. It is the lord who unifies moments, and sports by means of his age-old Yogic power. He is the leader of arrivals and departures (all sorts of movements and transits). He is the lord present everywhere in diverse ways.

35. He is the goal unto those who are endowed with piety. He is inaccessible to those of evil rites. He is the origin of the system of four castes and the protector of the same.

36-38. He is conversant with the four types of Vidyās (viz. Ānvīkṣikī, Trayī, Vārtā and Daṇḍanīti). He is the support of the four *Āśramas* (stages of life). He is the interstice of the quarters, Ether, Earth, waters, wind, fire, the two luminaries viz. moon and sun, he is identical with the lords of Yugas as well as the night-wanderers (demons?). He is reported as the greatest lord in the Vedas. He is spoken of as the greatest austerity. It is he whom they call the greatest one beyond darkness. He is the greatest one possessed of the Supreme Soul. He is the lord who is the foremost among Ādityas. He is the lord who is the cause of destruction of the Daityas.

He is the god of death during the closing periods of the Yugas and he is the annihilator of the destroyers of the worlds.

39-41. He is the bridge (or boundary) among bounds of the worlds (?); he is the holy sacrifice among those of middling holy rites. He is the Vedya (one who is to be known) to the scholars in Vedic lore. He is the lord of those who are of powerful souls. To the living beings, he is like the Soma (Moon). To those of fiery splendour he is like fire. Among human beings he is the Manu. He is the penance of sages, performers of penance. To those who are contented with good behaviour he is modesty, he is the splendid grandeur of those possessing glorious splendour.

42-44. He is the *Vigraha* (Body) of all the embodied beings. He is the velocity of those who are in speed (?)

Vāyu and *Ākāśa* (Ether) function as its source of origin. *Hutāśana* (fire) has *Vāyu* as its vital essence. Devas have their vital essence in fire. Madhusūdana is the vital essence of fire.

Blood takes its origin from *Rasa*[1] (a vital fluid constituent of the body) and it is said that the flesh originates from blood.

The source of fat is from the flesh. It is defined that the bone originates from the fat. From the bone the pith and marrow take their origin and the origin of Semen is from the marrow.

45-46. (?) Foetus originated from semen virile through its assimilative *rasa*—bodily fluid. It is there that water is mixed initially (?). This is called the *Saumya Rāśi*. The foetus

1. VV. 42-51 contain ancient ideas about embryology.

that is solidified [lit. born of *Aśman*, stone-solid] is called the second Rāśi. One should know that semen is of the nature of Soma and Menstrual blood is of the nature of fire.

47. These two Evolutes follow *Rasa*. In the Semen the moon and the fire are present. Semen belongs to the category of *Kapha* (a humour in the body) and Menstrual blood shall be in the category of *Pitta* (Bile, a humour in the body).

48. The place of *Kapha* is the heart. *Pitta* settles in the navel. The heart is in the middle of the body. It is remembered as the abode of the mind.

49. The navel is fixed in the belly and it is there that the shining gastric fire is present. Mind should be known as Prajāpati and *Kapha* is considered to be Soma.

50-51. *Pitta* is remembered as Agni (fire). Thus Universe is here of the nature of fire and the Moon.

Vāyu enters this foetus which is similar in size to jujube fruit and which begins to function. The Vāyu that enters, gets merged with the great Soul. It exists in the body in five forms and it makes the foetus grow.

52. The five vital airs are Prāṇa, Apāna, Samāna, Udāna and Vyāna. The vital air Prāṇa moves round developing the great soul.

53. *Apāna* develops the lower body. *Udāna* develops half of the soul, *Vyāna* is so called because it is scattered (i.e. spreads all over the body). *Samāna* is present in every Joint.

54-57. It then gets access to the element through the sense organs.

The five elements are *Pṛthivi* (earth), *Vāyu* (wind), *Ākāśa* (either), *Āpaḥ* (water) and the fifth one fire. These elements permeate the sense organs and begin their respective activity.

They call the physical body *Pārthiva* (having the characteristics of the element *Pṛthivi*).

The vital airs have the characteristics of wind. The pores of sense-organs have Ether as their source of origin.

It is from water element that there is liquid formation in the body. The fiery element is present in the eyes. Hence, these apertures are remembered after the names of elements.

It is to the virility of the supreme lord that these sense-organs function gathering their own respective objects.

Thus the eternal single Puruṣa creates all these.

58. How did Viṣṇu attain the state of being a man in this mortal world ? O intelligent one, this is our doubt. This is a great wonder, a miracle.

59. He is the ultimate goal of all who attain their goal. How did he assume a human body ? We wish to hear about the activities of Viṣṇu in due order.

60-61. Viṣṇu is the greatest miracle. He is mentioned so by even the lords of Devas.

O highly intelligent one, recount to us the origin (i.e. incarnation) of Viṣṇu which is very wonderful.

Let this wonderful and pleasing episode be narrated. Kindly recount the manifestations of the noble-souled one whose strength and prowess is well-known. The inherent power of Viṣṇu who has become miraculous on account of his activities is to be described here.

Sūta said :—

62-64. I shall recount unto you the manifestation of the noble-souled lord. I shall tell you. how the lord of great penance incarnated among human beings on account of the course of Bhṛgu, due to his fault of killing the wife of Bhṛgu. During the final periods of Yugas, he takes birth for the accomplishment of the task of the Devas. Understand the details of the divine person of Viṣṇu even as I recount.

65. When the yuga-dharma (the devout activities peculiar to a Yuga) becomes reversed, when the time becomes slack and ineffective, the lord is born among human beings in order to establish *Dharma* (Virtue). (These incarnations are) due to the curse of Bhṛgu brought about by the Devas and Asuras.

The sages enquired :

66. How did the lord become subject to this utterance—"brought about by the Devas and Asuras". This we wish to understand. What for and how did this incident of the Devas and Asuras take place.

Sūta explained :—

67-71. Understand all of you how this incident (of tussle between Devas and Asuras came about, even as I narrate the same.

Formerly, the Daitya (named) Hiraṇyakaśipu used to rule over the three worlds. Later on, the kingdom in the three worlds was presided over by Bali in due order.

There was great friendship between the Devas and Asuras. For a full period of ten Yugas, the universe was uninterrupted.

The Devas and Asuras used to abide by the behests of those two. But when Bali was bound over, a very terrible tussel arose. This caused horrible devastation to both Devas and Asuras. For the Dvīpas, many battles took place between them.

72. In this Varāha Kalpa, twelve ending with Saṇḍāmarka are remembered.[1] Even as I recount them listen to them succinctly by their names.

73. The first battle was fought by Narasiṁha (originating from the Man-lion incarnation of Viṣṇu). The second one (by) Vāmana (originating from the incarnation as a Dwarf). The third one is Varāha (originating from the Boar-incarnation of Viṣṇu) and the fourth battle (took place at the time of churning of the ocean of milk for the sake of nectar.

74. The fifth battle was a terrible one named Tārakāmaya caused by the abduction of Tārā by Candra. The sixth of those battles was (known as) the Āḍībaka and Traipura war is remembered as the seventh.

1. VV.72-126 describe the incarnations of Viṣṇu. The list of these is different in this Purāṇa. *vide*—Introduction—Vaiṣṇavism.

75. Andhakāra is the eighth one among them. *Dhvaja* is remembered as the ninth. *Vārtra* (pertaining to Vṛtra) is the tenth horrible battle. Halāhala is remembered as the battle thereafter (i.e. the eleventh).

76. Kolāhala, another terrible battle is remembered as the twelfth among them.

Hiraṇyakaśipu, the Daitya, was killed by Narasimha.

77-78. When the three worlds were measured up (by Vāmana's three steps) Bali was bound over by Vāmana. When the groups of the Devas were rejected, Hiraṇyākṣa was killed in a dual combat. That Daitya who had great strength and virility and who had never been defeated, was split into two by Varāha (Boar) with his curved teeth.

79-80. Prahlāda was defeated by Indra in the battle that followed the churning of the ocean for the sake of nectar Virocana who was the son of Prahlāda and who always attempted to slay Indra was killed by Indra himself by means of his exploits in the Tārakāmaya battle.

That Jambha who secured the boon of *Avadhyatā* (state of not being killed) from god Śiva along with special miraculous weapons was killed in the sixth battle by Viṣṇu in whom Indra had permeated.

81-83. When the Devas became incapable of enduring the great power of the Asuras, the demons were killed by Śiva in the course of Tripura battle.

Then Daityas, Asuras and Rākṣasas were conquered in the Andhakārika battle by the Devas and human beings. They merged with the manes.

With the help of Viṣṇu and magnified by him, Mahendra killed Dānavas along with Vṛtra, as they had joined together.

84-88a. In the battle called *Dhvāja*, Vipracitti who was accompanied by his younger brother, who was conversant with the Yogic practice and who had concealed himself by means of Māyā, was killed by Mahendra after penetrating a hundred thousand *Dhvajas* (banners).

In the battle Hālāhala, Vṛṣa (i.e. Indra) surrounded by the Devas conquered the Daityas and Dānavas who had gathered together.

In the battle called Kolâhala Raji surrounded by the Devas conquered the Daityas.

In the course of Avabhṛtha (valedictory bath after a sacrifice) Ṣaṇḍa and Marka were conquered by the Devas (and therefore the Daityas too were conquered).

88b. Thus, the twelve great battles between the Devas and Asuras took place. These battles caused ruin to both, the Suras and Asuras. They were inauspicious to the common people.

89. Hiraṇyakaśipu shone as the king and ruler of the three worlds for ten crores of years increased by seven million and two hundred and eighty thousand years.

90. As a hereditary ruler Ḅali reigned for ten crores thirty million and sixty thousand years (i.e. 13 crores and 60 thousand years).

91. In the company of Rākṣasas, Prahlâda reigned victorious for as many years as the period of administration of Bali.

92. These three were very famous as the Indras of the Asuras. They had great brilliance, strength and splendour.

The entire period of ten Yugas was under the Daityas.

93-95. Thereafter, Śukra cursed the realm extending to a period of ten Yugas. Then these three worlds of Bali were overrun by Mahendra.

When the kingdom of the three worlds of Prahlâda by inheritance was taken away by the efflux of time, it came over to the chastiser of Pāka (viz. Indra) by rotation.

Then the Yajña forsook the Asuras, and went over to the Devas. When the Yajña went over to the Devas those Asuras spoke to Śukra.

96. "Why has this happened? Even as we are widely awake, Yajña has abandoned our kingdom and gone to the Devas. We cannot stay here to-day. Let us enter Rasâtala".

97. On being told thus, Śukra became dejected. Consoling them with his words he said—"O Asuras, do not be afraid. I shall sustain you all by means of my spiritual brilliance.

98. Rainfall, medicinal herbs, *Rasā* (the world) and other things whatsoever—let all these things entirely remain with the Suras. The sin will be theirs (?)

99-101. "I shall give them all to you. It is being held up by me".

Thereafter, on seeing the Asuras supported by the intelligent preceptor Śukra, Devas became excited and frightened. With a desire to be victorious, they held consultations 'O, this preceptor is forcibly removing everything from us. Well, we shall hasten lest he should resuscitate and replenish them. After killing them forcibly in surprise attack we shall make the remaining ones go to Pātāla.

102. Thereafter, the excited Devas approached Dānavas and killed them. On being killed by them, Dānavas rushed to Kāvya himself.

103. On seeing them suddenly attacked by the Devas Kāvya protected the frightened sons of Diti from the Devas.

104-111. On seeing the Devas standing there steadily, Kāvya thought that it was fate. After meditating and remembering, the earlier happenings he said to Dānavas:—

"The entire area of the three worlds was conquered by Vāmana by means of three paces. Bali was bound over. Jambha was killed. Virocana was slain. The great Asuras were slaughtered by Suras in the twelve wars. Most of those who were very important were slain by means of different strategies. Only a very few of you remain now after the battle. I shall devise a plan for you. Let some period of time be waited for. I shall go to the lord Nīlalohita (i.e. Śiva), the great lord, for the sake of *Mantra* (holy spell etc.) and victory. The Hotṛ shall kindle and lit up the Fire by means of Mantras. It will burn. After returning here later I shall bless you all. Covered by means of bark garments, you do perform penance in the forest. The Devas shall not kill you till my return. After securing unrivalled and matchless Mantras from lord Maheśvara, we shall fight Devas once again. Thereby, you will attain victory".

112-114. After consulting (one another) the Asuras said to the Devas :—"We all have laid down our weapons.

All of you can pass on to the worlds (i.e. occupy them). Covered with bark garments we shall perform austerities in the forest".

On hearing these truthful worlds of Prahlāda, the Devas became delighted and free from ailments and worries. They returned. When the Daityas had drowned their weapons, they (the Devas) went back to their abodes whence they had come.

115-118a. Then Kāvya said to them—"Be patient to wait for some time without any undue enthusiasm for war. Be engaged in austerities. Time is the means of achieving your purpose. O Dānavas, stay in the hermitage of my father and wait". After giving directions to the Asuras, Kāvya, approached Mahādeva, bowed down to him and said thus to the lord, the source of origin of this Universe :—"O lord, I wish to secure those *Mantras* which are not in the possession of Bṛhaspati. I want them for the sake of defeating the Devas and according freedom from fear to the Asuras".

118b-120a. On being told thus, the lord said :—"If you wish to secure the *Mantras*, O Brāhmaṇa, observe the holy rite as instructed by me, remaining celibate and observing concentration and the purity of mind. With the head hanging down, if you inhale the smoke from the holy sacrificial pit for the full period of a thousand years, welfare unto you, you will secure the *Mantra* from me".

120b-121. On being told thus by the lord of the Devas, Śukra of great power of penance, touched the feet of the lord and said, "Certainly, O lord, I shall observe the holy rite as I have been directed.

122-125. Thereafter, Kuṇḍadhara was employed by the lord as the person producing the smoke for him.

When Śukra had gone for the welfare of the Asuras, when he was staying near Maheśvara observing celibacy for the sake of *Mantras*, the Devas understood by means of their diplomacy that the realm (? weapons) had been laid aside by the Asuras.

The Devas attacked them at that vulnerable point, with

great anger. The Devas with Bṛhaspati as their leader took up weapons and rushed at the Asuras.

125. On seeing the Devas taking up the weapons once again, all the groups of Asuras rose up suddenly. They became frightened.

126-128. (They thought thus) :—"When the weapons have been set aside, when freedom from fear has already been accorded, when our Ācārya (Preceptor) has undertaken holy rites and observances, these Devas have abrogated (unilaterally) the agreement. They are desirous of killing their enemies". (Then they told one another) :—"You are now devoid of an Ācārya. Welfare unto you. You had trusted them. We are all engaged in penance wearing bark garments and deer-skins. We are incapable of any action and are devoid of activities, properties and possessions. We are not at all competent to conquer the Devas in a battle. Without being engaged in battle we shall seek refuge in the mother of the preceptor".

129. Thereafter, those frightened Asuras resorted (to her). Freedom from fear (Assurance of protection) was granted by her to those frightened Daityas who sought freedom from fear.

130. Our seeing the Asuras being taken under her protection, the Devas pondered over their strength and weakness and then struck at the Asuras violently.

131. On seeing the Asuras being slain by the Devas, the infuriated gentle lady (the mother of the preceptor) spoke to them "I shall cause the destruction of Indra".

132-133. With great agitation and fury, she paralyzed Indra quickly and went away from that place. On seeing Indra benumbed and immobilised, the Devas became frightened. On seeing Indra thus brought under control, the Devas ran off from that place like deluded ones.

When the groups of Devas had gone, Viṣṇu spoke to Indra :—

134. "Enter me, O lord of Suras," said he. "Welfare unto you. I shall take you away".

On being told thus, Indra entered Viṣṇu.

135-136. On seeing that Indra was saved by Viṣṇu, the gentle lady became furious and spoke these words :—"I shall burn you, O Indra with my power along with Viṣṇu, even as all the living beings witness the same. Let the power of my penance be seen".

Those two Devas, Indra and Viṣṇu conspired thus on being attacked by her.

137-138. "How shall both of us get released together" said Viṣṇu to Indra." Indra then said—"O lord, kill her before she burns us. I shall be particularly attacked. Kill this lady. Do not delay". Thereupon Viṣṇu closely watched her and got ready for causing the death of that woman.

139-140. Thereafter, bearing in mind, that Indra was in trouble, lord the destroyer of the enemies of Suras, hastened Viṣṇu in his action. He wanted to be quicker than the mother of Kāvya who was also in a hurry. Viṣṇu was aware that what he was desirous of doing was a cruel deed. Becoming furious he pierced her head with his weapon and cut it into three parts.

141. On observing that horrible slaughter of a woman his wife, Bhṛgu the powerful one became angry. Then, due to the murder of his wife, Viṣṇu was cursed by Bhṛgu.

142. "Since a woman who should not be killed has been killed by you, though you are conversant with what is righteousness, you will have to take birth among human beings for seven times".

143. Thereafter on account of that curse the lord is born again and again among human beings here (in this world), for the welfare of all the worlds, whenever there is a destruction of piety and virtue.

144. After speaking to Viṣṇu, he himself took up the head and joined it to the body. After putting them together, he spoke these words :—

145-146. "I shall make you who have been killed by Viṣṇu actually regain your lost life. If the entire range of pious activities is known to me, if all virtuous holy rites have been performed by me, if I speak the truth, come back to life through the power of that truthfulness".

That gentle lady was then resuscitated on account of his truthful statement.

147-149. After sprinkling her with cool water he said "Come back to life". Then on seeing her get-up as though waking up from sleep, all living beings were surprised. Words and sounds of 'Well-done' of all living beings, of even invisible ones, echoed in the quarters.

150a. On seeing that noble lady resuscitated thus by Bhṛgu, even as all living beings were watching they thought that it was a miracle. On seeing his wife brought back to life by Bhṛgu who remained calm and composed, Indra was not at all happy. He became afraid of Bhṛgu.

150b-153a. Spending sleepless nights over this incident, Indra, the intelligent chastiser of Pāka, spoke to his daughter Jayantī, these words:—"This preceptor of Asuras is performing a severe penance for making the world devoid of Indra. Therefore, O my splendid daughter, I have been made very vexed and agitated although I am endowed with fortitude of mind. Go and honour him. Be alert and render service to him in various ways pleasing to his mind and dispelling his fatigue".

153b-157a. That lady of splendid activities, Jayantī, the daughter of Indra, assumed a decent form and went to the peceptor who had undertaken an ordinarily unbearable holy observance. She carried out everything in accordance with what had been mentioned by her father. Speaking sweetly and using agreeable words, she used to praise him. She served him at the proper time, massaging his limbs and giving pleasure to the sense of touch.

Serving him thus in an agreeable manner, she stayed with him for many years.

When the austere holy rite of inhaling smoke lasting for a thousand years, was concluded, Śiva who was much delighted, asked the preceptor to choose any boon he liked.

157b-160. "A holy vow such as this has been observed only by you and not by anyone else. Hence you will surpass all the Devas by the power of your penance, intellect, learning, strength and brilliance. O delighter of the members of the family of Bhṛgu, whatever mystic syllable and holy spell

(*Brahma*) I possess shall be revealed unto you along with its Aṅgas (ancillary adjuncts), and *Rahasya* (Esoteric secret). Whatever Yajña and Upaniṣads I have will be known to you. These things should not be mentioned to anyone. Thereby, O excellent Brāhmaṇas, you will become one who will excel every-one."

161. After granting this boon to that son of Bhṛgu, Bhava further gave him the status of a Prajāpati (patriarch), the status of being the presiding deity of wealth and immunity from death.

162. On securing these boons, the preceptor became highly delighted. Hairs over his body stood on their ends due to his excessive pleasure. On account of his delight, a divine eulogy of the great lord came out from his mouth.

Therefore, he stood aside and eulogised Nīlalohita.

163-166. Obeisance be to Śitikaṇṭha (the Blue-throated god), the foremost one among the Suras, *Suvarcas* (of excellent effulgence), *Lelihāna* (one who exhibits the mystic Mudrā of frequently licking with the tongue), *Lehya* (one who can be approached by the mystic Mudrā of licking up), *Vatsara* (the presiding deity of the year, *Jagatpati* (Lord of the Universe), *Kapardin* (having matted hair) *Urddhvaroman* (having the hairs standing up), Haryakṣavarada (the bestower of boons to Kubera), *Saṁstuta* (one who has been eulogised), *Sutīrtha* (who is a holy Tīrtha incarnate) Devadeva (Lord of the Devas), *Raṁhas* (Vehemence personified), *Uṣṇiṣin* (having a turban), *Suvaktra* (One of excellent charming face), *Sahasrākṣa* (God of thousand eyes), *Mīḍhvas* (Bountiful), *Vasureta* (Distributor of wealth), *Rudra* (one roaring terrifically), *Tapas* (one who performs penance), *Ciravāsas* (wearer of bark garments), *Nisva* (Devoid of possessions), *Muktakeśa* (one who has kept the tresses of hair loose), *Senānī* (commander-in-chief of the army of gods), *Rohita* (Red-coloured).

167-170. *Kavi* (Poet-Seer) *Rājavṛddha* (of excellent brilliance), *Takṣakakrīḍana* (One sporting with Takṣaka serpent), *Giriśa* (Lord of the mountain), *Arkanetra* (having the sun as an eye), *Yati* (Ascetic), *Ājyapa* (Imbibing the ghee offering), *Suvṛtta* (One of good conduct), *Suhasta* (a god having excellent hands), *Dhanvin* (wielder of a bow), *Bhārgava* (possessing radiance and effulgence) *Sahasra-Bāhu* (Thousand-armed), *Sahasrāmalacakṣus* (having a thousand eyes devoid of dirt), *Sahasrakukṣi* (having a thousand bellies), *Sahasracaraṇa* (having a thousand feet), *Sahasraśiras* (having a thousand heads), *Bahurūpa* (multiformed), *Vedhas* (Creator), *Bhava* (source of origin), *Viśvarūpa* (immanent in the universe), *Śveta* (the white one), *Puruṣa* (the Supreme man), *Niṣaṅgin* (possessing a quiver), *Kavacin* (wearing a coat of Mail), *Sūkṣma* (the subtle one), *Kṣapaṇa* (the destroyer).

171. *Tāmra* (the Copper-coloured one), *Bhīma* (the terrible one), *Ugra* (the formidable), *Śiva* (the benevolent one), *Mahādeva* (the great god), *Sarva* (Identical with everything), *Viśvarūpaśiva* (omnipresent and auspicious).

172. *Hiraṇya* (abounding in gold—so the bestower of gold) *Vasiṣṭha* (identical with sage Vasiṣṭha), *Varṣa* (causing rain), *Madhyama* (the middle one), *Dhāman* (the asylum), *Piśaṅga* (the tawny-coloured), *Piṅgala* (the reddish brown-coloured), *Aruṇa* (the pink-coloured).

173. *Pinākin* (wielding the bow Pināka), *Iṣumān* (possessing arrows), *Citra* (the variegated one, the miraculous one), *Rohita* (Maroon-coloured), *Dundubhya* (worthy of being honoured with the sound of wardrum), *Ekapāda* (having a single foot), *Arha* (the Deserving one), *Buddhi* (the intelligent one), *Mṛgavyādha* (one who had assumed the form of a hunter of deer in Dakṣa's sacrifice), *Sarva* (immanent in everything), *Sthāṇu* (standing steady), *Bhīṣaṇa* (the terrible one).

174. *Bahurūpa* (Multiple-formed), *Ugra* (the awful one), *Trinetra* (three-eyed), *Īśvara* (the Supreme Ruler), *Kapila* (Identical with sage Kapila or Tawny-coloured), *Ekavīra* (the sole hero), *Mṛtyu* (The god of Death), *Tryambaka* (the three-eyed).

175. *Vāstoṣpati* (Presiding deity and protector of buildings), *Pināka* (having the bow Pināka), *Śaṅkara* (one who brings happiness), *Śiva* (the auspicious one), *Āraṇya* (the forest-dweller), *Gṛhastha* (the house-holder), *Yati* (Ascetic), *Brahmacārin* (the religious student observing celibacy).

176. *Sāṅkhya* (approachable through the philosophy of *Sāṅkhya*), *Yoga* (Accessible through Yogic practice), *Dhyānin* (meditating one), *Dikṣita* (the initiated one), *Antarhita* (the

hidden one), *Sarva* (identical with every one), *Tapya* (worthy of being approached through penance), *Vyāpin* (the all-pervading lord).

177. *Buddha* (the enlightened one), *Śuddha* (the pure one), *Mukta* (the liberated one), *Kevala* (the single one), *Rodhas* (staying on mountain slopes), *Cekitāna* (the intelligent one), *Brahmiṣṭha* (the proficient one in Vedas), *Maharṣi* (Great Sage and Seer).

178. *Catuṣpāda* (having four legs), *Medhya* (the holy one), *Varmin* (having the armour), *Śighraga* (of fast movement), *Śikhaṇḍin* (having a tuft of hair), *Kapāla* (holding a skull), *Daṇḍin* (holding a staff), *Viśvamedhas* (of Universal intellect).

179. *Apratita* (Unobserved), *Dipta* (the illuminated one) *Bhāskara* (Creator of lustre), *Sumedhas* (of excellent intellect), *Krūra* (the cruel one), *Vikṛta* (the deformed one), *Bibhatsa* (the hideous one), *Śiva* (*the bestower of welfare*).

180. *Śuci* (the bright one), *Paridhāna* (the enveloping one), *Sadyojāta* (Newly born), *Mṛtyu* (God of Death), *Piśitāśa* (meat-eater), *Śarva* (the benign one), *Megha* (the cloud), *Vaidyuta* (the lightning).

181. *Dakṣa* (the skilful), *Jaghanya* (the lowest and last), *Lokānām Īśvara* (Lord of the worlds), *Anāmaya* (free from illness) *Idhma* (the sacred fuel), *Hiraṇya* (Gold), *Ekacakṣus* (single-eyed).

182. *Śreṣṭha* (the most excellent), *Vāmadeva* (A handsome god), *Īśāna* (the ruling master), *Dhimān* (Intelligent), *Mahākalpa* (the great sacred precept), *Dipta* (the shining one), *Rodana* (crying one), *Hāsa* (the laughing one).

183. *Dṛḍhandhanvin* (having a firm bow), *Kavacin* (having the coat of mail), *Rathin* (having a chariot), *Varūthin* (having an army), *Bhṛgunātha* (Lord of the Bhṛgus), *Śukra* (the bright one or identical with Śukra), *Gahvariṣṭha* (Resident of a cave), *Dhimān* (Sensible).

184. *Amogha* (never failing), *Praśānta* (tranquil), *Sadāviprapriya* (ever endearing to scholarly Brāhmaṇas), *Digvāsaḥ* (the nude one, lit. one having cardinal point as garment) *Kṛttivāsa* (wearing the elephant-hide); obeisance be to the slayer of Bhaga.

185. Obeisance to the lord of *Paśus* (Animals i.e. Individual Souls), to the lord of all elements, *Prabhu* (the lord), to Ṛk, Yajus, Sāman, Svāhā and Svadhā.

186. *Vaṣaṭkāratama* (Identical with that Vedic syllable *vaṣat*), obeisance to you the soul of all Mantras. Obeisance to the creator, the dispenser of destiny, the maker, the supporter and the destroyer.

187. Obeisance to you the lord of things of the past, present and future, to *Karmātman* (the soul of holy rites), to one identical with Vasus, Sādhyas, Rudras, Ādityas and Aśvinīdevas.

188. Obeisance to you identical with Viśvedevas, Marutas and the very soul of Devas, to you conversant with the process of *Agniṣṭoma*, to one identical with *Paśus*, Mantras and Medicines.

189. Obeisance to you identical with *Dakṣiṇā* (Monetary gifts), and *Avabhṛtha* (Valedictory bath after yajña), to *Tapas* (penance), *Satya* (Truth), *Tyāga* (sacrifice) and *Śama* (control of sense organs).

190. Obeisance to you the nonviolent one, to the covetous one (?), true of good dress and guise, to *Aniśa* (Devoid of night i.e. darkness), to one born of *Bhūtas* (living beings), to you the Soul of Yoga.

191-195. Obeisance to God who is identical with the Earth, the firmament, the bright light, the heaven; to the worlds Jana, Tapa and Satya, to you, identical with all the worlds, to the Unmanifest one, to the great one, to the great Element, to the great Sense-organ, to the *Tanmātra* (the subtle essence of elements), Bow to you identical with the Principles (*Tattvas*). Obeisance to you the eternal one, to the lord having no sex-distinction, to the subtle one, to the gross one, to the pure lord pervading all, to you identical with the eternal objects.

Salute to you in the three worlds beginning with the Earth and ending with Heaven. Obeisance be to you in the four worlds beginning with *Mahar* and ending with *Satya*.

O lord, favourable to the Brāhmaṇas, I have spoken erringly in the course of this *Namastotra* (Eulogy of repeating the names of god). Whatever has been mis-spoken in this, you deserve to forgive thinking "O ! he is my devotee."

CHAPTER SEVENTYTHREE

Description of the Glory of Viṣṇu

Sūta said :—

1. After propitiating Īśāna, Nīlalohita, the lord of the Devas, Śukra the preceptor of Asuras remained humble after prostrating at his feet. With palms joined in reverence, he spoke the words (indicating his wish).

2. After touching the body of the preceptor of the Asuras with his hand, the delighted lord, Hara, manifested himself to his view adequately and then vanished there itself.

3. When the lord, along with his followers, had vanished Śukra the preceptor spoke these words to Jayantī who was standing there with palms joined in reverence.

4. "O gentle lady of great fortune, whom do you belong to ? Who are you who underwent misery when I was in misery? Why are you vying with me who am endowed with great power of penance.

5. O lady of exquisite hips and excellent complexion, I am highly pleased with this constant (unwavering), devotion, humility, self-control and affection.

6. O beautiful lady, what do you wish ? What desire of yours is to be fully gratified ? Even if it be very difficult to get, I shall get it fulfilled for you".

7. On being told thus she said :

"It behoves you to know it by means of your power of penance, O very learned and pious one, you alone will know definitely what I have desired to do".

8-10. On being told thus Śukra the preceptor of Asuras observed every thing by his divine vision and said to her :— "O excellent lady, you are the daughter of Mahendra. You have come here for my welfare. O Beautiful lady of excellent hips, you wish to be in touch with me for ten years without being seen by any living being. O gentle lady with the shining lustre of the blue sapphire, O excellent lady of bright eyes, choose this desire from me, O lady of sweet speech. Let it be so, O lady with the majestic gait of the elephant in its rut we shall go home".

11-12. Thereafter, the holy lord Bhārgava reached his house accompanied by Jayantī. He lived there with her for ten years invisible to all living beings, after being covered by Māyā (Magical power of illusion).

13. After coming to know that Śukra had returned with his object realised, all the sons of Diti became delighted. Desirous of seeing him, they went to his house.

14-16. After going in when they did not see their preceptor because he had been concealed by Jayantī, they understood that it was the sign (of his not having returned.) They went back in the manner they had come.

Bṛhaspati understood that Śukra had been restrained by Jayantī for ten years for the sake of pleasure, due to the boon granted to her as well as due to her desire for the welfare of the Devas.

Considering that as a good opportunity, Bṛhaspati was urged through a secret council of the Devas. He assumed the form of Śukra and addressed the Asuras.

17-18. On seeing them assembled, Bṛhaspati said to them :—

"Welcome to you for whose sake I perform sacrifices. I have come back for your welfare. I shall teach you all the Lores acquired by me".

Thereupon they became delighted in their minds and approached him for the sake of *Vidyās*.

19-21. At the end of the stipulated period of ten years, Śukra, the preceptor of Daityas, suddenly remembered that ten years had been completed. He decided to look after his *Yājyas*.

Śukra said :—

"O gentle lady of pure smiles, I am going to see mine *Yājyas* O chaste lady with broad eyes of three colours, O lady of rolling eyes".

On being told thus, the gentle lady said—"O sage of great holy rites, resort to your devotees. This is the holy virtuous *dharma* of good people. I will not make you err from your duty".

Sūta said :

22-25. After going there, he saw that the Asuras had been deceived by the intelligent preceptor of the Devas in the form of Śukra. Thereupon, he spoke these words :—

"Know ye all that I am Śukra. This is the Aṅgirasa (i.e. Bṛhaspati). O Dānavas, you have been cheated even as I continue to be attached to you all".

On hearing him speak in that manner, the Daityas became confused and bewildered. They saw both of them sitting firmly and smiling pleasantly. Thereupon, all of them stood there utterly deluded. They did not take up anything. (They did not do anything).

26-29. When they were confused, Śukra spoke to them again :—"This is (evidently pointing to himself) indeed your preceptor; this is (pointing to Bṛhaspati) Aṅgiras, the preceptor of the Devas. All of you follow me. Leave off this Bṛhaspati."

On being told thus, they closely looked at both of them. The Asuras could not find out any difference between these two.

When without any excitement, Bṛhaspati said to them—"This man is Aṅgiras indeed. O Daityas, I am Śukra, your preceptor. This is Bṛhaspati in my guise.

O Asuras, this man makes you confounded though my form".

30-33. On hearing his words they consulted one another and spoke these words—"This holy lord has been imparting instructions to us for the last ten years. Indeed he is our preceptor. This Brāhmaṇa is some-one (else) desirous of securing an opportunity". Then all those Dānavas bowed down and made obeisance to Bṛhaspati. Deluded by the lore imparted by him, they accepted his words (as true) Those Asuras became angry with their eyes turning red and they spoke to him (i.e. Śukra).

"This is our well-wisher and preceptor. You may go. You are not our preceptor. Whether he be Bhārgava or Aṅgirasa, let him alone be our preceptor. We shall abide by his command. Well, you may go. Do not delay".

34-36. After saying thus, all the Asuras accepted Bṛhaspati as their preceptor and resorted to him.

When the Asuras did not pay heed to his beneficial utterance, Bhārgava became furious with their arrogance. Then he said thus :—

"Although apprised and instructed by me, you do not resort to me. Hence, you will lose your sense and attain defeat and destruction."

37-38. After saying thus to them, Śukra went back the way he had come. On coming to know that the Asuras had been cursed by Śukra, Bṛhaspati became delighted that his object had been fulfilled. Knowing that the Asuras were doomed, he became pleased. He then re-assumed his form and disappeared from that place.

39-40. When he vanished, the Dānavas became perplexed. They spoke thus to one another. "O fie upon us. We have been deceived due to our affection. We have been made disinclined towards piety by the Creator. We have been doomed in our own activities through fraud, and application of Māyā (Illusion)".

41. Thereafter, the Asuras became afraid of the Devas. Hence, they hastened to follow Śukra, keeping Prahlāda as their leader.

42. After approaching Śukra, they stood around him with their heads bent down. On seeing that his *Yājyas* had approached him again, Śukra said to them :—

43. "You have been cautioned at proper time by me. But, since you did not pay heed to me or approve me you have met with discomfiture on account of that arrogance".

44-46. Prahlāda then said to him :—"Do not forsake us, O Bhārgava, we are your own *Yājyas*. We have resorted to you. We are your special devotees. When you were not seen, we were deluded by that preceptor of the Devas. It behoves you to protect us after understanding everything with your divine vision of long range. If you do not favour us, O son of

Bhṛgu, we are cursed mentally by you. So we shall enter Rasātala".

Sūta said :—

47. On understanding the facts as they were in reality, Śukra was soon pacified on account of his great compassionate nature. Then he ceased to be angry.

48. He said this :—"You need not be afraid. There is no necessity to go to Rasātala. This event was inevitable. Hence, it befell you even when I was alert.

49. Destiny is very powerful. It cannot be changed. As for the loss of your sense, you can regain it as you please.

50. "Has the time of succession come ?" said Brahmā. It was due to my favour that the glorious realm of the three worlds has been enjoyed by you all.

51. A long period of time reckoned as ten Yugas, has been completed since you had attacked the Devas and ruled over their head. Brahmā had declared that much as the period of your rule.

52. In the Sāvarṇika Manvantara, you will have the suzerainty once more. Your grandson Bali will become the future lord of the worlds.

53. This period and the over-lordship of your grandson have been declared by Brahmā himself. Therefore, we did not have any sorrow when the worlds were recaptured.

54. Since Bali's activities were not prompted by personal love or passion, Brahmā had become pleased and the kingdom had been bestowed upon him in the Sāvarṇika Manvantara.

55. Īśvara (lord Śiva) has told me that the kingdom of the Devas should pass on to Bali. Hence, he remains waiting for the proper time. He is invisible to all living beings.

56. (Defective text). Immortality has been granted to you by the delighted self-born lord Brahmā. Hence why should you be lacking in enthusiasm regarding the succession by turns ? You get agitated suddenly.

57. It is not possible for me to make it. Predestined

course of events move on beforehand. I have been prohibited by Brahmā who knows the future, O lord.

58. These two are my disciples. They are on a par with Bṛhaspati. They will support you when you are overwhelmed by or engaged in conflict with the Devas".

Sūta said :—

59. On being told thus by Śukra of indefatigable activity, Prahlāda and other descendants of Diti went along with those two priests.

60-62. On hearing about that inevitable matter, the descendants of Diti and Danu, commended at once the Victory spoken of by Śukra. Wearing the armours and wielding the weapons, all of them challenged the Devas for a fight. On seeing the Asuras readily advanced for battle, the Devas made preparations for the same and fought with them.

This battle between Devas and Asuras lasted a hundred years. In it the Asuras defeated the Devas. The distressed and afflicted Devas spoke among themselves.

The Devas said :—

63. It is on account of the great power of Ṣaṇḍa and Marka that we have been conquered by the Asuras. Hence, by declaring a Yajña, something should be done conducive to our own welfare.

64. We shall invite them for a sacrifice and thereby conquer the Asuras. Then the Devas invited both Ṣaṇḍa and Marka.

65-66. They were invited to the sacrifice and told thus :— O Brāhmaṇas, let the Asuras be abandoned. After conquering Dānavas, we shall make you receive a share. In this manner Ṣaṇḍa and Marka left off the Asuras then.

67. Thereafter, Devas gained victory and the Dānavas met with discomfiture. After vanquishing the Asuras, the Devas approached Ṣaṇḍa and Marka (?).

68. (The Dānavas) who had no support, who were overwhelmed by the curse of Kāvya and who were once again harassed by the Devas entered Rasātala.

69. Thus the Dānavas were rendered inactive by Indra as well as due to the curse originating from Śukra.

70. When the cult of sacrifice became slack, lord Viṣṇu incarnated again and again in order to destroy Sin and re-establish *Dharma* (Piety).

71. Lord Brahmā pronounced that those Asuras who did not abide by the directions of Prahlāda were sure to be killed by human beings.

72. Hence, Nārāyaṇa was born of Dharma in the Cākṣuṣa Manvantara. The son of Vena (i.e. Pṛthu) made *Yajña* function in the Vaivasvata Manvantara.

73-74. When the son of Vena came into being, Brahmā himself was *Purohita* (Priest).

In the fourth reckoning of period of time called Yuga, when the Suras were in distress, he was born within the ocean (? the Varāha incarnation of Viṣṇu ?)

In the case of slaying Hiraṇyakaśipu he became Narasiṁha (Man-lion), a second Rudra, with his son (? Prahlāda) placed in front.

75. When Bali, the lord of Daityas and the son of Virocana, was performing a sacrifice, he became a Brāhmaṇa, the delighter of the family of Aditi and spoke thus to Bali at an auspicious time :—

76. "You are the king of the three worlds. Everything is vested in you. It behoves you, O king, to give me three paces of land. so said the lord.

77. "I shall of course give", said the king Bali the son of Virocana. Thinking him to be only a Dwarf he became glad and offered the same.

78. That Vāmana, O excellent Brāhmaṇas, the lord covered the entire Universe by means of three paces, viz. heaven, ether and Earth.

79. The lord *Bhūtātmā* (the immanent soul of all living beings) excelled even the sun by means of his refulgence. The glorious lord illuminated the quarters and interstices.

80. After taking away the Royal splendour of Asuras, the mighty-armed Viṣṇu of great prowess, brightened the worlds and shone.

81-85. He drove the Asuras along with their sons and grandsons to Pātāla. They were Namuci, Śambara and Prahlāda.

The cruel ones among them were killed by Viṣṇu. Completely shaken, the other Asuras fled to all directions.

The lord Mādhava, the immanent soul of all living beings, O Brāhmaṇas, showed a great miracle to the great elements along with the special forms as well as to Bali along with his army.

The entire universe saw itself in his physical body.

There is nothing in all the worlds which is not pervaded by the lord.

Devas, Dānavas and human beings became enchanted and deluded on seeing that form of Upendra (i.e. Vāmana). They were fascinated by the splendour of Viṣṇu.

Bali was bound with great nooses along with his kins—men and groups of friends.

86-87. The entire family of Virocana was confined to Pātāla.

Thereafter, lord Viṣṇu bestowed to the noble-souled Indra the wealth and glory of immortal beings (i.e. Devas). These three incarnations are remembered as his splendid divine manifestations. Then, the lord of great prowess appeared among human beings.

88-90. He had seven incarnations as human being. Understand them along with the leader (i.e. the priest or preceptor).

In the tenth Tretā Yuga, when Dharma became adversely affected, he assumed the fourth manifestation of Dattātreya. Mārkaṇḍeya was his preceptor.

In the fifteenth Tretāyuga, the fifth incarnation took place as Māndhātā, the Emperor. Utathya was his preceptor.

In the nineteenth Tretāyuga, the lord was born as the son of Jamadagni with Viśvāmitra as his preceptor. He annihilated all the Kṣatriyas. This was the sixth manifestation.

91-92. In the twentyfourth Tretā Yuga, the lord took his seventh incarnation as Rāma, the son of Daśaratha, for killing Rāvaṇa, and had Vasiṣṭha as his preceptor.

In the twenty-eighth Dvāpara Yuga, the lord had his eighth incarnation as Vedavyāsa. He was born of Parāśara with Jātukarṇya as his preceptor.

93-98. The lord Viṣṇu who was born of Aditi and Kaśyapa in the Vāmana incarnation took birth (as Kṛṣṇa) the son of Devakī and Vasudeva, with Gārgya as his preceptor.

The lord is incomprehensible. He is one who cannot be ordered about. He has perfect control over his senses. He has restrained his Kāma (Love).

The lord sports in the world like a child with his toys. This powerful lord Viṣṇu cannot be comprehended.

There is nothing which is more excellent or greater than this lord of cosmic form.

At the close of the twenty-eighth Dvāpara Yuga, when Dharma was adversely affected, lord Viṣṇu was born in the family of Vṛṣṇi in order to carry out the annihilation of Asuras and to re-establish piety and virtue. The lord of Yogic power fascinates all living beings by means of his Yogic Māyā. Assuming human form, the Lord moves about on the Earth in a concealed form or disguise.

99-101. For the sake of his divine sport, the Lord took his incarnation among human beings with Sāndīpani also as his preceptor. During this incarnation the lord of great virility killed the Daityas who had taken up human bodies, such as Kaṁsa, Śālva, the great Asuras, Dvivida, Ariṣṭa, Vṛṣabha, Pūtanā, Keśī who came as a horse, the elephant Kuvalayāpīḍa, the athlete (Cāṇūra etc.), the lord of Rājagṛha (Jarāsandha) etc. The thousand arms of Bāṇa were cut off by the lord of miraculous activities.

102. Naraka was killed. So also the extremely powerful Yavana. All the valuable gems of the kings were taken away by him along with their splendour and glory.

103. The heroic warriors of the Kuru race were killed by him. So also the kings who were in the Rasātala.

These were the exploits of the Supreme Soul for the welfare, of all the worlds.

104. In this Kali Yuga itself, when the *Sandhyā* (Junction) period is yet to lapse, the lord will be born under

the name Kalki and Viṣṇuyaśas. He will have great exploits and belong to the family of Parāśara.

105. It is the tenth incarnation which is yet to take place. Yājñavalkya will be his preceptor. He will be taking behind him an army full of horses, elephants and chariots.

106-109. He will be surrounded by hundreds and thousands of Brāhmaṇas who have taken up weapons. The powerful lord will put an end to the Mlecchas with the followers functioning duly. He will go round among the *Udīcyas* (Northerners), *Madhyadeśas* (Middle lands), other sides of the Vindhyas, Dākṣinātyas (Southerners), Draviḍas along with the Siṁhalas (those who stay in Laṅkā), Gandhāras, Pāradas, Pahlavas, Pavanas, Śakas, Tubaras, Śabaras, Pulindas, Baradas, Vaśas, Lampākas, Āndhrakas, Puṇḍras, and Kirātas. He will chastise those who are not very pious and in some places those who hate piety and devotion.

110-111. He will wander over the whole of the Earth without being seen by any living being. He will be born as a human being as the son of Devasena the intelligent.

The lord Viṣṇu who had been born in the previous birth as a powerful one, Pramiti by name, will be born in the Gotra of Candramas when the Kaliyuga is complete.

112-115. Thus these ten incarnations of the lord are remembered. He accepts different wombs in the three worlds partially, adopting at different periods of time, different physical bodies, and different purposes for the manifestations. He will be born in the twentyfifth Kalpa. For twenty-five years he will be exterminating the living beings and all human beings (?). With this cruel act, he will render the Earth left with only the seeds. He will subdue Vṛṣalas (low caste people) and almost those evil-doers.

Thereafter, Kalki will become contented along with his army.

116. Those who are not killed in this action, those who achieve something, will become deluded suddenly and fight with one another.

117. After the annihilation of all those, on being urged by the

inevitable future events, he will establish himself in between Gaṅgā and Yamunā, along with his followers.

118-123. When Kalpa comes to a close, the kings will be destroyed along with their soldiers. Then the subjects will become free from restraint. When the arrangement for defence recedes, they will kill one another in battle. They will remove the wealth and property of one another. They will not have any pleasure in doing so. They will be excessively dejected. They will forsake cities and villages (and stay elsewhere). All their holy rites and devotional observances will become upset. They will have stunted growth. They will not live long. They will be staying in the forests like this resorting to rivers and mountains. They will have only leaves and roots to eat. They will be wearing bark garments, leaves or deer skin. They will be undergoing the terrible difficulties due to mixture of castes. They will be short-lived. Their means of sustenance such as agriculture etc. will be affected. They will have to face many harassments and obstacles. They will be miserable.

In this miserable plight, during that period of *Kalisandhyāṁśa* (Residual period of the close of the Kali Yuga), the subjects will become reduced in number. They will be affected along with the Kali Yuga.

124-126. When Kali Yuga lapses completely and when the Kṛtayuga begins to function once again, the people will resume once again every thing by nature and not otherwise.

Thus the entire activity of the Devas and Asuras has been recounted to you. In the context of the description of the race of Yadu, the great reputation of Viṣṇu has been recounted.

I shall now narrate the lines of Turvasu, Pūru, Druhyu and Anu.

CHAPTER SEVENTYFOUR

Royal Dynasties

Sūta said :—

1. Vahni was the son of Turvasu. Gobhānu was the son of Vahni.[1] Trisānu, the unvanquished hero, was the son of Gobhānu.

2. Karandhama was the son of Trisānu. Marutta was his son. Marutta, the son of Āvikṣit mentioned before, was another king.

3. It is heard that, that king Marutta was issueless. He adopted Duṣyanta the son of Pūru, as his son.

4. It is said that thus, in view of the former curse of Yayāti in the context of the transference of old age, the race of Turvasu got merged in the family of Pūru.

5. The successor of Duṣkanta (? Duṣyanta) was the king named Sarūpya.[2] Āṇḍīra was born of Sarūpya. He had four sons.

6. They were Pāṇḍya, Kerala, Cola and Kulya. Their realms were Pāṇḍyas, Keralas, Colas and Kulyas.

7. The two sons of Druhyu, viz. Babhru and Setu were renowned warriors. Aruddha was Setu's son and Ripu is mentioned as the son of Babhru.

8. This strong king fought a great battle with Yauvanāśva for full fourteen months. Due to great strain, he was killed in that battle by Yauvanāśva.

9. The heir and successor of Aruddha was the king named Gandhāra.[3] The great realm of Gandhāra is named after him.

10. The horses born (bred) in the country of Gāndhāra are excellent horses. Dharma was the son of Gāndhāra. Dhṛta was his son.

---

1. AIHT.p.144 records Garbha as the descendent of Vahni and Gobhānu comes after Garbha.

2. The same as Sarūtha in Vā.P. But Bharata is regarded as the son of Duṣyanta and Śakuntalā in Mbh. etc.

3. It means Druhyu dynasty ruled over a part of Afghanistan.

11. Durdama was born as the son of Dhṛta. Pracetas was his son. Hundred sons were born to Pracetas. All of them were kings.

12. They were the rulers of the Mleccha territories in the northern quarter.

Anu had three sons. They were great heroes and extremely pious.

13. They are renowned by the name of Sabhānara, Kālacakṣus and Parākṣa.

The son of Sabhānara was Kālānala, the scholarly king.

14. Sṛñjaya was the son of Kālānala. He was righteous and famous. The heroic son of Sṛñjaya was Purañjaya by name.

15. This king was on a par with Indra. His fame became established even in heaven. Mahāmanas, the righteous one, was the son of that Mahāśāla (the great householder).

16. King Mahāmanas was the lord of the seven continents. He became an emperor of great renown. He begot two well-reputed sons.

17. They were Uśīnara who was conversant with piety and Virtue and Titikṣu who was righteous. Uśīnara had five wives who hailed from the families of saintly kings.

18-20. They were Nṛgā, Kṛmī, Darvā, Navā and the fifth one Dṛṣadvatī. Uśīnara had from them five daughters who supported the family. After performing severe penance when he became old, the following virtuous sons were born to him.

Nṛga was the son of Nṛgā. Nava was the son of Navā. Kṛmi was the son of Kṛmī. The virtuous son named Suvrata was the son of Darvā. Śibi (famous as) Auśīnara. O Brāhmaṇas, was the son of Dṛṣadvatī.

21. The city of Śibi became well known as Śivapura.[1] That of Nṛga was Yaudheya; that of Nava was Navarāṣṭra and the city of Kṛmi was Kṛmilā.

---

1. The following are the locations of places mentioned here :
   i. Śivapura—The country of Siaposh; it included Kafiristan (De 211)
   ii. Yaudheya—Located between Hydaspes and Indus (De 215).
   iii. Navarāṣṭra—Nausari in Baroach Dist. Gujarat (De 139)
   iv. Kṛmilā—untraced.

22-23. The city of Suvrata was Ambaṣṭā.[1] Now understand the sons of Śibi.

Śibi had four sons honoured in the world. They were known as Śibis. They were Vṛṣadarbha, Suvīra, Kekaya and Madraka. Their territories were flourishing viz. Kekayas, Madrakas, Vṛṣadarbhas and Suvīras.

Listen to the children of Titikṣu

24-25. Titikṣu became famous as the king in the Eastern quarter. The mighty Uśadratha was his son. Hema was his son. Sutapas was born to Hema and Bali was the son of Sutapas.

26. The noble-minded Bali who was bound by Vāmana was a great Yogin and he took birth in human womb being desirous of children, as the family was nearing extinction due to absence of issues.

27-28. He begot sons who established the disciplined life of four castes. He begot Aṅga, Vaṅga, Suhma (? Puṇḍra), Yuddha (?) and Kaliṅga. This group is called Bāleya Kṣatra (i.e. Kṣatriya dynasty of Bali). Brāhmaṇas too known as Bāleyas perpetuated the line of that lord.

29-32. Many boons were granted to the intelligent Bali by Brahmā who had become pleased. They were—*Mahāyogitva* (State of being a great Yogin); longevity extending to one Kalpa; invincibility in battles; ability to visit the three worlds, prominence in the matter of progeny due to his power of piety and devotion, state of being unrivalled, ability to understand the principle of *Dharma* (Devotion, Virtue and Piety). (He was told thus)—"You will establish the four castes duly". On being told thus by the lord (Brahmā), Bali, the king, attained great tranquility. After a long time the scholarly king attained his own region.

33. Their territories viz. Aṅgas, Vaṅgas, Suhmakas, Puṇḍras and Kaliṅgas were very flourishing. Understand their genealogy.

34. All those sons of his were *Kṣetrajas* (born of his wife to another). They were born to a sage. Those sons of great prowess were born to Sudeṣṇā by Dīrghatamas.

---

1. The country of the tribe of Ambutai who lived in northern Sindh at the time of Alexander. (De 6)

The Sages said:—

35. How were the five sons of Bali begot as *Kṣetrajas*, O holy Sir, by the sage Dīrghatamas. Kindly recount this to us who ask you.

Sūta said:—

36. Formerly, there was a well- renowned and intelligent Sage named Uśija. The wife of this noble-souled sage was Mamatā by name.

37. The younger brother of Uśija was the priest of heaven-dwellers named Bṛhaspati. He had a great deal of effulgence. He approached Mamatā.

38. Mamatā who did not like Bṛhaspati said to him—"I am the wife of your elder brother and I am pregnant too.

39. This child in my womb, O Bṛhaspati, yells constantly practising the recitation of the Vedas along with their Aṅgas (ancillary subjects).

40. You too are *Amogharetas* (one whose semen never goes in vain). It does not behove you, O lord, to approach me on this occasion or in the manner you think."

41-42. Though told thus clearly Bṛhaspati of great effulgence could not resist the passionate impulse of himself, although he was a noble soul.

The righteous-souled Bṛhaspati did indeed have sexual intercourse with her. Even as he was discharging the seminal fluid, the child in the womb spoke to him.

43. —"Do not discharge semen O Bṛhaspati. There is no space here for two. You are one whose semen never goes in vain. But I have come here before."

44. On being told thus, the exalted sage Bṛhaspati, became infuriated then. He cursed the son of his brother Uśija, though he was yet in the womb.

45. "Since, out of delusion, you told me thus, at a time eagerly desired by all living beings, you will enter a period of prolonged darkness".

46. Thereupon, due to the curse, the son of Uśija became a sage named Dīrghatamas. He earned great reputation

and he was on a par with Bṛhaspati by means of his splendour and prowess.

47. He was an *Ūrddhvaretas* (a person abstaining from sexual inter-course). He lived in the hermitage of the brother (of his father). He heard *Godharma* (the *dharma* of the cattle) from a lordly bull, the son of Surabhi.

48. His father's brother built a house for him. While he was staying, the bull came there casually.

49. The son of Surabhi grazed the Darbha grass spread in the yard for the *Darśa* rites (the holy rites to be performed on the New moon day). Dīrghatamas caught hold of him by the horns even as he was struggling to free himself.

50-51. On being held by him, the bull did not move even a step. Then he told the sage—"Leave me, O most excellent one among the mighty beings. O dear one, a mighty person like you, I have never come across anywhere. I am the vehicle of lord Tryambaka, and am born now on the Earth. Therefore, O excellent one among the mighty beings, release me. Acquire my affection in return and choose a boon."

52-53. On being told thus, he spoke to him (the Sage said to the bull)—"Where will you go alive away from me ? Hence, I will not leave you though a quadruped, (because) you have eaten other's property. Then the bull replied to Dīrghatamas.

54-55. "O we do not incur anything like the sin of theft, O dear one. We do not distinguish between what should be eaten and what should not be eaten or what should be drunk and what should not be drunk. O Brāhmaṇa, we do not differentiate between what should be done and what should not be done or what should be approached and what should not be approached. We are not at all sinners, O Brāhmaṇa. This Dharma of kine is well known."

56. On hearing the name of cows, he became bewildered and released him. With his devotion and desire to hear the bull's words he propitiated the son of the cow.

57. By the grace of the leading bull he accepted *Godharma*[1]

---

1. This obscure rite is mentioned by Buddha in derision. Mbh. attests to the existence of this practice—MW 365A

(law of cattle). He retained it in his mind. Being eagerly devoted to it, he became one like the Bulls.

58. Thereafter, as ill luck would have it he became deluded in his mind and so he sexually desired the wife of his younger brother (or son ?) Autathya, although she struggled and cried in protest.

59. It was by resorting to *Godharma* that he desired his daughter-in-law. Śaradvān did not brook it, as he considered it an outrage and insult.

60-62. On seeing this perversity, the noble-souled Śaradvān thought over it deeply. He understood the future consequences. With the eyes turned red due to anger, he disparagingly said to Dīrghatamas—"You do not distinguish between what should be approached and what should not be approached. Adopting *Godharma*, you have desired your own daughter-in-law. Since you are ill-behaved, I abandon you. You may go along with your evil action. Since you are blind and old (I considered) that you should be sustained, but you have acted in a vile manner. Therefore, you are forsaken. I consider you as one of evil conduct."

***Sūta said*:—**

63-64. Therefore, he (i.e. Śaradvān) thought of a cruel activity. He rebuked him in many ways, caught hold of him with both arms and put him in a sealed box. Then he cast it off in the waters of Gaṅgā.

65-67. The sealed box was carried by the current and was wafted here and there for seven days. A king named Bali[1] saw it. He was conversant with the principles of piety and matters concerning wealth. He was accompanied by his wife. He saw the box sinking and floating. When it came near the bank the pious king Bali, the son of Virocana, took it. He propitiated Dīrghatamas with different kinds of foodstuffs and

1. The text has mixed up Bali, the great rival of Indra and this Bali, the king of East India. The story of having Aṅga, Vaṅga, Kaliṅga, Puṇḍra, Suhma as the sons from Dīrgha-tamas to his queen Sudeṣṇā is of a different Bali and not of Indra's rival. See MLBD. PE. pp.104-105.

kept him well-looked after, in the harem. On being delighted due to that, he (the sage) asked Bali to choose a boon.

68-69. The leading Dānava who was desirous of sons, chose the boon thus.

Bali said :—

O sage of exalted dignity and fortune, O bestower of honour, I am desirous of progeny. It behoves you to beget sons of my wife, sons endowed with virtue and wealth.

On being told thus, the sage said to him—"So be it".

70. The king sent his wife named Sudeṣṇā to the sage. On seeing him blind and old, the queen did not go to him.

71-73. She beautified her maid with ornaments and sent her to him. The sage of great Self-control with a pious soul begot two sons viz. Kakṣīvān and Cakṣus of her in the womb of a Śūdra lady. The two sons Kakṣīvān and Cakṣus had great prowess. On seeing them well learned in the Vedas in accordance with the injunctions, and on observing them to be masters of everything and expounders of Vedic lore, on finding that they have achieved spiritual enlightenment and that they had become the most excellent ones, Bali, the son of Virocana, said to the sage—"These two are my sons".

74-75. He (the sage) said—"No". Thereafter, he said again—"These are my sons. They are excellent Brāhmaṇas born of Śūdra womb, the servant of yours.

Considering me blind and old, Sudeṣṇā your chief Queen sent her Śūdra maid to me thereby insulting me.

76-77. Thereupon, Bali propitiated the excellent sage once again. Bali, the lord rebuked his wife Sudeṣṇā. He made her bedecked in ornaments and offered her to the sage.

78-79. The sage Dīrghatamas then said to the Queen—"O splendid lady, I will be completely smeared with curd mixed with salt and I will remain nude. Without any feeling of revulsion you must lick my body from head to the sole of foot. Thereby, O gentle lady, you shall attain sons as desired by you.

80. The Queen carried out his behest but coming to the anus she had feelings of revulsion and so she avoided it.

81-82. Then the sage told her, "Since, O splendid lady, you avoided the anus, you will have the eldest of your sons without anus.

Thereupon, that queen replied to Dīrghatamas—"O exalted one, it does not behove you to give me a son like this"

The sage said :—

83-84. "O Queen, this is your own fault. It cannot be otherwise. O Queen of good holy rites, I shall grant you a grandson like this; Even without the anus, he will have capability.

Touching her belly Dīrghatamas said thus :—

85-86. "O lady of pure smiles, since the curd has been licked by you from my body, your conception is complete. Your womb is filled like the ocean on the full-moon day.

Five sons comparable to the sons of Devas will be born to you.

They will be lustrous and virtuous. They will have exploits. They will be oppressors of their foes. They will be performing sacrifices.

87. Then Aṅga was born as the eldest son of Sudeṣṇā. Thereafter, Vaṅga, Kaliṅga, Puṇḍra and Suhma were born.

88. These five sons were born of the wife of Bali and they perpetuated the line. It was thus that these sons were formerly given to Bali by Dīrghatamas.

89-90. In view of certain reasons, progeny of Bali had been prevented by Brahmā, saying—"Let there not be any offspring of this noble-souled king by his own wives. That was why he begot children of human womb.

The delighted cow Surabhi spoke these words to Dīrghatamas.

91. "O sage, you pondered over *Godharma* and did like this. Therefore, I am pleased with your single-minded devotion to us.

92-94. Hence, I shall dispel your chronic darkness. You will be able to see. By sniffing and inhaling the air from your body, I shall dispel the sin of curse imprecated by Bṛhaspati, which lingers yet in your body. I shall dispel the fear of old age and death in you."

The moment he was sniffed and smelt, he became competent to see as the darkness was dispelled. He became a young man endowed with longevity and power of sight. He became Gautama because his *Tamas* (darkness) was removed by a cow.[1]

95. Kakṣīvān went to Girivraja along with his father and performed elaborate penance as directed by him.

96. After the lapse of a great deal of time, he became sanctified through austerities. The saintly lord got rid of his defects. He attained the status of a Brāhmaṇa along with his younger brother Caksus.

97. Then the father said to him :—"O lord, now I am one endowed with son. With you as my famous son, O dear one, I am now contented and happy.

98-99a. Thereafter, he engaged himself in Yogic practice and attained the abode of Brahmā.

After attaining the status of a Brāhmaṇa, Kakṣīvān begot a thousand sons. Those sons are remembered as Kūṣmāṇḍas and Gautamas.

99b-100a. Thus the mutual contact of Dīrghatamas and Bali the son of Virocana, has been recounted. Their children have been enumerated.

100b-101. After performing the coronation of his five sinless (meritorious) sons, lord Bali became satisfied. Resorting to Yogic power and having communion with the Supreme Soul, he moves about in the world biding his time. He is invisible to all living beings.

102. King Dadhivāhana was the son of the saintly king Aṅga. Due to the fault of Sudeṣṇā, that king was called *Anapāna* without anus.

103. King Diviratha is remembered as the son of Anapāna. The learned king Dharmaratha was the son of Diviratha.

104-106. These are said to be the descendants of Ikṣvāku. They will be born in the Kaliyuga in the family of Bṛhadbala.

---

1. A popular etymology of Gautama.

They shall be endowed with great vigour and exploit. They will be heroic, learned and truthful. They will conquer the sense-organs.

In this context the following verse regarding the family is cited by the people who know future events.

—"This family of Ikṣvākus shall continue upto Sumitra. Having reached Sumitra in the Kali Yuga it will become extinct."

107-110. Thus the Kṣatriya clan originating from Manu and Aila (Pururavas) has been recounted. Henceforth, I shall narrate to you the lineage of king Bṛhadratha of Magadha, especially the kings of the past, present and future[1] born in the race of Jarāsandha, in the family of Sahadeva, in accordance with their importance.

Understand the same as I recount.

Sahadeva was vanquished and killed in the Bhārata battle. The saintly king Somāpi was his son. He ruled the kingdom of Girivraja for fifty-eight years.

111. His son Śrutaśravas ruled for sixty-seven years. His son Ayutāyu ruled the kingdom for twenty-six years.

112. Nirāmitra enjoyed the Earth for a hundred years and went to heaven.

Sukṣatra held sway over the Earth for fifty-six years.

113. Bṛhatkarman ruled the kingdom for twenty-three years. Senājit is reigning at present. The following kings of the future will rule the kingdom for the period (mentioned against their names).

114-115. Śrutañjaya will rule for forty years. The mighty king Ripuñjaya of great intellect and exploit will rule over the Earth for thirtyfive years.

Śuci will stay in the kingdom (as a ruler) for fiftyeight years.

---

1. VV. 107-203 give the brief history of different 'Future' dynasties. The dynasties mentioned here are (1) Bārhadratha, (2) Pradyota, (3) Śiśunāga (4) Nanda, (5) Maurya, (6) Kāṇva and (8) Āndhra.

For the discussion of these historical dynasties, see Introduction "Historical Tradition in Bd.P."

116. Kṣema will be the king for full twenty-eight years. The vigorous king Suvrata will retain the kingdom for sixty-four years.

117-118. (?) Dharmanetra will be five years old when he becomes a king. He will enjoy (the kingdom) for fifty-eight years. Suśarmā will reign over the kingdom for thirty-eight and protect the Earth after exterminating the Kṣatriyas, due to the force of inevitability of the future.
Dṛḍhasena will be a king for forty, ten and eight years (i.e. 58 years).

119. Then Sumati will obtain and rule the kingdom for thirty-three years. Thereafter, king Sunetra will enjoy (the kingdom) for forty years.

120. Satyajit will rule over the Earth for eighty-three years. After obtaining the kingdom Viśvajit will rule over it for twenty-five years.

121-124. Ariñjaya will retain the Earth (as a king) for fifty years. Thus there will be twentytwo kings (called) Brhadrathas. They will retain the kingdom for full thousand years.

When the Bṛhadrathas pass away, when there will be no slayers of heroes, Śunaka will kill his master and crown his son. Even as all the Kṣatriyas remain watching, he will kill his master the king and crown his son Pradyoti by his might.

He will be made to do like this by the (inevitability of the) future. All the vassal kings will bow down to him. That excellent person will rule as a king for twenty-three years.

125. Thereafter, Pālaka will be the king for twenty-four years. Viśākhayūpa will be the king for fifty years.

126. Ajaka will have the kingdom for twenty-one years. His son Nandivardhana will be the king for twenty years.

127-129. These five kings called Pradyotas (Descendants of (Pradyoti) will rule for one hundred and thirtyeight years. Śiśunāga will dispel their entire glory and become (king) in Vārāṇasī. His son will go to Girivraja. Śiśunāga will be the king for forty years; Kākavarṇa, his son, will be the king for thirtysix years. Thereafter, Kṣemadharmā will be the king for twenty years.

130. Then Kṣatraujas will obtain the kingdom and rule for forty years. Vidhisāra will be king for thirtyeight years.

131. Ajātaśatru will be the king for twentyfive years. Darbhaka will be the king for thirtyfive years.

132-133. Afterwards Upayi will become king (and rule) for thirty-three years. On the fourth day that king will build an excellent city named Kusumapura (now Patna in Bihār) on the Southern bank of Gaṅgā. Nandivardhana will be the king for forty years.

134-135. Mahānandi will be the king for forty-three years.

Thus Śiśunāga and his descendants will be the kings for three hundred and sixty years. Kings of the family of Śiśunāga are thus only ten. They are all Kṣatriyas by caste. Other kings will rule thereafter for an equal period.

136-138. There will be twenty-four kings in the dynasty of Ikṣvāku, twenty-five (rulers of) Pāñcālas, twenty-four Kālakas, twenty-four kings in Haihaya dynasty, thirtytwo rulers in Ekaliṅga dynasty, twentyfive kings in Śaka race, thirty six rulers in the Kuru dynasty and twenty-eight kings of Mithilā; the Śūrasena rulers were twenty-three, the Vītihotra rulers twenty. Thus all these kings will be contemporaries (?)

139. Mahānandi's son, begot of a Śūdra woman, will become the king by force of Time (circumstances). (He will be called) Mahāpadma. He will be an exterminator of all Kṣatriyas.

140-141. Thereafter, all the future kings will be born of Śūdra wombs. Mahāpadma will be a single ruler of great power, the sole Emperor. He will rule for eighty-eight years

142. Thereafter, his eight sons will be kings for twelve years in due order, in the family of Mahāpadma.

143. The leading Brāhmaṇa Kauṭilya will exterminate all of them. That leading man will enjoy* the Earth for a hundred years.

---

*As suggested by Pargiter (DKA p.26) *bhuktā mahī* 'the earth that was enjoyed' (for 100 years etc) was a better reading.

144. Kauṭilya will instal Candragupta. He will be king for twenty-four years.

145. Bhadrasāra (?) will be king for twenty-five years. The king will accord contentment to Aśoka (by installing him as a king) for thirty-six years.

146. His son Kulāla (Kuśāla, Kuṇāla) will be king for eight years. Bandhupālita, the son of Kuśāla, shall enjoy the kingdom for eight years.

147. Indrapālita will be the heir and successor of Bandhupālita. [For Ten years' as emended in DKA p. 29]. Devavarmā shall become the ruler of men for seven years.

148-149. His son shall be the king Śatadhanu. Bṛhadratha shall be the king for seven years. Thus these nine Mauryas will enjoy the Earth for full hundred and thirtyseven years. From them the kingdom will go to the Śuṅgas.

150. Puṣyamitra the commander-in-chief will overthrow Bṛhadratha and rule the kingdom for sixty years.

151. Agnimitra will be the king for eight years. Thereafter, Sujyeṣṭha will be the king for seven years.

152. Vasumitra will then become king and reign for ten years. Then Bhadra will be the ruler for two years.

153. Thereafter, Pulindaka will be the king for three years. Thereafter, Ghoṣa will be the king for three years.

154. Vajramitra will be the king for seven years. Bhāgavata will be the king for thirtytwo years.

155-157. His son Devabhūmi will be the king for ten years. Thus these ten kings of the family of Śuṅgas will enjoy the Earth for full one hundred and twelve years. From them, the kingdom will go to the Kaṇva family. The Minister Vasudeva will kill king Devabhūmi who will be indulging in vice from childhood onwards. He will become the king in the realm of the Śuṅgas. He will be a Kāṇvāyana (Belonging to the family of Kaṇva) and will reign for five years.

158. Bhūmimitra, his son, will be the king for twenty-four years. After him Nārāyaṇa will be the king for twelve years.

159-161. His son Suśarmā will be the king for four years. The kings called Kāṇvāyanas shall be four and they will reign for fortyfive years and enjoy the Earth. Then the kingdom will pass on to the Āndhras.

Sindhuka belonging to the Andhra race will uproot by force, Suśarmā the Kāṇvāyana and hold sway over the Earth.

Sindhuka will be the king for twentythree years.

162-163. Kṛṣṇa, his brother, will be the king for ten years after him. His son, Śrī-Śāntakarṇi [Śātakarni] will be a great king; Śāntakarṇi will be the king for fifty-six years. His son Āpolava will be the king for twelve years.

164. Paṭumān will be the king for twenty-four years. Aniṣṭakarmā will be the king for twenty-five years.

165. Then for a full year, Hāla will be the king. The extremely powerful king named Pattallaka will be the king for five years.

166. Purīṣabhīru will be the king for twentyone years. Śātakarni will be the king for a year.

167. Śivasvāti will be the king for twenty-eight years. Gautamīputra will be the king for twenty-one years.

168. Then Yajña-Śrī·Śātakarṇi will be the king for nineteen years. After him Vijaya will be the king for only six years.

169-170. His son Daṇḍaśrī Śātakarṇi will be the king for three years. pulomāri (?) shall be the king for seven years.

Thus these thirty Andhra kings will enjoy the Earth for four hundred and fiftysix years.

171. Five families of Āndhras have passed away. Those belonging to their families are seven in the future (?) Thereafter there will be ten Ābhīra kings.

172. Gardabhin kings are seven. Then the Śaka rulers are ten. There will be eight Yavana families and fourteen Tuṣāras.

173. There will be thirteen Guruṇḍas and eleven Maunas. Āndhras will enjoy the Earth for three hundred years.

174. The ten Ābhīras will be kings for sixty-seven years. The seven Gardabhins will enjoy the Earth for seventy-two years.

175. Śakas will enjoy the Earth for three hundred and eighty years.

Yavanas will enjoy the Earth for one hundred and sixty years.

176-177. Tusāras will retain the kingdom for five hundred years. The thirteen Guruṇḍas who belong to Mleccha tribes will enjoy the Earth for three hundred years (?) along with Vrsalas.

The eleven Maunas will reign for three hundred years.

178. When they are exterminated by force of time, the clan of Kilakila shall rule. After the Kilakilas, Vindhyaśakti will be the king.

179. He will retain the Earth for ninety-six years. Understand, henceforth, the kings of the future belonging to the land of Vidiśā.

180-181. The serpent-king Sadācandra, the son of Śeṣa, the king of Serpents, will conquer the city of Suras.* He will uplift the race of Nāgas (serpents).

The second king will be Candrāṁśu. Thereafter, Nakhavān will be the king. The fourth one born in this family will be Dhanadharmā.

182. Bhūtinanda shall succeed him as ruler in Vidiśā. His younger brother will be Nandiyaśas by name.

183. In his family, there will be only three kings. His daughters' son shall become the king in Pūrikā.

184. Vindhyaśakti's son, a heroic warrior named Pravīra will enjoy the city Kāñcanakā for sixty years.

185. He will perform Vājapeya sacrifices after distributing excellent Dakṣiṇās at the conclusion. His four sons will become rulers.

186-187. Three of them by marriage alliance with Vindhyakas** shall become kings. Supratīka and Gabhīra

---

**Surapurañjaya* but *Svarapūrñjaya* in Vā. P. 99.368.

***vindhyakānāṁ kulānāṁ te nṛpā vaivāhikās trayaḥ*. the word *vaivāhika* renders the meaning obscure if not absurd. Vā. P. 99.372 reads : *vindhyakānāṁ kule 'tīte nṛpā vaivāhikās trayaḥ*.

'when the dynasty of Vindhyaka was terminated, there were three kings of the *Agni-kula* (the race of the Fire god).

shall enjoy the kingdom for twenty years.

King Śaṅkamāna will become the ruler of Mahiṣī. There shall be six Puṣyamitras and thirteen Strīmitras (*Paṭṭamitras* in Vā. P.)

188. There will be seven kings ruling over Mekalā for seventy years. The kings in Komalā will be very powerful.

189. They are called Meghas and they are very intelligent. There will be nine kings in that line. All the Naiṣadhas will be great kings, and the family will last till the close of Manvantara.

190-193. They are born in the family of Nala. They will be vigorous and extremely powerful.

Viśvasphāṇi will be the king of Magadha. He will be very vigorous. After uprooting all the kings, he will create other castes viz. Kaivartas, Madrakas, Pulindas and Brāhmaṇas. Those kings will establish the people in different lands. Viśvasphāṇi will be extremely powerful and noble. In battle he will be as brilliant as Viṣṇu. The king Viśvasphāṇi, it is said, will appear like a eunuch. After exterminating the current Kṣatriyas, he will create other Kṣatriyas.

194. Nine Nāga kings will rule over the city of Campāvatī. Seven Nāga kings will enjoy the beautiful city of Mathurā.

195. The descendants of those seven families will enjoy the territories around Gaṅgā such as Prayāga, Sāketa and Magadha.

196. They will enjoy the following territories abounding in jewels and food-grains viz. Naiṣadha, Yaduka, Śaiśīta and Kālatoyaka.

197. Devarakṣitas (those guarded by Devas) will rule over the territories of Kosala, Āndhra, Pauṇḍra, Tāmralipta and Sāgara as well as the charming city of Campā.

198. Guha will protect the following territories viz. Kaliṅga, Mahiṣa and Mahendranilaya.

199-200. Kanakāhvaya (one named Kanaka) will

enjoy the territories of Strīrāṣṭra (realm of women) and Bhojaka.

All these kings will be contemporaries. There will be Yavanas (Yavana kings) who will be difficult to please and quick in being furious. They will be untruthful and unrighteous in the affairs of Virtue, Love and Wealth.

201. Those kings will not be regularly consecrated with the ritualistic sprinkling of holy water over the head. Those kings will be evil in their conduct, due to the evil influence of the Yuga.[1]

202. Those persons will become kings by turns after the lapse of some time. They will be devoid of Dharma. They will be base and mean in the matter of love and wealth.

203. On account of them all the territories will become inter-mixed. They will follow the customs and conventions of the Mlecchas. They will act in contravention of established principles of religion and ruin the subjects.

204-206. When their turn comes, when the era becomes abounding in women, the kings will be greedy, miserly and untruthful. The subjects will slowly and little by little decline and decay in regard to length of life, features of the body, physical strength and learning. When the subjects thus reach the lowest point (of deterioration) the kings and emperors will be over-whelmed by *Kāla* (God of Time. or death) and they will be ruined. Struck down, by Kalki, all the Mlecchas will face destruction.

207. Similarly, all those who are unrighteous and extremely heretic will face destruction.

Even the name 'king' will vanish, when only the *Sandhyā* period of junction between two Yugas in the Kali Yuga remains.

208. The few people who survive till that period will face various hardships, as *Dharma* (virtue) has become discredited. They will become destitutes without possessions

1. VV.201-241 depict the gloomy picture of the Kali Age. This description is common to other Purāṇas also. R. C. Hazra, in PRHRC states that such was probably the condition of Hindu society from 200 B.C. to A.D. 200.

and belongings. They will not have proper means. Their wealth and assets will be taken away and destroyed. They will be afflicted by sickness, miseries and sorrows.

209. They will be ruined due to drought and absence of rain and by killing one another.

210. They will have none to support them. Due to great fear, they will desert their profession and places of work. They will become still more miserable. They will leave off cities and villages. They will begin to dwell in forest.

211-212. Thus, when all these things are destroyed, the people will abandon their houses and resort to rivers and mountains. When the feelings of affection are lost, they will become miserable with all their friends devoid of friendship. They will err and deviate from the discipline and duties of the four castes and stages of life. They will have a mixed caste with intermarriages etc. and it will be an awful state of affairs.

213-217a. They will resort to rivers, marshy places in the foreshores of seas as well as mountains. Men will resort to Aṅga, Kaliṅga, Vaṅga, Kāśmīra, Kāśī, Kosala and large lakes and ponds around the mountain Ṛṣikānta.

The noble people along with the Mlecchas will go to the shores of the salty sea and to the top of Himavān and the forests in between.

Men will sustain themselves with the meat of deer, fishes, birds and beasts of prey as well as sugar-cane plants, honey, greens, fruits and roots.

Like the sages of olden days, they will make for themselves different garments of leaves, barks of trees and hides of deer and wear them.

217b-220. With wooden spikes they will attempt to ferret out seeds and other edible things from beneath the ground. With great effort, they will keep goats, sheep, donkeys and camels. Men will resort to the rivers for the sake of water and sustenance. The kings will be harassing one another by means of their evil dealings. They will think highly of themselves. They will be devoid of progeny. They will not maintain cleanliness or good habits and conventions. Men will be like this, engaged fully in sinful activities. The common people will have to obey people of mean and base nature, evil conduct and depressed condition.

221-222. No one will live beyond a life span of twenty-three years. They will be weak and oppressed by old age. They will be sick and fatigued on account of sensuous attachment to worldly objects. They will be taking in leaves, roots and fruits as their food and will wear barks of trees and hides of antelopes for dress. Desirous of means of sustenance and occupations for livelihood, they will be roaming over the Earth.

223-225. By the time the subjects reach this situation, the Kali Yuga will come to a close. Kali Yuga consisting of a thousand years according to divine reckoning, will lapse and along with the Kali Yuga, the people will also pass away. When the Kali Yuga lapses completely along with the Sandhyāṁśa (period of junction or transition), Kṛta Yuga will dawn.

When the Sun, Moon, Bṛhaspati (Jupiter) and Tiṣya constellations meet together in one *Rāśi* (sign of zodiac), the Kṛta Yuga will set in.

226. The genealogy and the order of succession of the kings of the past, present and future, has been completely recounted to you.

227. It should be known that the period beginning with the birth of Parīkṣit and ending with the coronation of Mahānanda consists of a thousand and fifty years.

228-229. (Defective Text). It is possible to mention proof (?) for the fact that the period after Mahāpadma and ending with the Āndhra kings is remembered as comprising eight hundred and thirty-six years. This has already been mentioned. This period has been calculated by well-known sages conversant with Purāṇas.

230-231. The stellar zone consists of twentyseven stars. The Saptarṣis are seven sages (Ursa Major). During the period of Parīkṣit the Saptarṣis were in the *Pitrya* constellation (i.e. Maghā) where they stayed for a hundred years. They will stay for a hundred years in each of the contellations by twins. Hence, the period of dynasty of Āndhras will be two thousand seven hundred years.

232-234. This Yuga of Saptarṣis, it should be known is in accordance with the divine reckoning. The numbers of months calculated in accordance with the divine reckoning are remembered as six and the divine years are seven. From them the divine period begins to function ($360\times7\frac{1}{2}=2700$) The first two (stars) of the *Saptarṣis* are seen in the sky in the north. Between them, a constellation is seen. It should be known that the *Saptarṣis* are in conjunction with that star. This period of contact will last for a hundred years.

235-238. This is the basis for the contact of the Ṛṣis and the stars. The Saptarṣis in contact with Maghā constellation were there for hundred years in the age of Parīkṣit.

(?) Hundred years will be completed with the twenty-fourth (king) in the line of Āndhras.

The subjects will violently attack the *Prakṛtis* (ministers etc).

When the holy rites laid down in Śrutis and Smṛtis fall into disuse and become slack, when the discipline of life in the four stages and castes becomes upset, the subjects will be oppressed by falsehood in regard to virtue, wealth and love. They will be deluded and morally weak. They will become involved in *Saṁkara* (inter-mixture of castes). The Śūdras will have alliance with the Brāhmanas (and other "twice-born" people.).

239. Brāhmaṇas will perform *Yāgas* (sacrifices) on behalf of Śūdras. Śudras will be the source of origin of Mantras. Brāhmaṇas will resort to them and attend on them with a desire to get some base means of livelihood.

240. Their subjects will be falling away from *Dharma* little by little. At the end of the Yuga, the subjects will be utterly destroyed.

241. Kali Yuga began on the day when Kṛṣṇa passed on to heaven. Understand how it is calculated.

242-243. Three hundred and sixty thousand years (3,60,000) according to human reckoning constitute the Kali.

Yuga. That is the period of a thousand years according to divine reckoning. The two periods of its conjunction have already been mentioned. When the entire period lapses, Kṛta Yuga sets in.

244. The two dynasties viz. that of Aila and that of Iksvāku have been recounted along with their different clans and subdivisions. The solar dynasty of Ikṣvāku is remembered as ending with Sumitra.

245-246. Persons conversant with the lunar dynasty know that the Kṣatriya race of Aila ends with Kṣemaka. These renowned descendants of the Sun of the past, present and future have been glorified. They are remembered to have been born as Brāhmaṇas, Kṣatriyas, Vaiśyas and Śūdras.

247-248. Thousands of noble souls have passed on in different Yugas. Their number is legion. Many names are repeated. Hence, the kings are not fully enumerated familywise. In this Vaivasvata Manvantara, Nimi's race comes to an end.

249. I shall mention those persons from whom the Kṣatriya race begins in this Yuga. Even as I recount it try to understand the same.

250. Devāpi, the king belonging to the family of Pūru, and Maru who belongs to Ikṣvāku family, these two are endowed with great Yogic power. They occupied the village called Kalāpa.

251-253. In the twenty-fourth *Catur-Yuga* (set of four Yugas) these will be the persons responsible for the functioning of Kṣatriya race. A son named Suvarcas will be born to Ikṣvāku in the twentyninth Yuga. He will be the founder in the racc. Paula shall be the first person in the Aila dynasty of Devāpi. These two will be the persons who set the Kṣatriya race function in the set of four Yugas. The same principle regarding the perpetuation of the line should be understood everywhere. When the Kali Yuga lapses, they will be born in the Kṛta Yuga.

254-259. In the first Tretā Yuga, along with the Saptarṣis, they will set the *Gotras* of Brāhmaṇas and the families of Kṣatriyas function. With a part of Dvāpara, the Kṣatriyas will stay behind along with the sages. It is for the sake of the nucleus of the races of Brāhmaṇas and Kṣatriyas in the future creation of the Kṛta Yuga.

In the same manner, the Saptarṣis stay behind among the Asuras along with the kings in every Yuga for the perpetuation of the line. The relationship of the Kṣatriyas with the Brāhmanas is remembered as one of extermination (?)

The progeny of the seven Manvantaras has been heard by you. The origin of the Yugas as well as of the race of Brāhmaṇas and Kṣatriyas is mutually interdependent (?)

The origin and destruction of these, how these function and how they meet with destruction after beginning to function,—only the Saptarṣis know this because of their longevity.

260-261. In this order, O Brāhmaṇas, the families—Aila and Ikṣvāku are originated in the Tretā and destroyed in the Kali Yuga. They will follow the Yuga, till the close of the Manvantara.

162. When the Kṣatriyas were completely exterminated by Rāma son of Jamadagni, this entire Earth was rendered confused by the Kṣatriya kings.

263-264. I shall recount the original cause of the two races. Understand it. The origins of the family of Aila and that of Ikṣvāku are different (Sun and Moon).

The kings and other Kṣatriyas come in a series (?). Just as those belonging to the family of Aila, so also those of Ikṣvāku are well renowned kings.

265. Hundred and one families belonging to them have been accorded coronation. The extent of the Bhojas is remembered as twice.

266. (Defective Text). Three-fourths of the Kṣatriyas, become established. The other one-fourth is scattered here and there in various directions (?). Undersand even as I recount those who are equal (?) to those who are of the past.

267. There are hundred descendants of the Prativindhyas, hundred Nāgas along with Haihayas, hundred and one Dhṛtarāṣṭras and eighty Janamejayas.

268-269. Hundred Brahmadattas, hundred Śārins and Vīrins and hundred Paulas, Śvetas, Kāśyas, Kuśas and others who have gone by and Śaśabindus are a thousand. All of them performed horse-sacrifices distributing millions of coins as monetary gifts.

270-271. Thus there had been hundreds and thousands of saintly kings in the past in the current Manvantara of Vaivasvata Manu. Many of the children born to them are remembered. But understand that it is impossible to describe them in detail and in the proper order even in hundreds of years.

272-274. Twentyeight sets of four Yugas have gone by in the Vaivasvata Manvantara along with these saintly kings. Understand those that yet remain. Forty-three sets of four Yugas are yet to come in the future along with the future kings. Thereafter, the Vaivasvata Manvantara will come to a close, thus everything has been mentioned to you either succinctly or in detail.

275-278. On account of the innumerable repetitions it is impossible to mention all completely along with the Yugas.

These five families of the sons of Yayāti are beneficial to the people. They have been recounted. They have passed by sustaining the worlds.

By retaining in memory and by listening to the description of the five families of great intellect one acquires five excellent and rare worldly benefits viz. long life, reputation, wealth, children and heavenly bliss for an indefinite period.

Thus, O Brāhmaṇas, the third *Pāda* (section) has been recounted to you in detail as well as in the proper order.

What else shall I describe?